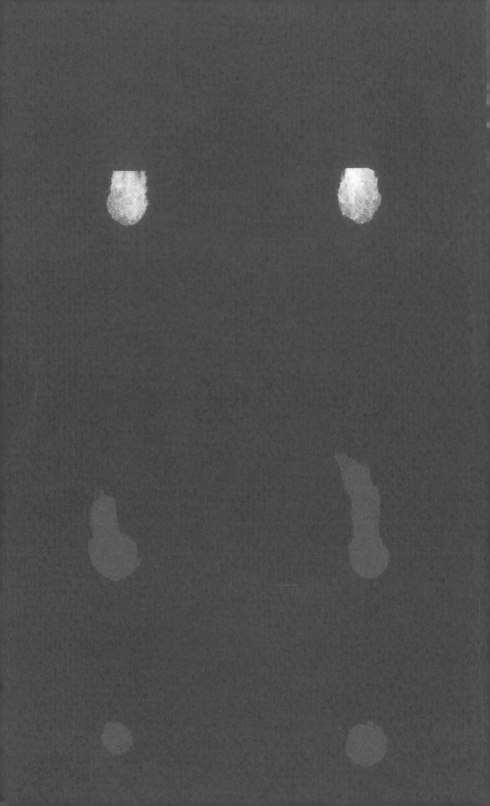

The True Genius of Oliver Goldsmith

The World is wider to a Poet than to any other Man, and new follyes and Vices will never be wanting any more than new fashions.

Swift, *Letter to John Gay* (1729)

To be more serious, new fashions, follies, and vices, make new monitors necessary in every age. An author may be considered as a merciful substitute to the legislature; he acts not by punishing crimes, but preventing them; however virtuous the present age, there may be still growing employment for ridicule, or reproof, for persuasion, or satire.

Goldsmith, *An Enquiry into the Present State of Polite Learning in Europe* (1759)

. . . I awoke, and received no other benefit from my imaginary journey, than a certain conviction that a shallow understanding generally aspires at the reputation of wit; but true genius ever chooses to wear the appearance of good sense.

Goldsmith, "A Dream" (1760)

THE TRUE GENIUS OF
OLIVER
GOLDSMITH

ROBERT H. HOPKINS, *1930* —

The Johns Hopkins Press
Baltimore

Standard Book Number 8018–1016–7
Copyright © 1969 by
The Johns Hopkins Press
Baltimore, Maryland 21218
All rights reserved

Manufactured in the
United States of America

Library of Congress
Catalog Card Number 69–15760

The Thomas Rowlandson illustration on the
end papers, published in the 1832 edition
of Goldsmith's *The Vicar of Wakefield,* is
reproduced by permission of the Huntington
Library, San Marino, California.

Quotations from *The Collected Works of
Oliver Goldsmith,* ed. Arthur Friedman,
5 vols. (Oxford, 1966), and from James
Boswell, *Life of Johnson,* ed. G. B. Hill, rev.
L. F. Powell, 6 vols. (Oxford, 1936–64), are
reprinted by permission of the Clarendon
Press.

Quotations from James Clifford, *Young Sam
Johnson* (New York, 1955), are reprinted
by permission of McGraw-Hill Book
Company.

For Vicki

PREFACE

A reviewer of Paul Fussell's *The Rhetorical World of Augustan Humanism* (*TLS*, February, 1967) shrewdly observes that while Goldsmith is placed in an optimistic counterhumanistic tradition, all of the examples Fussell later quotes show Goldsmith to be "clearly wearing the humanist jersey." My critical reading of Goldsmith offered in this book seeks to present a different view of Goldsmith from the one commonly found in literary histories. I see Goldsmith at his best to be a master of comic satire and refined irony. I see him at other times to be a lesser master of the craft of persuasion. I do *not* see Goldsmith as a muddling sentimentalist but as a remarkable writer committed to a conservative view of the fallibility of human nature and of literature as a species of virtue. If I tend to interpret Goldsmith as antisentimental, I hope that my interpretations do not distort the meanings of his work so as to fit an inflexible thesis. Although I frankly question the value of Goldsmith's poetry insofar as it tends toward excessive didacticism, if not propaganda, I deal with *The Traveller* and find that it is indeed complex and poetic. As for *The Deserted Village*, Earl Miner and Ricardo Quintana have both published excellent essays on the poem that would render an additional criticism of mine superfluous. Similarly, because Goldsmith's plays present no special problems and because Quintana has published two relatively recent comprehensive essays on them, I see no reason for writing on the plays. The very selection of which works I chose to interpret obviously has its own bias. I should hope, however, that my critical readings offer fresh insights into each work and that the over-all pattern of such insights corresponds to what is actually there in the texts.

Although close explication happens rarely to have been applied to Goldsmith's prose, with the exception of *The Vicar of Wakefield,* and although I still happen to favor such close explication as a legitimate critical endeavor, I have tried to place my interpretations in a framework of cultural context and literary history. I am very grateful to Arthur H. Scouten and Maurice Johnson for having taught me what the eighteenth century was like and what some of its crucial central issues were. I am even more grateful for their interest in my interpretation of *The Vicar of Wakefield,* which is, in my opinion, both the most important and most controversial chapter in my study. I owe much to Frederick W. Hilles for his cogent criticisms. Even now in 1969 there is still too little sophisticated literary criticism of Goldsmith's comic craft. By default, we have allowed his status as a major writer to diminish. Perhaps now that Friedman's edition has established the canon and given us the most accurate text of any eighteenth-century writer yet published, we can get on with a dialogue and place Goldsmith back on the pedestal where he properly belongs.

All quotations from Goldsmith's works, unless otherwise stated, will refer by volume and page number to *The Collected Works of Oliver Goldsmith,* ed. Arthur Friedman, 5 vols. (Oxford, 1966).

CONTENTS

The True Genius of Oliver Goldsmith

INTRODUCTION

Oh how hard it is to be shallow enough for a polite audience!

JOHN WESLEY

"The great misery of writers proceeds from their multitude," wrote Samuel Johnson with a mock projector's voice in "A Project for the Employment of Authors" (1756). Literature had become a business such that writers had become "retailers of knowledge."[1] In the 1750's and 1760's the writer was at the mercy of the booksellers, who were themselves at the mercy of a middle-class reading public. Before his confinement for mental illness Christopher Smart was the chief writer for John Newbery, one of the most successful booksellers of his age. Smart had left the comfortable patronage of Pembroke College, Cambridge, to plunge into the literary whirlpool of London, to write and compile, to become seriously ill several times, and finally to develop a religious mania which society chose to call madness. Although one may be reluctant to sentimentalize Smart's plight, especially when the plight was partly of Smart's own making, nonetheless, Smart became the symbol to his contemporaries of the exploited writer going mad and breaking down under the anxieties and pressures of the bookseller's deadline while trying to cater to a shallow reading public. So it was that in 1754 Arthur Murphy complained that "a Treatise on

[1] *The Works of Samuel Johnson, LL.D.*, 11 vols. (Oxford, 1825), V, 358–59, hereinafter cited as *Works of Johnson*.

[1]

Cribidge, or a Calculation of the Chances at Whist, is sure of being better received at present, than such a perform- ance as the *Analysis of Beauty,* or any other Work of distinguished Genius," and that while "a *Smart* subsists among us, I cannot help thinking it an indelible Reproach to the Age, that he has not any where found a Me- caenas. . . ." [2] So it was that Johnson, elsewhere sympa- thetic to the narrow profit margins of booksellers, was reported to have cited Smart's contract with Gardner, the bookseller, as an "excellent instance" of the "oppression of booksellers towards poor authours." [3]

John Newbery's next chief writer was Oliver Goldsmith. Goldsmith's own attitudes toward the decline of patronage and the problem of a writer's integrity in a bookseller's market were early expressed in *An Enquiry into the Pres- ent State of Polite Learning in Europe* (1759): "When the link between patronage and learning was entire, then all who deserved fame were in a capacity of attaining it" (I, 310). But when Sir Robert Walpole was prime min- ister and a *nouveau riche* merchant class began buying its way into the Whig aristocracy, patrons became incapable of judging a writer's true worth, the link between patrons and genuine learning was "entirely broken," and a "jockey, or a laced player," supplied "the place of the scholar, poet, or the man of virtue" (I, 311). When, therefore, the writer is "unpatronized by the Great," he "has naturally recourse to the bookseller," a recourse which can hardly be imag- ined as "more prejudicial to taste": "It is the interest of the one [the bookseller] to allow as little for writing, and of the other [the writer] to write as much as possible; accordingly, tedious compilations, and periodical maga- zines, are the result of their joint endeavours. In these

[2] *The Gray's Inn Journal,* no. 19 (Feb. 2, 1754), p. 111.
[3] James Boswell, *Life of Johnson,* ed. G. B. Hill, rev. L. F. Powell, 6 vols. (Oxford, 1936–64), II, 345, hereinafter cited as *Life.*

circumstances, the author bids adieu to fame, writes for bread, and for that only" (I, 316). Under these circumstances the writer loses his integrity and "turns to profit," finding "that money procures all those advantages, that respect, and that ease, which he vainly expected from fame" (I, 316). In spite of this, given the situation of ill-bred, shallowly educated, dilettante aristocrats and patrons, Goldsmith like Johnson would prefer the freedom of a literary market dependent on booksellers and the taste of the public, which "collectively considered, is a good and a generous master" (II, 344).[4]

In view of our lack of information about reading audiences in the mid-eighteenth century, one could do worse than to turn to the recently published materials in *The London Stage 1660–1800*. Arthur H. Scouten cites evidence to show "that the reading public for whom Swift and Pope wrote and the theatre-goers who applauded the plays of Congreve and Gay were yielding to a new audience affected by a recrudescence of English Puritanism," and he praises Winton Dean's study of Handel for its "excellent, heavily documented account of the intrusion of the didactic and anti-aesthetic views of the new middle class made prosperous by the world of commerce."[5] One might suggest that the English novel as a uniquely middle-class narrative form reaches an artistic peak in the hands of Fielding, Sterne, and Smollett insofar as it ridicules the anti-aesthetic, materialistic values of that class. By the 1760's this prose line of wit is being smothered by a line of sensibility and delicacy and does not surface again until the era of Robert Bage and Jane Austen. It

[4] Johnson's recognition of the benefits of commerce is discussed by John H. Middendorf, "Johnson on Wealth and Commerce," in *Johnson, Boswell and Their Circle: Essays Presented to Lawrence Fitzroy Powell* (Oxford, 1965), pp. 47–64.

[5] *The London Stage 1660–1800: Part 3: 1729–1747*, ed. Arthur H. Scouten, 2 vols. (Carbondale, Ill., 1961), I, clxix.

will be one purpose of this study of Goldsmith's writings to focus on his works that belong in this prose line of wit and sense and to suggest that his other works in the line of sensibility are magnificently controlled rhetoric, but, nonetheless, rhetoric.

It is, then, a fact of English literary history that most of the great eighteenth-century novels were written between 1740 and 1771. By 1762 Goldsmith could already complain that "the plan" of the novel "even is quite exhausted": "The manner in which one reputation is lost, exactly resembles that by which another is taken away. The gentleman begins at timid distance, grows more bold, becomes rude, till the lady is married or undone; such is the substance of every modern novel . . ." (III, 321–22). Tobias Smollett provides an explanation within the context of *The Expedition of Humphry Clinker,* when Jerry Melford concludes his description of the members of a London society of authors with the "most facetious member," little Tim Cropdale, a literary con man:

> . . . he had happily wound up the catastrophe of a *virgin* tragedy, from the exhibition of which he promised himself a large *fund of profit* and reputation. Tim had made shift to live many years by writing novels, at the rate of five pounds a volume; but that *branch of business* is now *engrossed* [in commercial discourse, to monopolize goods already on the market] by female authors, who publish merely for the propagation of virtue, with so much ease and spirit, and *delicacy,* and knowledge of the human heart, and all in the serene tranquillity of high life, that the reader is not only enchanted by their genius, but reformed by their morality.[6]

If "retailers of knowledge" had been Johnson's 1756 phrase to refer to hack writers participating in a ruthless com-

[6] *The Expedition of Humphry Clinker,* ed. Lewis M. Knapp, Oxford English Novels (London, 1966), pp. 127–28. Italics mine.

mercial enterprise, Jerry Melford's witty play on commercial metaphors to depict the corruption of fiction suggests that Smollett was in substantial agreement with Johnson's earlier assessment. Via Melford's account Smollett also suggests that much of the century's later fiction was becoming sentimentalized by an overemphasis on "delicacy" as a prime value. Such emphasis on delicacy as "exquisite fineness of feeling" and a "refined sense of what is becoming, modest or proper" (*O.E.D.*) would stress sensibility or a cult of hedonistic feeling.[7] A theoretical basis for the popularity of delicacy had been laid in Edmund Burke's *A Philosophical Enquiry into the Origin of Our Ideas of the Sublime and Beautiful.* As J. T. Boulton shows, Burke had so distinguished between the sublime and the beautiful that beauty was left a "weak and sentimentalized conception"—a "mere prettiness." By devoting an entire section to delicacy as a quality of the beautiful, Burke had defined beauty in terms of an "uncompromising sensationism."[8] Essentially, Burke merely articulated in formal terms what was a gradual cultural transformation in literature, art, and religion. Mrs. Thrale had observed it in connection with a rather feeble imitation of Swift when she remarked that "*as our Piety grows less fervid, it becomes more delicate.*"[9] Similarly, Johnson's heroic refusal to take religion complacently was enigmatic to the later eighteenth century that thought his concern with death (harking back to a seventeenth-century mode) slightly morbid, if not itself a sign of loss of faith.

[7] *The Oxford English Dictionary*, 13 vols. (Oxford, 1933), III, 160. See also C. J. Rawson, "Some Remarks on Eighteenth-Century 'Delicacy', with a Note on Hugh Kelly's *False Delicacy* (1768)," *Journal of English and German Philology*, LXI (1962), 1–13.

[8] Edmund Burke, *A Philosophical Enquiry into the Origin of Our Ideas of the Sublime and Beautiful,* ed. J. T. Boulton (London, 1958), pp. lxxv, lxxii.

[9] *Thraliana: The Diary of Mrs. Hester Lynch Thrale, 1776–1809,* ed. Katharine C. Balderston, 2d ed., 2 vols. (Oxford, 1951), II, 758. Italics mine.

Here then is one key to later eighteenth-century irony and satire. Goldsmith and Smollett are both defending the finest values of the disintegrating English Augustan world so graphically illustrated in Hogarth's last print, "Tailpiece, or the Bathos" (April, 1764), which has been aptly called "the epilogue to the Augustan age." [10] On the one hand, Smollett uses the nauseating, sense-shocking, graphic, and concrete descriptions of London and Bath life by Matthew Bramble to make the surface-level, "delicate sensationism" of superficial fiction totally untenable. On the other, Goldsmith with a superb, graceful deftness uses subtle irony to undermine "delicate" sensibility as a primary literary norm. Smollett's magnificent rendering of Matthew Bramble's grotesque descriptions looks back to—and indeed deliberately echoes—Swift's corrosive humor, "odd, grotesque, and wild" ("To Mr. Delany"). Goldsmith's technique is to appear to join the enemy and then to bore from within. His achievement is an extraordinary *refinement* of irony—an achievement that, like Smollett's, also looks back to Swift, who was "born to introduce" irony—"Refined it first, and shew'd its use" (*Verses on Dr. Swift*).

John Wesley, whose life spanning the century makes his *Journal* a valuable index to the age, continually worried that his missions might succeed too well—that Methodist societies by practicing Christian virtue might in the process become so affluent as to endanger the strength of their faith. One can see Wesley's concern increase as his preaching succeeded. In 1747 Wesley could be amazed at the number of fine people in a congregation to which he preached: "Surely God is working a new thing in the earth. Even to the rich is the gospel preached!" [11] Ten

---

[10] Vivian De Sola Pinto, "William Hogarth," in *From Dryden to Johnson*, ed. Boris Ford (Baltimore, 1957), p. 287.

[11] *The Journal of the Rev. John Wesley, A. M.*, ed. Nehemiah Curnock, Bicentenary Issue, 8 vols. (London, 1938), III, 289.

years later Wesley could refer in a sermon to "the gross ignorance" he had "observed in the rich and genteel people throughout the nation," at which point his prosperous congregation "drew near, and showed as serious an attention as if they had been poor colliers." [12] Why backsliding was more probable among the affluent than among those lower middle classes on the make was never more graphically stated by Wesley than in June, 1758: "How unspeakable is the advantage, in point of common sense, which middling people have over the rich! There is so much paint and affectation, so many unmeaning words and senseless customs among people of rank, as fully justify the remark made seventeen hundred years ago: *Rarus enim ferme sensus communis in illa Fortuna*" ["For in such an elevated condition of life, common sense is generally very rare"] (Juvenal *Satires* viii. 73)." [13] In 1763 Wesley gave his brethren "a solemn caution not to 'love the world, neither the things of the world' " because this was precisely "their grand danger. . . . As they are industrious and frugal they must needs increase in goods. This appears already. In London, Bristol, and most other trading towns, those who are in business have increased in substance sevenfold, some of them twenty, yea, an hundredfold." [14] But the classic statement occurs in 1771 when Wesley preaches to a Welsh congregation in Monkton Priory church: "Many of them were gay, genteel people: so I spake on the first elements of the gospel. But I was still out of their depth. *Oh how hard it is to be shallow enough for a polite audience!*" [15] There is no reason to doubt that Wesley's problem was that of the man of letters as well. Indeed, there would seem to be a complex of an increasingly wealthy middle class, an expanding

[12] *Ibid.*, IV, 222.
[13] *Ibid.*, 276–77.
[14] *Ibid.*, V, 30–31.
[15] *Ibid.*, p. 429. Italics mine.

reading public supporting the increase in circulating libraries, and an increase in bland shallow works of imaginative literature. Wesley's problem was Goldsmith's— how to maintain one's artistic, intellectual, and ethical integrity without losing that integrity by becoming "shallow enough" for the taste of a "polite audience."

If Swift, Gay, Pope, and Fielding had maintained their integrity by means of an irony depending on a dual audience of dunces and perceptive insiders, this dual audience was perhaps no longer quite so pronounced in the 1750's and 1760's.[16] A larger "polite audience" would dictate literary modes and taste to the extent that refined and sophisticated irony would become increasingly difficult because it would have to become more subtle. Furthermore, a writer like Goldsmith, owing much to Swift and Pope, would find that he would be competing against the collected works of these authors who were now enshrined as classics. If Juvenal and Horace were Roman models for the early eighteenth-century Augustans, Swift and Pope were, if not replacing the Roman writers, certainly receiving equal status as indigenous models for the writers of Goldsmith's generation. If Goldsmith and his contemporaries were to be at all original, they could not therefore merely imitate the matter or forms of their predecessors. Hence, it was Charles Churchill and other radicals who imitated Swift and Pope too closely, whereas Goldsmith and Johnson, who would be thought to have more in common with the "Tory" line of wit, took great pains not to imitate them.

[16] For a perceptive discussion of the dual audience, see Ian Watt, "The Ironic Tradition in Augustan Prose from Swift to Johnson," in *Restoration and Augustan Prose,* William Andrews Clark Memorial Library Seminar Papers (Los Angeles, 1956). For tangible evidence of such a dual audience at the theater, see George Winchester Stone's discussion of the Chinese Festival riot of November, 1755, at Drury Lane, in *The London Stage 1660–1800: Part 4: 1747–1776,* 3 vols. (Carbondale, Ill., 1962), I, clxxxvi.

Irony, then, becomes increasingly subtle and complex in later eighteenth-century literature. In connection with both Sterne and Goldsmith there is considerable debate over whether the author's point of view favors sense or sensibility or whether the author even when he intends to favor sense is in his actual achievement favoring sensibility. If there is such doubt among literary critics who are experts in the period, there is even the question whether such doubt is itself evidence of a failure of achievement—whether the ambiguity of a work stems from the author's failure to control his materials or from his failure to communicate his viewpoint with clarity. Or, there is the possibility that in the nature of the compromise the writer has to make in writing to the bookseller's demands and pleasing the taste of his reading audience, he might have sold himself out and appeased the public by catering to their shallow taste. None of these possibilities need apply to Goldsmith. If many of his contemporaries failed to understand his irony, it was not because he had failed to plant the signposts.

There is one excellent illustration of how at least one contemporary completely misunderstood Goldsmith's irony. It was Richard Cumberland who found Goldsmith's prose "uncommonly sweet and harmonious" and so "clear, simple, easy to be understood" that "we never want to read his period twice over, except for the pleasure it bestows." [17] Coming from Cumberland, of all critics, this assessment is ludicrous! Goldsmith's sketch of Cumberland in *Retaliation* reads as follows:

> Here Cumberland lies having acted his parts,
> The Terence of England, the mender of hearts;
> A flattering painter, who made it his care
> To draw men as they ought to be, not as they are.
> His gallants are all faultless, his women divine,

[17] *Memoirs of Richard Cumberland*, 2 vols. (London, 1807), I, 351.

And comedy wonders at being so fine;
Like a tragedy queen he has dizen'd her out,
Or rather like tragedy giving a rout.
His fools have their follies so lost in a croud
Or virtues and feelings, that folly grows proud,
And coxcombs alike in their failings alone,
Adopting his portraits are pleas'd with their own.
Say, where has our poet this malady caught,
Or wherefore his characters thus without fault?
Say was it that vainly directing his view,
To find out mens virtues and finding them few,
Quite sick of pursuing each troublesome elf,
He grew lazy at last and drew from himself?

(IV, 355–56)

Recalling Goldsmith in his *Memoirs,* Cumberland was overwhelmingly grateful to Goldsmith for including him in the poem: "I conclude my account of him with gratitude for the epitaph he bestowed on me in his poem called Retaliation." [18] Obviously, Cumberland thought the epitaph to be personally complimentary even though sentimental drama was being attacked. James Boaden records for posterity, however, a valuable piece of oral tradition on this very point: "The excellent Mrs. Piozzi [Mrs. Thrale] used to give, as an instance of the danger of *irony,* the character of Cumberland in Goldsmith's Retaliation; which had, by all who did not know the doctor, been taken for serious commendation. He drew the characters which were to mend the *hearts* of the community, not from his contemporaries, but *himself.*" [19] Mrs. Thrale's observation shows that Goldsmith's irony was misunderstood both by the individual against whom the satire was

[18] *Ibid.,* p. 359.
[19] *Memoirs of the Life of John Philip Kemble, Esq.,* ed. James Boaden, 2 vols. (London, 1825), I, 438.

directed as well as by others. It shows that many of Goldsmith's contemporaries were unable to accept his anti-sentimental attitudes on a subject even though there was unmistakable evidence elsewhere ("An Essay on the Theatre; or, a Comparison between Laughing and Sentimental Comedy") as to what his real attitude was. Such misunderstanding can be precisely irony's strength. That the victim of Goldsmith's satire was completely fooled by the technique of blame by praise must have been a very rich source of amusement to Goldsmith's closest friends who, like Mrs. Piozzi, understood perfectly well what was going on.

Goldsmith attacked Cumberland's hypocrisy and above all his self-centered egotism, an egotism that Goldsmith associated with sentimental drama. The last line, "He grew lazy at last, and drew from himself," appears on the surface to mean that Cumberland sought models of virtue in other men in order to draw his stage characters but, finding few such models, ended by drawing from his own character, which was a paragon of virtue. This is clearly how Cumberland interpreted the line. But the line is seen in its true satirical light as an echo of lines 71–72: "And coxcombs alike in their failings alone, / Adopting his portraits are pleas'd with their own." *Ergo*—Cumberland himself is a coxcomb! One may suggest that this instance of mistaken irony by a sentimentalist like Cumberland prefigures the nineteenth-century view of Goldsmith—a view that by critical default has lingered well into our time.

This is not to say that Goldsmith's artistry is at fault because he has been misunderstood. It was not too many decades ago that Swift was misunderstood because of similar nineteenth-century views lingering into the twentieth century. Swift himself provides us with a defense of satire even when it is misunderstood by the age in which it was written:

> There are two Ends that Men propose in writing Satyr; one of them less noble than the other, as regarding nothing further than the private Satisfaction, and Pleasure of the Writer; but without any View towards *personal Malice:* The other is a *publick Spirit,* prompting Men of *Genius* and Virtue, to mend the World as far as they are able. And as both these Ends are innocent, so the latter is highly commendable. With regard to the former, I demand, whether I have not as good a Title to laugh, as Men have to be ridiculous; and to expose Vice, as another hath to be vicious. If I ridicule the Follies and Corruptions of a *Court,* a *Ministry,* or a *Senate,* are they not amply paid by *Pensions, Titles,* and *Power;* while I expect, and desire no other Reward than that of laughing with a few Friends in a Corner? [20]

"Private Satisfaction and Pleasure" and the reward of "laughing with a few Friends in a Corner"—these are the motives for a satirist who knows in advance that he may be misunderstood, possibly condemned, or even worse taken as a defender of the very values he is attacking. Ultimately, the ironic satirist may write for himself; he may write for the "private Satisfaction" of aesthetic fulfillment; he may write in hopes that other kindred, likeminded souls will in future eras come to see what he was getting at. He will *not* in the end compromise his art or his integrity.

Surprisingly enough, it was Goldsmith's compiling for the booksellers, his knowing which continental sources to borrow and translate from, and his graceful introductions

---

[20] *The Intelligencer, Number III, Irish Tracts 1728–1733,* ed. Herbert Davis (Oxford, 1955), p. 34. For the function of private irony in satire, see Maximillian E. Novak, "Defoe's *Shortest Way With The Dissenters,* Hoax, Parody, Paradox, Fiction, Irony, and Satire," *Modern Language Quarterly,* XXVII (1966), 402–17.

and prefaces that enabled him to maintain his integrity. Goldsmith's era was one of utility, of applying the truths of new discovery (science) to the welfare of mankind (art). Encyclopedias, histories, dictionaries, and other sundry reference works were what the bookseller could count on for steady profits. Had Goldsmith depended merely on his creative work of essays, fiction, poetry, and drama, he might have gone the way of Smart. As in all ages, imaginative *contemporary* literature appeals to and is supported by a minority. The translations of the Greek and Roman authors could be counted on to sell, but *The Citizen of the World, The Good Natured Man, The Vicar of Wakefield,* and *The Traveller* were highly speculative publishing and commercial ventures. To the very end Goldsmith maintained his compilation work—for it was this that enabled him to survive in the rat race that was London long enough to establish his reputation, and then to live in the style which that reputation demanded. It was this that enabled him to remain independent of "the promises of great men" or of writing political tracts for the ministry.[21] The ludicrously sentimentalized view of Goldsmith as the Thomas Wolfean, pre-Romantic, home-sick Irishman, who wanted to but could not "go home again," will not do. Like Johnson, Goldsmith knew where his bread and butter was, and where his source of strength was—in the marvelous microcosm of the age that was London. The booksellers invested in Goldsmith himself as a commodity and got their money's worth many times over. But Goldsmith could play their game too. There is a world of ambiguity in Johnson's admiring exclamation at the end of the following passage: "Of poor dear Dr. Goldsmith there is little to be told, more than the papers have made publick. He died of a fever, made, I am afraid,

[21] James Prior, *The Life of Oliver Goldsmith, M. B.,* 2 vols. (London, 1837), II, 68–69, 278–79.

more violent by uneasiness of mind. His debts began to be heavy, and all his resources were exhausted. Sir Joshua is of the opinion that he *owed not less than two thousand pounds. Was ever poet so trusted before?*" [22] The strange perversities of this commercial era in which one man could run up a debt for £2,000 while another could be hanged at Tyburn for stealing a loaf of bread may be epitomized in Boswell's account of the Reverend William Dodd, who after forging Lord Chesterfield's name to a bond fell "a victim to the dreadful consequences of violating the law against forgery, *the most dangerous crime in a commercial country.*" [23] What counted, whether in lobbying for sinecures and plural livings in the church, for a commission in the army, or for empire, were credit, currency, and prestige. It was a game Goldsmith knew how to play —and, more importantly, to satirize.

This might suggest that Goldsmith was a hypocrite. But we too live in a commercial era with its own peculiar legal perversities and, with few exceptions, we too in our daily affairs are all hypocrites. Swift and Pope attacked such hypocrisy, and so did Goldsmith and Blake. The nineteenth century at its great peak of British commerce and empire found it convenient to dismiss Swift as insane, Pope as a vindictive hunchback, and Blake as an unreadable mystic. By our day, a group of dedicated eighteenth-century specialists has established Swift as the greatest satirist of all time, Pope as a major English poet of the first rank, and Blake as a profound but lucid prophet of all the ills of contemporary civilization. But these same specialists have been ill at ease around Goldsmith and have thus remained strangely silent. One reason for this silence has been the lack of a fixed canon and definitive edition. Another may be that our scholars and

[22] Boswell, *Life*, II, 280. Italics mine.
[23] *Ibid.*, III, 140. Italics mine.

critics were thrown off the scent by the Victorian critics who chose to misread Goldsmith by making him one of their own. If these nineteenth-century journalists could not comprehend the irony of Swift, Pope, and Blake, is it any wonder that they would fail to comprehend the irony of Goldsmith? That they themselves took a surface-level view of his work when it was that very genteel view that Goldsmith was attacking? It is time to return to the works of Goldsmith himself and read them in the order that he wrote them in their cultural context. It is best to divorce Goldsmith's private life—about which we really know very little except that he was wildly extravagant—from his imaginative, objective craft. F. Scott Fitzgerald could write damningly about self-pitying alcoholics—and still be one himself. It is quite possible, as Frederick W. Hilles has suggested, that Goldsmith could satirize in his fiction his own personal foibles.[24]

I have already suggested that for a writer of Goldsmith's generation one of the central problems was to write something original or new without imitating too closely Swift, Pope, or Fielding. But there was surely still much to satirize. The political secularization of the Church of England threatened to turn it into a moribund institution. Swift had once written to the Reverend Thomas Sheridan: "It is safer for a Man's Interest to blaspheme God, than to be of a Party out of Power, or even to be thought so." [25] The eccentric William Whiston tells of an Italian who, coming to England in hopes of finding true religion, protested: *"No religion in* Italy: *No religion in* England: *all politicks, politicks."* [26] Whiston quotes an-

[24] *Portraits by Sir Joshua Reynolds,* ed. Frederick W. Hilles (London, 1952), p. 41.
[25] *The Correspondence of Jonathan Swift,* ed. Harold Williams, 5 vols. (Oxford, 1963), III, 93.
[26] *Memoirs of the Life and Writings of Mr. William Whiston. Containing, Memoirs of Several of his Friends also. Written by Himself. The Second Edition Corrected,* 2 vols. (London, 1753), I, 225.

other observer of ecclesiastical affairs as saying: "Happy is
that man who is not made a worse Christian by being made
a bishop, and thrice happy that man who is not made
a much worse Christian by being made an archbishop."
J. H. Plumb's account of how Walpole subtly "secured a
closer control of the hierarchy and the church than any
ministry had enjoyed since the Revolution" is revealing.[27]
Religious vocation in the higher echelons had become
civil service. The one extreme of the dormant Anglican
church presented in Hogarth's *The Sleeping Congregation*
(1736) or the other extreme of nonconformity in *Enthu-
siasm Delineated* (1761) were hardly appealing alternatives. When Lord Chesterfield wrote to a clergyman
explaining why he did not want to apply to the Duke of
Newcastle for a bishopric for him, he wittily turned to a
commercial metaphor: "There is a sort of *commerce* at
Courts which a man must not engage in without a certain
stock to answer calls, and I am known to be too poor to be
able to *deal* by way of *truck or barter*." [28] Meanwhile, life
goes on, and true men of God like Goldsmith's brother
lived out their life-spans in provincial obscurity. David
Garrick pleads for one such parson in a letter to John
Fitzwilliam. The "honest Vicar of Egham," Thomas Beigh-
ton, "is oblig'd to undergo more labour, & fatigue, than
he can possibly support another Winter: He has not only
the severe duty of Egham upon him, but besides that, he
is obliged to ride five or six Miles thro' much water &

[27] *Sir Robert Walpole* (Boston, 1961), p. 97. In all fairness, a strong
case can be made for the theological and pastoral vitality of the Church
of England in the eighteenth century. The pessimistic view that I present here, as I shall show later, is akin to Goldsmith's own personal view
expressed in his works. As such, Goldsmith's "mythical" view should
not be mistaken for historical reality. John Wesley was, after all, an
Anglican clergyman who was only one of many figures involved in
"Anglican Evangelicalism." And Jonathan Swift's own exemplary role
as a priest in Ireland demonstrates the Church's pastoral vitality.

[28] *The Letters of Lord Chesterfield,* ed. Bonamy Dobrée, 6 vols. (London, 1932), V, 2326–27. Italics mine.

often to swim his horse, for the sake of about thirty pounds a year—this to a gouty Man, & turn'd of Sixty, is a terrible consideration!" [29] It is typical of the period that Garrick asks only for a curate for the vicar, that Fitzwilliam replies saying that the Duke of Cumberland promises a chaplainship as soon as "desk is put into the chapel," that nothing comes of the promise, and that the Duke dies the next year. Meanwhile, the Vicar?

Goldsmith found out about other-directedness and conspicuous consumption 250 years before Thorstein Veblen, David Riesman, and Vance Packard. The desire of the *nouveau riche* Whig aristocracy to prove that it had arrived took some incredibly bizarre forms and violated what had hitherto passed for neoclassical decorum. It was a trend Alexander Pope had bemocked in his *Epistle to Burlington,* particularly in his satire on George Bubb Dodington (described by Pope's Twickenham editor as "a clever, cynical Whig politician"):

> See! sportive fate, to punish aukward pride,
> Bids Bubo build, and sends him such a Guide:
> A standing sermon, at each year's expense,
> That never Coxcomb reach'd Magnificence!

As if this were not enough, the middle classes began to imitate the eclectic taste of the Whig aristocracy as well. Bad taste encouraging bad art, and bad art imitating bad morals, would provide Goldsmith with more than enough material for ironic criticism and satire. And, since his Chinese letters appeared in the *Public Ledger,* his subtle but unmistakable satire on middle-class mores might have a salutary effect. Indeed, the whole significance of Goldsmith's essays appearing in the *Public Ledger; Or, Daily Register of Commerce and Intelligence* has only recently

[29] *The Letters of David Garrick,* ed. David M. Little and George M. Kahrl, 3 vols. (Cambridge, Mass., 1963), II, 470.

been brought out by Robert Haig in his study of the *Gazetteer* (1735–97). As Haig observes, the *Public Ledger* "was aimed at appealing to commercial London, a public with which the *Gazetteer* had long sought favor." The impact of Goldsmith's essays appearing on the front page may be analogous to that of the *Wall Street Journal* suddenly featuring *New Yorker*–caliber fiction on its front page. As Haig suggests, "A threat to the circulation of long established dailies must have been felt almost at once." [30]

Perhaps the key word summarizing middle-class conspicuous consumption and other-directedness is *genteel.* Earlier, *genteel* was an honorific word representing good manners and good taste. By the time Goldsmith is finished with the word, it is thoroughly pejorative. As Gregory Glenn, the narrator of Robert Bage's *Hermsprong* (1796), sarcastically writes about his brief sojourn in London: "Instead of an opening for the exercise of my talents, I found one in my purse, through which had flowed, in eight little months, the sum total of my legacy: such is the force of genteel company, genteel clothes, and genteel reckonings." [31] Middle-class readers were dominated by the quantitative values that were making them affluent; and, as Goldsmith knew, these same values threatened the qualitative values that constitute the essence of humanity— and the essence of great imaginative literature.

The greatest value of Goldsmith's irony is that once it is comprehended, it forces readers to look into themselves. Indeed, as we shall see, Goldsmith focuses again and again on first-person "unreliable narrators" (Wayne Booth's phrase) whose failure to examine themselves can-

[30] *The Gazetteer 1735–1797* (Carbondale, Ill., 1960), pp. 43, 44.

[31] *Hermsprong or man as he is not,* The Folio Society (London, 1960), p. 11. For an interesting discussion of the complexities of the genteel, see C. J. Rawson, "Gentlemen and Dancing-Masters: Thoughts on Fielding, Chesterfield, and the Genteel," *Eighteenth-Century Studies,* I (1967), 127–58.

didly and to *act* accordingly is the source of much comic amusement and ultimately symbolic. The literary technique itself is converted into meaning so that a discerning point of view becomes synonymous with moral insight. On the other hand, a middle-class audience prefers to find scapegoats, to project its own depravity onto others, in brief, to rationalize away its own shortcomings by refusing to admit their existence. A classic example of this is given in the autobiography of Alexander Carlyle. In 1769 Carlyle visited the Mary Magdalen Hospital for Reformed Prostitutes:

> It being *much the fashion* to go on a Sunday evening to a chapel of the Magdalen Asylum, we went there on the second Sunday we were in London, and had difficulty to get tolerable seats for my sister and wife, the crowd of *genteel* people was so great. The preacher was Dr. Dodd, a man afterwards too well known. The unfortunate young women were in a latticed gallery, where you could only see those who chose to be seen. The preacher's text was, "If a man look on a woman to lust after her," &c. The text itself was shocking, and the sermon was composed with the least possible delicacy, and was *a shocking insult on a sincere penitent,* and fuel for the warm passions of the hypocrites. The fellow was handsome, and delivered his discourse remarkably well for a reader. When he had finished, *there were unceasing whispers of applause,* which I could not help contradicting aloud, and condemning the whole institution, as well as *the exhibition of the preacher,* as *contra bonos mores,* and a disgrace to a Christian city.[32]

It is doubtful if a more spectacular example of the pathology of middle-class sensibility is to be found in all of eighteenth-century culture. A self-centered wallowing in a state

---

[32] *Autobiography of the Rev. Dr. Alexander Carlyle* (Edinburgh, 1860), pp. 503–4.

of euphoria, a pharisaical projection of guilt onto scape-goats, and a kind of titillating undercurrent—accentuated for us by what eventually happened to the "handsome" Dr. Dodd who himself chose to look on a woman and do more than merely lust—all combine to show that the lessons of Swift and Pope, Gay and Fielding, were being glossed over. For Goldsmith's ironic vision, then, there was a need. How that need was fulfilled is the subject of this study.

Chapter One

AUGUSTANISMS AND THE MORAL
BASIS FOR GOLDSMITH'S ART

Maurice Johnson asks, "Just as we have learned, through Lovejoy and others, to read in terms of romanticisms, should we not more often be aware of Augustanisms too?" [1] In recent years there has been considerable skepticism toward a literary history that in seeking for the common denominator of a certain group of writers results in leveling out the unique or best qualities of the individual writer. Nonetheless, one may appeal to the experience of artists in any age who begin their careers by imitating or rebelling against the idioms of their predecessors, who usually tend to be highly self-conscious of their own originality, and who in retrospect may be grouped into several distinct conventions. William K. Wimsatt, Jr., has referred to the "comfortable relation" of the sublime in the eighteenth century—its "less precise versification of the Miltonic influence," its "'philosophic' vocabulary," its "newly pervasive benevolence," and its "apple-bearing landscape without original sin"—with "the softening, the tenderly emotive trend of the age, the sentimentalizing of comedy," and "the subsiding of tragedy." Working against this convention, according to Wimsatt, is "Augustan poetry at its best," the "last stand of a classic mode of laughter against forces that were working

[1] Review, *Philological Quarterly*, XXXIII (1954), 259.

OLIVER GOLDSMITH

for a sublime inflation of ideas and a luxury of sorry feeling." [2] Certainly, it has long been recognized that in the early eighteenth century there was a critical Augustanism based on a Christian Augustinian view of human nature, which expressed itself in the forms of protest, assessment, and satire, and which we associate with Arbuthnot, Swift, Gay, and Pope, and later with Fielding and Johnson.[3] Certainly there has long been recognition of

[2] *Hateful Contraries* (Lexington, Ky., 1965), pp. 162, 164. Ralph Cohen, however, sees a single poetic mode for English poetry from 1660 to 1750 in his essay "The Augustan Mode in English Poetry," *Eighteenth-Century Studies,* I (1967), 1–32. If one accepts the possibility of ever defining a literary period style that is the common denominator of several distinct poetic conventions (such definition is more easily accomplished in art history), the importance of Cohen's essay is apparent. I do not see, however, that Cohen necessarily invalidates Wimsatt's distinction between the satiric and sublime modes. Wimsatt's discrimination is based on the real ideological differences expressed contextually in whole poems. There *is* a difference between the sublime and the antisublime, between an idiom and a parody of that idiom. Both may well share common syntactical patterns and rhetorical figures, yet the major significance resides not in similarity but in dissimilarity, and this dissimilarity exists in the writer's attitude toward his materials, in what we commonly call "tone." Is it not possible that both Wimsatt and Cohen are right, that there is a common Augustan period style or mode within which at least two often antithetical Augustanisms are functioning?

[3] See Louis Bredvold, "The Gloom of the Tory Satirists," in *Pope and His Contemporaries: Essays Presented to George Sherburn,* ed. James L. Clifford and Louis A. Landa (Oxford, 1949), pp. 1–19. For a brilliant discussion of Christian Augustinianism as the basic theology of Swift and Johnson, with important aesthetic implications as well, see Donald J. Greene, "Augustinianism and Empiricism: A Note on Eighteenth-Century English Intellectual History," *Eighteenth-Century Studies,* I (1967), 33–68.

Paul Fussell has listed twelve characteristics of Augustan humanism in *The Rhetorical World of Augustan Humanism* (Oxford, 1965). These are: (1) doubts about the probability of any moral or qualitative progress; (2) doubt that most human problems can be ultimately solved; (3) emphasis on the symbol-making power as the focus of man's uniqueness; (4) an evaluative habit of mind, hierarchical and vertical rather than egalitarian and horizontal; (5) reverence for the experience of the past; (6) belief in the close alliance of ethics and expression; (7) belief that man's primary obligation is the strenuous determination of moral questions; (8) belief that human nature is irremediably flawed and corrupt at the core so that self-distrust becomes a central experience and another Augustanism based on an optimistic view of human nature, which expressed itself in the forms of affirmation, sentimental drama, and fiction, and which we associate with Addison, Steele, the pastoral poets of Button's Coffee-house, and later with the fiction of Richardson. Unfortunately, Goldsmith has been linked to this sentimental and benevolent Augustanism rather than to the more tough-minded tradition, largely on the basis of an interpretation of *The Vicar of Wakefield* as a sentimental novel, a biographical interpretation of *The Deserted Village*, and the failure to integrate Goldsmith's critical values with his creative artistry.

One need not force a modern view of these two Augustanisms through an external interpretation onto Goldsmith's critical views: Goldsmith himself was aware of such a distinction and expressed his allegiance to the critical tradition of Swift and Pope. By his very use of the term "Augustan" to define the literature of the Age of Queen Anne, Goldsmith shows a fatalistic view of contemporary literature; the political patronage and high

satire a central literary action; (9) a tendency to assume that the world of physical nature is morally neutral; (10) suspicion toward political and ethical theories which appear to scant the experienced facts of man's mysterious complexity; (11) an assumption that man's relation to literature and art is primarily moral; and (12) a belief that man is absolutely unique as a species (pp. 4–10). These characteristics seem to me to be applicable to Goldsmith even though, as I have already noted in my preface, Fussell places Goldsmith in the optimistic counterhumanistic tradition. I have some reservations about Fussell's use of *humanism* to identify the conservative tradition and about his using the opinion of Samuel Johnson to place Henry Fielding in the optimistic camp. I agree with Wimsatt that Fielding was among "the last of the triumphantly comic Augustans" (*Hateful Contraries*, p. 164). Both Fielding and Goldsmith belong in the Swift-Pope tradition, whatever name we choose to call it.

See also Bertrand A. Goldgar, *The Curse of Party: Swift's Relations with Addison and Steele* (Lincoln, Neb., 1961), pp. 3–27; and Robert J. Griffin's "Goldsmith's Augustanism: A Study of His Literary Works" (Ph.D. diss., University of California, Berkeley, 1965). Professor Griffin stresses the hard edge of Goldsmith's works as I had done earlier in my University of Pennsylvania dissertation of 1961.

moral tone of letters associated with a ruler worth celebrating in literature were no longer available to Goldsmith and his contemporaries under the Hanoverian reign,
and English letters were felt to be in a state of decline.[4]
Goldsmith's interest in the Age of Queen Anne was expressed in his essay "An Account of the Augustan Age in
England," in *An Enquiry into the Present State of Polite
Learning in Europe,* and in his lives of Bolingbroke and
Parnell; but for our purposes his most significant statement is in *The History of England in a Series of Letters
from a Nobleman* (London, 1764), in the letter entitled
"Literature in the Reign of George I." After praising Addison and Steele for their style, Goldsmith writes of Swift:
"Dean Swift was the professed antagonist of both Addison
and him [Steele]. He perceived that there was *a spirit of
romance* mixed with all the works of the poets who preceded him; or, in other words, that *they had drawn nature on the most pleasing side.* There still, therefore, was
a place left for him, who careless of censure, should describe it just as it was, with all its deformities . . ." (p.
345; italics mine). Here Goldsmith clearly recognizes the
two Augustanisms and praises Swift for his critical realism, with which he identified. In a letter to his brother,
Goldsmith advises him to never let his nephew "touch a
romance, or novel, those paint beauty in colours more
charming than nature, and describe happiness that man
never tastes."[5] Goldsmith's skepticism extended, however, beyond a warning against romances; he was more
aware of the underlying philosophical issues than the
facile view of him as a mere amuser would indicate. In
The History of England in a Series of Letters Goldsmith
praises the Earl of Shaftesbury among moral writers for

[4] See James W. Johnson, "The Meaning of Augustan," *Journal of the
History of Ideas,* XIX (1958), 521.
[5] *The Collected Letters of Oliver Goldsmith,* ed. Katharine C. Balderston (Cambridge, 1928), p. 60.

his elegance, while pointedly commenting on his "want of solidity" (p. 344). The "want of solidity" in Shaftesbury's philosophy would be for Goldsmith an optimistic view of human nature and a failure to recognize the innate depravity of human nature.

In the late 1750's and early 1760's, as in the earlier Augustan age, the battle line between the tough-minded and optimistic views of human nature was clearly drawn. For example, an anonymous reviewer of Helvétius' *L'Esprit* objected to Helvétius' thesis that interest alone directs man's judgment. Identifying himself "with the elegant Shaftesbury," he flatly insists that the social instinct or desire for public welfare motivates social actions.[6] On the other side was James Ralph, who, in *The Case of Authors by Profession or Trade* . . . , warns that "original Sin," called by some a "Defect of Nature," by others a "Principle of Perverseness," and "left in the human Composition, like Sterility in the Soul, purposely for Man to exercise his Wits and Virtues upon, is always fermenting so strongly, and operating so busily and subtily, that all the Wisdom and all the Power of Government must be incessantly imploy'd, to restrain it from pervading and vitiating the whole Mass."[7] For Ralph, society's failure to recognize man's underlying depravity is part of the contemporary failure to accept the reality of essences or a philosophy of absolute values: *"Essences are superior to Forms, tho' the World is so made, that Forms govern it— But then Forms are satisfy'd with Forms; and if we bow the Knee to Majorities, our Hearts are at Liberty to bestow themselves."*[8] In aesthetics, there was a parallel ten-

---

[6] *Critical Review,* VI (1758), 503.
[7] James Ralph, *The Case of Authors by Profession or Trade* . . . (London, 1758), p. 46.
[8] *Ibid.,* Dedication, "To the Few." See Robert W. Kenny, "Ralph's *Case of Authors:* Its Influence on Goldsmith and Isaac D'Israeli," *PMLA,* LII (1937), 104–13.

dency toward subjective systems (psychologism) and away from formal objective criteria, and in his *A Philosophical Enquiry into the Origin of our Ideas of the Sublime and Beautiful*, Edmund Burke placed even more emphasis on the physiological and less on essences.[9] In his review of *A Philosophical Enquiry* for the *Monthly Review*, Goldsmith praises Burke's originality but objects in a footnote to Burke's account of beauty as the cause of love of society. This footnote reveals another phase of Goldsmith's tough-mindedness. Burke's analysis seemed dangerous to Goldsmith on two levels: ethically, it seemed to favor the innate moral-sense theory that man was naturally benevolent; aesthetically, it seemed to place beauty too much in the realm of sensual perception and, by removing the element of the rational (judgment, understanding) from the dominant role, to separate the ethical function from the aesthetic and threaten the traditional neoclassical theorem that art was a species of virtue. "Self-interest, and not beauty, may be the object of this passion," writes Goldsmith. After giving several examples of the role of reason in locating the beauty of objects by the criterion of fitness, he repeats his thesis more emphatically: "Hence a great part of our perceptions of beauty, arises not from any mechanical operation on the senses, capable of producing positive pleasure, but from a *rational inference* drawn with an eye to self-interest, and which may, in many instances, be deduced from self-preservation" (I, 30; italics mine).[10] Goldsmith's footnote is crucial. It places him squarely against the benevolent tradition of Shaftesbury and Hutcheson when he sees the object or the motive of the passion for the social instinct

[9] For a discussion of the general background, see Ernest Tuveson, *The Imagination as a Means of Grace* (Berkeley and Los Angeles, 1960).

[10] Herbert A. Wichelns does not sufficiently stress Goldsmith's footnote in his "Burke's Essay on The Sublime and Its Reviewers," *Journal of English and Germanic Philology*, XXI (1922), 654.

to reside not, as Burke says, in beauty, but rather in self-interest; when he asserts that "reason, not sensation, certainly suggests our ideas of this species of beauty." It indicates that Goldsmith's aesthetics is grounded on an ethical view of man in which taste or the total response to beauty is ultimately determined by reason; and coupled with his previously quoted assessment of Swift, it fixes Goldsmith where he properly belongs—in a tough-minded Augustan tradition.[11]

It is unfortunate that Goldsmith's *An Enquiry into the Present State of Polite Learning in Europe* (April, 1759) received little acclaim and failed to establish his reputation as a man of letters. Although in terms of influence the work was of little effect, the *Enquiry* articulates self-consciously Goldsmith's assumptions about criticism and literature. Instead of cogently analyzing its ideas and structure, John Forster compares the *Enquiry* to Ralph's *The Case of Authors by Profession* and writes it off autobiographically as a complaint. Following this approach, George Sherburn tends to dismiss the *Enquiry* as one of a "long series of complaints made by writers that their art is both unappreciated and unrewarded" and to find many of the positions taken in the work as "not thoroughly considered."[12] Only Ronald S. Crane, in what still remains the best short account of English neoclassical criticism, rates the *Enquiry* highly by placing it in a

[11] Goldsmith's emphasis on reason as a moral power is based on traditional faculty psychology. For a good brief summary of this psychology, see Miriam Starkman, *Swift's Satire on Learning in A Tale of a Tub* (Princeton, 1950), pp. 35–39. Donald Greene, however, has warned against confusing such emphasis on reason with neo-Stoicism. "Augustinianism and Empiricism," *Eighteenth-Century Studies*, I (1967), 62–67. And long ago Edward N. Hooker showed how the English Augustan tradition (a Christian one) strives for a balance and reconciliation between reason and passion. *The Critical Works of John Dennis,* ed. Hooker, 2 vols. (Baltimore, 1943), II, xci–xcix.

[12] "The Periodicals and Oliver Goldsmith," in *A Literary History of England,* ed. Albert C. Baugh (New York, 1948), pp. 1057–58.

group of writings that deal with the question of criticism itself and finds "the most notable of these" to be Goldsmith's work, Pope's *Essay on Criticism,* and Gibbon's *Essai sur l'étude de litterature.*[13] Even so, the neglect of the *Enquiry* continues. In *A History of Modern Criticism 1750–1950,* René Wellek quotes once from the *Enquiry* and again cites Goldsmith to illustrate the new historicism that came to dominate literary criticism in the late eighteenth century. Yet in his chronological lists of important critical works in the appendix, Wellek omits the *Enquiry.*[14]

The assumption that the *Enquiry* was hastily written and lightly thought out is a dangerous one. Such an assumption ignores the fact that the *Enquiry* was published by Robert Dodsley, the most distinguished publisher of his day and a shrewd businessman, who, as his biographer observes, "never allowed his personal interest in a manuscript to warp his commercial judgment."[15] Dodsley's publication of the *Enquiry* was not an act of charity but a calculated business venture. In 1754 he had published John Gilbert Cooper's *Letters Concerning Taste* (anonymously), and by 1757 it had reached its third edition.[16] The contemporary interest in aesthetics was further shown by the success of Burke's *Philosophical Enquiry,* which reached its second edition in 1759. Insofar as Goldsmith's work dealt with aesthetics, then, it would have appeared to Dodsley to be a good risk. Insofar as the *Enquiry* criticized contemporary culture as a whole, Dodsley could hope that it would meet with the tremendous success of

[13] "Neo-Classical Criticism," in *Dictionary of World Literature,* ed. Joseph T. Shipley (Paterson, N.J., 1953), p. 117.

[14] *A History of Modern Criticism 1750–1950,* 5 vols. (New Haven, 1955———), I, 124, 343.

[15] Ralph Straus, *Robert Dodsley* (New York, 1910), p. 266.

[16] See the reprint of this third edition with an introduction by Ralph Cohen, The Augustan Reprint Society, no. 30 (Los Angeles, 1951).

John Brown's *An Estimate of the Manners and Principles of the Times,* which, published by a rival in 1757, had run through five editions in one year and had reached the seventh by 1758. In fact, Brown's militant tone and boldly stated thesis provided the contrast against which Goldsmith intended his more coolly detached and seemingly philosophical approach to be measured. Finally, one of the original titles proposed by Goldsmith in a letter and retained in part in the book, "The Present State of Taste and Literature in Europe," links the *Enquiry* to another of Dodsley's more successful publishing ventures, John Campbell's anonymously published political history, *The Present State of Europe,* which in expanded form had reached its fifth edition by 1756. Dodsley may well have thought that Goldsmith's brief cultural history of Europe might form a companion piece to Campbell's political history and, if successful, might also be expanded in successive editions. Certainly, there was almost no counterpart in English publications to the compact, quarto encyclopedic summaries and sketches of the French world of letters compiled by Formey. As a fusion of aesthetics, a critical estimate, and a cultural history, there was every reason to hope for the success of the *Enquiry.* That it was not a publishing success may be due not so much to defects in the book as to saturation in the market of previous similar works and to Kendrick's sarcastic treatment of it in the *Monthly Review.*

The *Enquiry* is neither a complaint nor an elaborately detailed analysis of European culture. It is an apology for a point of view toward culture and literature that is thoroughly neoclassical. It is also a carefully constructed attack and defense against what seemed to Goldsmith to be the aberrations in the taste of his age. In his first major work, and incidentally one of his most original ones, Goldsmith attempts with some success to reconcile the neoclassical quest for the universal found in the uniformity of human nature in all epochs and all cultures with the neoclassical concern for the here and now. This reconciliation was of great importance to the problem of taste in Goldsmith's day. In the ethical realm human nature remains the same; Goldsmith pleads, in his chapter on English and French learning, for critics and the learned to "look beyond the bounds of national prejudice" and become "citizens of the world." But in the realm of art every nation has its own set of manners, which makes each nation's literature organically native to that nation. For a critic, then, to impose his own cultural standards while interpreting another nation's poetry would be a violation of the neoclassical belief in decorum. Conversely, for the poet of one country to attempt to import artificially the idioms and forms of another country and to make them the basis of a new mode of poetry would be another violation of decorum. Goldsmith's entire argument or apology in his *Enquiry* is subtly directed against the fad in the mid-eighteenth century for the Gothic and for *chinoiserie* in fashions and for the exotic innovations in poetry associated with Gray and Warton.

In 1746, through a fictitious letter-essay, John Gilbert Cooper deplored the ostentation of contemporary art and its failure to make "use" the end of its endeavor.[17] This letter is followed by another in which the writer mocks the "unmeaning Glitter, the tasteless Profusion, and monstrous Enormities" that he observes in suburban London villas: "In one Place was a House built from an aukward [*sic*] Delineation plundered from an old *Indian* Screen, and decorated with all the Monsters of *Asia* and *Africa*, inhospitably grinning at Strangers over every Door, Win-

[17] *Letters concerning Taste. The Fourth Edition. To Which Are Added Essays on Similar and Other Subjects. The Second Edition* (London, 1771), p. 51. A note to Letter VIII explains that it was first published in a 1746 periodical (p. 49).

dow, and Chimney-Piece. In another we found an old *Gothic* Building encrusted with Stucco, sliced into Grecian Pilasters, with gilded Capitals; superbly lined with Paper disfigured all over with the fat Deities of CHINA, and the heterogeneous Animals that exist only in the aerial Regions of UTOPIA" (pp. 57–58). The writer attributes this prostitution of taste to a "distempered *Fancy*" and jests sarcastically that these villas would make one think that "the new Gentry of the City, and their Leaders the well dressed Mob about St. *James's* were seized the very Moment they left the Town-Air, with a *Chinese* Madness. . . ." [18] In his *Estimate of the Manners and Principles of the Times* (1757), John Brown noted that not even Hogarth had been able to "keep alive the Taste of Nature, or of Beauty": "The fantastic and grotesque have banished *both*. Every House of Fashion is now crowded with Porcelain Trees and Birds, Porcelain Men and Beasts, cross-legged Mandarins and Bramins, perpendicular Lines and stiff right Angles: Every gaudy *Chinese* Crudity, either in Colour, Form, Attitude, or Grouping, is adopted into fashionable Use, and become the Standard of Taste and Elegance." [19] Even Alexander Gerard, in *An Essay on Taste* (1759), felt compelled to criticize the manner in which men eschewed "real beauty" and "imitate the Chinese, or revive the Gothic taste" merely for "the pleasure of novelty." [20]

Perhaps the best illustration to reveal Goldsmith's underlying strategy in the *Enquiry* is to be found in Edmund Burke's *Annual Register* for 1758. Under "Literary and Miscellaneous Essays" there was first a translation of Montesquieu's article on taste written for the *Encyclo-*

[18] *Ibid.*, p. 58.
[19] *Estimate of the Manners and Principles of the Times*, 4th ed. (London, 1757), pp. 47–48.
[20] *An Essay on Taste*, introduction by Walter J. Hipple, Jr. (Gainesville, Fla., 1963), p. 7.

pédie, followed by Sir William Chambers' article "Of the art of laying out gardens among the Chinese." Among other remarks, Montesquieu refers to a Gothic building as "a kind of aenigma to the eye" that embarrasses the soul "as when she is presented with an obscure poem," [21] and in the light of his anti-Gothic point of view it comes as a surprise that his essay is followed by one on Chinese gardens. It comes as a surprise because in the pejorative criticisms of Cooper, Brown, and Gerard, the Gothic and Chinese fads are seen as synonymous. As B. Sprague Allen suggests, "different" as the "obvious physical characteristics" are between Gothicism, *chinoiserie,* and the rococo, there exists between them "no fundamental opposition": "These three modes of artistic expression possessed in common qualities of design—asymmetry, movement, variety, freedom, spontaneity—by virtue of which the influence of one reinforced that of the others. Singly and together they militated against the classical ideals of repose, sobriety, and discipline." [22] It would seem strange, then, that the *Annual Register* would print side by side an anti-Gothic treatise and one on the art of laying out a Chinese garden. The solution is to recognize the irony of Burke's editorial introduction to Chambers' essay: *"It will not be the less agreeable, that the observations are drawn from a country, which while it is so remote from us in situation, manners, and customs, preserves so strong a conformity in this article, with the best ideas, which the improvement of taste has introduced amongst us in England."* [23] If this interpretation of the editorial comment as ironic is accurate, one should then compare Burke's "improvement of taste" with the comments of Cooper, Brown, and Gerard. The crux of the irony is that

[21] *Annual Register for 1758,* 9th ed. (1795), I, 313.
[22] *Tides in English Taste* (1619–1800), 2 vols. (New York, 1958), II, 102.
[23] *Annual Register for 1758,* I, 318–19.

one could substitute the term *Gothic* for *Chinese* in Chambers' article and never know the difference. But there is more. After his description is finished, Chambers concludes with a warning that "the art of laying out grounds after the Chinese manner is exceedingly difficult, and not to be attained by persons of narrow intellects: for though the precepts are simple and obvious, yet the putting them in execution requires genius, judgment, and experience, a strong imagination, and a thorough knowledge of the human mind. . . ."[24] It is this final warning that drives the *Annual Register's* point home. Englishmen should be cosmopolitan and study the customs and manners of other nations, but to attempt to graft these alien customs and manners onto an indigenous English culture is a potential corruption of taste.

The operative structural metaphor of the *Enquiry* is the organic equation of learning with a plant. "Learning, when *planted* in any country, is transient and fading, nor does it *flourish* till slow gradations of improvement have *naturalized it to the soil*" (I, 261; italics mine). Consistent with this metaphor is Goldsmith's cyclical view of history that, while human nature is constant, individual cultures can and do vary in degree of excellence: "The *seeds* of excellence are *sown* in every age, and it is wholly owing to a wrong direction in the passions or pursuits of mankind that they have not received the proper *cultivation*" (I, 260; italics mine). The importation of foreign cultures under the reign of illustrious rulers, while commendable, usually fails in time because such importations are artificial and the cultures do not become indigenous after the demise of the patrons: "While in the *radiance* of royal favour, every art and science seemed to *flourish*, but when that was withdrawn, they quickly felt the rigours of a *strange climate*, and with *exotic constitutions perished* by

[24] *Ibid.*, p. 323.

neglect" (I, 262; italics mine). Thus the Netherlands and the Berlin Academy of Letters fail in not having indigenous learning. This organic metaphor of culture is sustained throughout the entire work even to the point of comparing incompetent critics and commentators to plant pests: "the *insect-like* absurdities, which were *hatched* in the schools of those specious idlers . . . encreased as learning improved, but *swarmed* on its decline" (I, 267; italics mine). The controlling point of view of the *Enquiry* is that of the medical doctor examining the pathology of a culture not merely to make a diagnosis but to prescribe the remedy. Unlike Brown in his *Estimate* and Ralph in his *Appeal*, Goldsmith deliberately establishes the empirical, philosophical tone of his work on a high plane so that instead of destructive analysis leading to a kind of fruitless atomism there will be an organic synthesis leading to a cultural therapy. To emphasize this synthesis, he states his central position in the beginning: "True learning and true morality are closely connected; to improve the head will insensibly influence the heart, a deficiency of taste and a corruption of manners are sometimes found mutually to produce each other" (I, 259). As in his earlier footnote to Burke's treatise, Goldsmith is concerned in the *Enquiry* with reaffirming the concept of art as a species of virtue, with eschewing pure sense perception or the emotive while recognizing its importance as the physical basis for aesthetics, and with establishing the primary locus of aesthetic response in reason. His definition of taste as *"the exhibition of the greatest quantity of beauty and of use, that may be admitted into any description without counteracting each other"* (I, 296), follows Hume's distinction between the physiological perception of beauty ("bodily taste") and the mental conception of beauty which ultimately involves reason, which Hume termed "mental taste" and Goldsmith termed "use." [25] Good taste for Goldsmith, as for Hume, meant a fusion of sensual perception *and* reason in which the locus resides in the ethical golden mean determined by judgment. If we were to substitute for Goldsmith's "use" one of the traditional terms "utility" or "fitness," we would more readily see that in his definition he is following an orthodox position. He is saying that since what constitutes the useful varies from country to country, one must study each national culture on its own terms. Rather than being parochial, Goldsmith is, on the contrary, working against a critical chauvinism that measures one literature through the bifocals of its own. He returns explicitly to his formerly implicit metaphor of the enquirer as doctor when he writes: "Critics should, therefore, imitate physicians, and consider every country as having a peculiar constitution, and consequently requiring a peculiar regimen" (I, 297).

Goldsmith's use of the medical metaphor applied to an organic context allows us to understand more accurately his interest in the zoological studies of Buffon and the theory that climate had much to do in determining a nation's culture. There has been perhaps a tendency to consider Goldsmith as an English *philosophe*, but such a belief distorts his conservative position.[26] Not only were

[25] Hume's 1757 essay on the standard of taste would in all probability have been known to Goldsmith. For discussions of Hume's essay, see Walter J. Hipple, Jr., *The Beautiful, The Sublime, and The Picturesque in Eighteenth-Century British Aesthetic Theory* (Carbondale, Ill., 1957), pp. 44–48; and Ralph Cohen's "David Hume's Experimental Method and The Theory of Taste," *ELH*, XXV (1958), 270–87.

[26] See Sherburn, *A Literary History of England*, p. 1057. See also the discussion by Ronald S. Crane, *New Essays by Oliver Goldsmith* (Chicago, 1927), pp. xxxvii–xxxviii. Crane seems to favor Cazamian's view that Goldsmith was a *philosophe* in his manner. Of course Cazamian could not have known that Goldsmith was borrowing from Buffon, as Crane shows. Arthur Lytton Sells, on the other hand, thinks of Goldsmith as more the conservative and in some respects a reactionary. See his *Les Sources Françaises de Goldsmith* (Paris, 1924), pp. 204–5.

there precedents in classical theory for the influence of climate on the manners of nations, but to Goldsmith, Buffon's researches would seem to show modern science verifying not only a time-honored theory but also the traditional neoclassical principle of decorum.[27] To show that Goldsmith was merely pouring old wine into new casks, one need only place these three quotations in chronological order:

> *You* then whose Judgment the right Course wou'd steer,
> Know well each ANCIENT's proper *Character,*
> His *Fable, Subject, Scope* in ev'ry Page,
> *Religion, Country, Genius* of his *Age:*
> (POPE, *Essay on Criticism,* ll. 118–21)

We can never completely relish, or adequately understand, any author, especially any ancient, except we constantly keep in our eye, his climate, his country and his age.
(JOSEPH WARTON, *Essay on Pope* [1756], I, 5.)

Criticism must understand the nature of the climate and country, &c. before it gives rules to direct Taste. In other words, every country should have a national system of criticism.
(GOLDSMITH, *An Enquiry,* I, 296.)

Nor should Goldsmith's use of organic metaphors glibly be thought to represent an underlying urge toward romanticism hidden by a mechanical framework of standard neoclassical platitudes. By now it is surely clear that the

[27] That Goldsmith's reliance on Buffon's science is not radical is shown in F. T. H. Fletcher's chapter "Climate and Law," in his *Montesquieu and English Politics 1751–1800* (London, 1939), pp. 93–103. Fletcher reminds us that there were precedents in classical literature for the influence of climate on the character, laws, and manners of men (p. 93). And Wellek recognizes that the influence of environment could be used to reinforce "the classical recommendation of a proper regard for decorum and circumstance." See his *A History of Modern Criticism 1750–1950,* I, 124. Goldsmith's physician-health metaphor and the idea of culture as an organism requiring a suitable environment come as much from Plato's *Republic* as from Buffon.

mechanistic-organistic dichotomy often used to distinguish neoclassicism from romanticism is a hideous parody of the major neoclassical writers themselves. A careful reading of Pope's *An Essay on Criticism* (disregarding the analytical table at the beginning, quite probably not of Pope's making) would show that, like Goldsmith, Pope was pleading for an organic, creative, and synthetic (rather than merely analytical) criticism. Goldsmith's thesis that the decay of politeness is caused by all such critics who *"judge by rule, and not by feelings"* (I, 287), should not be lifted out of context and made the basis for a view of Goldsmith rebelling against so-called neoclassical dogmas. As we have already seen, his theory of taste retains the dominant role of the rational faculty, and his emphasis on feeling merely reiterates that genius must possess the imaginative capacity for creativity and that critics should respond accordingly. As Pope had warned: "Survey the *Whole*, nor seek slight *Faults* to find, / Where *Nature moves*, and *Rapture warms* the Mind." [28]

In his specific comments on the decline of learning in the various European nations, Goldsmith is actually criticizing what he thought were contemporary abuses of taste in English letters. The key semantic term is *obscure*. In his *Philosophical Enquiry* Burke had so praised the obscure as a source of the sublime that he actually wrote: "A clear idea is therefore another name for a little idea." [29] When Reynolds in his *Discourses* followed Burke in permitting the obscure because of its connection with the sublime, William Blake retorted: "Obscurity is Neither the Source of the Sublime nor of any Thing Else." [30]

[28] *An Essay on Criticism*, ll. 235–36. *The Poems of Alexander Pope*, gen. ed. John Butt, Twickenham Edition, 10 vols. (London, 1939–1967), I, 266.

[29] *A Philosophical Enquiry into the Origin of our Ideas of the Sublime and Beautiful*, ed. J. T. Boulton (London, 1958), p. 63.

[30] *Ibid.*, p. cii. See William Blake, *Complete Writings*, ed. Geoffrey Keynes (London, 1966), p. 473.

Goldsmith's deliberate repetition of *obscure* in his *Enquiry* is surely a parody of Burke. Like Samuel Johnson, Goldsmith is concerned with literature that is clear in its commitment to an audience of literate, intelligent men, not to the esoteric few. The artist must mediate between the timeless moral truths and the unique manners of each age and of each culture. The work of art itself is the balanced mean between these two demands. In Chapter Three, "*A view of the obscure ages*," Goldsmith avoids a frontal attack on the "Gothic" and instead uses *obscure* as a pejorative synonym. It is a slanted view designed to undermine the medieval revival of the poems and treatises of Gray and Warton. Thus, later in the *Enquiry* when Goldsmith criticizes the English poetry of his contemporaries, he refers to "the affected *obscurity* of our odes, the tuneless flow of our blank verse, the pompous epithet, laboured diction, and every other deviation from common sense . . ." (I, 317; italics mine). Paradoxically, though we now think of Gray as an innovator in his metrical experiments, Goldsmith's earlier high praise of Dante as an innovator who followed nature forces one to see contemporary poetics as derivative in its imitations of artifacts and as frowning on "novelty, one of the greatest beauties in poetry" (I, 317). The point is, then, that Goldsmith's impressions of European letters are slanted and opinionated, but slanted to a purpose. His attack on the artificial pastoral poetry of Italy is really an attack on the stale mid-eighteenth-century pastoral magazine verse of the English periodicals. He is insidiously using the Swiftian technique of criticizing English taste by reflecting and distorting its worst excesses in the literatures of other countries. His centripetal position is based on an idealistic view of art in which the artist is not alienated from society but united with it in his use of rhyme and choice of themes. His defense of rhyme is that it restricts the thought of a good poet and thereby "often lifts and encreases the vehemence of every sentiment" (I, 318). Rhyme itself is a social and aesthetic convention whereby right feeling is rationally controlled and correctness measured. When in 1770 Goldsmith's *Life of Parnell* appeared, he reiterated almost identically his critical position of 1759. As in the *Enquiry* Goldsmith used the great poets of the past to indict his contemporaries, so in the *Life* Parnell is the measure used to judge current poetic abuses. While modern poets, Goldsmith complains, heap "up splendid images without any selection," restore "antiquated words and phrases," indulge in "the most licentious transpositions, and the harshest constructions," and adopt "a language of their own," Parnell was a "studious and correct observer of antiquity," who set himself to "consider nature with the lights it lent him," who was "ever happy" in "the selection of his images," and in "the choice of his subjects," who considered "the language of poetry as the language of life," and who conveyed "the warmest thoughts in the simplest expression" (III, 422–23). Over the brief span of his creative career, Goldsmith's critical views did not change from his original position in the *Enquiry*. Not a complaint and not a learned treatise, *An Enquiry into the Present State of Polite Learning in Europe* is still one of the last highly stylized, tough-minded Augustan pleas for a moral view of art in which right reason will prevail, for an organic literary culture in which tradition and originality will be in harmony, and for artists and critics who will reconcile through their creative work a universal ethical view of human nature with the particular and unique manners of the country in which they live.

Chapter Two

THE CRAFT OF PERSUASION

The Adornment of Prose

Johnson said it all in Goldsmith's epitaph: "OLIVARII GOLDSMITH, / *Poetae, Physici, Historici, / Qui nullum fere scribendi genus, / Non tetigit, / Nullum quod tetigit non ornavit*" (Oliver Goldsmith, Poet, Naturalist, Historian; who touched almost every kind of writing, and touched none that he did not adorn). There has never been any doubt about Goldsmith's prose achievement. Even Mrs. Thrale, who presents such a prejudiced account of his character, recognized the effectiveness of his style: "I have heard Mr. Evans observe that all which Dr. Johnson says in his last page concerning Addison's Prose—would if reversed, form an exact description of his own: this Remark is acute, if the Observation is not accurate, I would add that the Praises given to Addison would suit Goldsmith whom however he does not resemble: Johnson's Panegyrick on Goldsmith is notwithstanding both pointed in Expression, and perfect in Description—In *His* Works I think is found at last, the true Standard of English Prose." [1] Prior makes the same analogy between Addison and Goldsmith by placing them both in the rhetorical category of the middle style: "Three natives of Ireland, and the circumstance is not unworthy of remark, stand nearly, if not

[1] *Thraliana*, II, 621–22.

quite, at the head of our prose literature as regards their styles, though each as different in manner as he was in genius; these are Swift in what is called the plain style, Goldsmith in the middle or more elegant style, and Burke in that of the higher order of eloquence. . . . the claims of Goldsmith to take rank as one of the first, if not the very first of the elegant writers of our country, must not be passed unnoticed." [2] If Addison's English has more "purity" than Goldsmith's, Goldsmith, according to Prior, "has equal ease, greater perspicuity, more variety, and more strength." [3] Middle style is primarily a mean between extremes, between ornate diction on the one hand and referential diction on the other, between a writer's idiom that calls attention to itself and another idiom that is hardly recognized as an idiom. The difficulty of such a style is that it tends to defy definition and is almost synonymous with what some would call a "natural style" (a contradiction in terms). Whereas Johnson's prose style is highly individualistic so that personal imprint can be and has been successfully defined, Goldsmith's prose, except for his tendency to repeat certain phrases throughout his works, gives the appearance of being highly conventional. There is, however, great virtue in Goldsmith's style, and the point of view expressed by the late Edward Sapir would justify Mrs. Thrale's conviction that Goldsmith had achieved "the true Standard of English Prose." Sapir believes that the major characteristics of style "are given in the language itself" and that "a truly great style" cannot "seriously oppose itself to the basic form patterns of the language." From his point of view Sapir considers Carlylese as not a style but "a Teutonic mannerism" and Milton's prose as "semi-Latin done into magnificent English words." "It is strange," Sapir observes, "how long it has

[2] Prior, *Life of Goldsmith*, II, 556.
[3] *Ibid.*

[41]

taken the European literatures to learn that style is not an absolute, a something that is to be imposed on the language from Greek or Latin models, but merely the language itself, running in its natural grooves, and with enough of an individual accent to allow the artist's personality to be felt as a presence, not as an acrobat." [4] Sapir's concept of a true prose style is not, of course, definitive: many critics could point to the virtues of a language that can successfully incorporate a Latinate style and a Teutonic style—styles not easily imitated but certainly functional to the individual writers to whom they belong. What is of the greatest importance, however, is that Sapir's criteria of a genuine prose style, "ease and economy," are precisely the characteristics of Goldsmith's style.

Still, ease and economy are hardly sufficient to explain adequately the nature of Goldsmith's prose. One theory of modern stylistics, based on the analysis of a writer's choices measured by the total possible number of alternatives available to the writer, suggests that before one can define an individual writer's personal idiom, one needs to know the possible variations in the total linguistic system in which the idiom occurs. [5] Such knowledge is at present difficult, if not impossible. Fortunately, there is another method whereby one can measure Goldsmith's choices. A few of his borrowings from *English* sources reveal variations within the sentence that give us genuine insights into the nature of his prose. The most significant passages occur in Goldsmith's *Life of St. John, Lord Viscount Bolingbroke*, the biography being for the most part plagiarized or adapted from the biography of Bolingbroke in *Biographia Britannica: or, the lives of the most eminent*

[4] *Language* (New York, 1949), pp. 226–27.
[5] See Stephen Ullmann, *Style in the French Novel* (Cambridge, 1957), pp. 1–39.

persons who have flourished in Great Britain and Ireland,
Volume V (London, 1760). Goldsmith's indebtedness to
this source, first accurately assessed by Arthur Friedman,
was considerable; and yet his stylistic variations reveal
his creative artistry, which can be measured by placing
Goldsmith's text and the text of his source side by side:[6]

Goldsmith	Biographia Britannica
. . . he accordingly pitched upon a seat of lord TANKER-VILLE's, at Dawley, near Uxbridge in Middlesex, where he settled with his lady, and laid himself out to enjoy the rural pleasures in perfection, since the more glorious ones of ambition were denied him. With his resolution he began to improve his new purchase in a very peculiar style, giving it all the air of a country farm, and adorning even his hall with all the implements of husbandry.	. . . he pitched upon a seat of Lord Tankerville's, at Dawley near Uxbridge in Middlesex, where he settled with his lady, and indulged the pleasure of gratifying the politeness of his taste, by improving it into a most elegant villa, finely picturesque of the present state of his fortune, and there amused himself with rural employments.
(III, 464.)	(V, 3575.)

Although Goldsmith expands his source, it is instructive to
perceive his preference for the shorter sentence. Whereas
Goldsmith's passage contains seventy-seven words as con-
trasted to the fifty-five-word sentence of his source, the
seventy-seven words are broken into sentences of forty-
two and thirty-five words. The addition of "accordingly"

[6] All of the passages herewith quoted in my text from the *Biographia*
were originally cited by Friedman to show Goldsmith's indebtedness,
not to illustrate the characteristics of his style. See "Goldsmith's Life
of Bolingbroke and the *Biographia Britannica*," *Modern Language
Notes*, L (1935), 25–29.

to the first sentence adds to the continuity of the entire passage by looking back to the preceding sentence and by establishing a cause and effect sequence. That Goldsmith here is far from artless is to be seen in the ending of the first sentence, which consists of a perfect antithesis that points the sentence and that is both comic and illuminating, showing Bolingbroke's political ambitions to be still very strong in spite of his long exile in France. This in turn adds to the humor of the second sentence by showing that Bolingbroke's rustic interior decoration was itself a stroke of self-conscious irony. The second sentence is more concrete than its source, and it is characteristic of Goldsmith's "natural" style that he prefers the short, concrete, and more vivid "country farm" to the more formal, Latinate, and fastidious "elegant villa." The total effect of his variations is to endow the passage with more color and with a comic tone completely lacking in the source.

Goldsmith's effect of verbal ease in writing is demonstrated in these passages:

Goldsmith	*Biographia Britannica*
We have a sketch of his way of living in this retreat, in a letter of POPE's to SWIFT, who omits no opportunity of representing his lordship in the most amiable points of view.	We have a sketch of his Lordship's way of life at this retreat, in a letter to Dr. Swift by Mr. Pope, who omits no opportunity of representing his Lordship in the most amiable colours.
(III, 464.)	(V, 3575–76.)

By omitting the formal titles "Dr." and "Mr." Goldsmith makes the passage more personal and less formal; by omitting the first "Lordship" he also avoids the redundancy of the source, in which "Lordship" is repeated toward the end of the sentence. The most characteristic variation is the change in word order from "a letter to Dr. Swift by

Mr. Pope" to "a letter of POPE's to SWIFT." The word order of Goldsmith's passage reflects functionally the actual transmission of the letter in time and space from the letter-writer to the recipient. There is no better example in all of Goldsmith's prose to demonstrate what we mean by his ease in writing and his "natural" style, which when compared with the source is seen to be far from natural. One could justify the source by asserting that "Pope" must follow "Swift" in order to avoid ambiguity in the following relative clause by showing that "who" refers to Pope and not to Swift. But in the over-all context there is no real ambiguity since a passage in Pope's letter is quoted both in the source and in Goldsmith's *Life* only one sentence later. A *too close* attention to avoidance of possible grammatical ambiguities within the sentence is characteristic of Goldsmith's source and by contrast explains his effect of verbal ease. John Langhorne accuses Goldsmith of a "false, futile and slovenly style" characterized by an "*utter neglect of grammatical precision and purity.*" [7] By avoiding the picayune grammatical literalism called for by Langhorne and by relying instead on the semantic context of the whole passage, Goldsmith's prose gains considerable freedom and versatility—qualities ideal for ironic nuances.

Another comparison will demonstrate Goldsmith's fondness for compound sentence structure, for an economy of words made possible by parallel structure, and for the Swiftian emphasis on proper words in proper places:

Goldsmith	Biographia Britannica
With the graces of an handsome person, and a face in which dignity was happily blended with sweetness, he had a manner of address	With the graces of a handsome person, in whose aspect dignity was happily tempered with sweetness, he had a manner and ad-

[7] *Monthly Review*, XLIV (1771), 108. Italics mine.

that was very engaging. His vivacity was always awake, his apprehension was quick, his wit refined, and his memory amazing: his subtilty in thinking and reasoning were profound, and all these talents were adorned with an elocution that was irresistible.

(III, 438–39.)

dress that was irresistibly engaging; a sparkling vivacity, a quick apprehension, a piercing wit, were united to a prodigious strength of memory, a peculiar subtlety of thinking and reasoning, and a masterly elocution. . . .

(V, 3560.)

By changing "aspect" to "face" Goldsmith is more specific; by changing "tempered" to "blended" he is more accurate, since there need not be any incongruity between dignity and sweetness such as is implied in "tempered." By changing "manner and address" to "manner of address" Goldsmith reveals his dislike of co-ordinate phrases used carelessly without emphasis. Again he expands his source but uses a shorter sentence. The second sentence not only illustrates his fondness for compound sentence structure but is also artistically superior to the accumulation of adjectives in the source which tend to cancel one another out by overstatement. Goldsmith emphasizes each of the admirable traits of Bolingbroke's character by recasting the adjective-noun construction into the more forceful noun–verb–predicate adjective construction so that by means of parallel structure he is able to leave the verb out of "his wit refined" and "his memory amazing." This construction is more effective than the source in that the adjectives "refined" and "amazing" are now in the more emphatic position of following the nouns they modify. In Goldsmith's passage there is also a pattern of increasing emphasis climaxed by the praise of Bolingbroke's elocution. Whereas "irresistibly" was buried internally in the source, Goldsmith converts it to a predicate adjective and saves it for the most effective position of all for rhetorical stress —the very end of the sentence.

One more example of Goldsmith's stylistic variations is worthy of analysis:

Goldsmith	Brooke's *Natural History*
When a woodpecker, by its natural sagacity, finds out a rotten hollow tree, where there are worms, ant's eggs, or insects, it immediately prepares for its operations. Resting by its strong claws, and leaning on the thick feathers of its tail, it begins to bore with its sharp, strong beak, until it discloses the whole internal habitation. Upon this, either through pleasure at the sight of its prey, or with a desire to alarm the insect colony, it sends forth a loud cry, which throws terror and confusion into the whole insect tribe. They creep hither and thither seeking for safety; while the bird luxuriously feasts upon them at leisure, darting its tongue with unerring certainty, and devouring the whole brood.	When a Wood-pecker, by its natural sagacity, finds out a rotten or hollow tree, where there are worms and other insects, it immediately repairs to it, resting on its strong claws, and leaning on the thick feathers of the tail; after which it bores the tree with its sharp strong beak, which done, he thrusts it into the hole, and sends forth a great cry, with a design to alarm the insects; for after this they creep hither and thither, and the woodpecker darts out its tongue into the bodies of these small animals, and draws them into its mouth to devour them.[8]

[8] Goldsmith, *An History of the Earth, and Animated Nature*, 1st ed., 8 vols. (London, 1763), V, 251; Richard Brookes, *A New and Accurate System of Natural History*, 2d ed., 6 vols. (London, 1772), II, 82. See Winifred Lynskey, "The Scientific Sources of Goldsmith's *Animated Nature*," *Studies in Philology*, XL (1943), 33–57.

Once more Goldsmith expands his source (one sentence of 103 words) while shortening sentence structure to 4 sentences of 27, 30, 36, and 28 words respectively. Once more he shows his dislike for co-ordinate phrases by changing "rotten or hollow tree" to "rotten hollow tree." But the most striking variation is the manner in which Goldsmith endows the woodpecker and the insects with human motivations. The loud cry of the woodpecker can be both for pleasure and to alarm the insect colony; and the insects, terrorized and confused, "seek for safety." Such additions contribute a considerable narrative interest to an otherwise mediocre description of animal life, and this concentration on minute, vivid details explains in part the *liveliness* of Goldsmith's prose. Although more frequently than not he merely borrowed whole pages of material without making any changes, the passages we have discussed are ideal in that they exemplify the characteristics of Goldsmith's style in his original work.

Goldsmith's preference for the shorter sentence and the familiar word indicates that he was writing more in the Augustan prose tradition of Swift, Addison, and Steele than were his contemporaries Johnson and Gibbon—a tradition that stressed readability as a primary virtue. Few will disagree with James Sutherland's thesis that later eighteenth-century prose moved away from an idiomatic prose based on cultured, colloquial discourse to "a more strictly scholarly phraseology and sentence-structure," but not once does he mention Goldsmith's prose, which will not fit into this general trend.[9] In terms of sentence structure Goldsmith possesses a distinctive characteristic among the major writers of the latter half of the century. His main clauses consistently outnumbered his subordi-

[9] "Some Aspects of Eighteenth-Century Prose," in *Essays on the Eighteenth Century Presented to David Nichol Smith* (Oxford, 1945), pp. 94–110.

nate clauses.[10] Such a characteristic has important implications if we are to understand the nature of Goldsmith's artistic technique. In the first place, the preponderance of independent clauses is characteristic of colloquial discourse; that Samuel Johnson talked as he wrote in complex sentence structure is an exception to the rule and a remarkable demonstration of the self-discipline of his intellect. Why such main-clause sentence structure is associated with conversation has been explained very ably by the late H. J. Chaytor: "Early language is inclined to avoid subordinate clauses; the elaboration of the Ciceronian period is but little attempted, for the reason that auditors with acoustic, but with no visualising capacity, are likely to lose the thread of a lengthy sentence, unless it is presented to them in co-ordinate clauses." [11] Ideally suited to oral discourse, Goldsmith's prose is remarkably flexible as it shifts from narrative to exposition to dramatic dialogue. An anecdote often cited to show the reverberance of Johnson's prose is in reality even more illuminating in respect to the expressionism of Goldsmith's:

> Goldsmith, however, was often very fortunate in his witty contests, even when he entered the lists with Johnson himself. Sir Joshua Reynolds was in company with them one day, when Goldsmith said, that he thought he could write a good fable, mentioned the simplicity which that kind of composition requires, and observed, that in most fables the animals introduced seldom talk in character. "For instance, (said he,) the fable of the little fishes, who saw birds fly over their heads, and envying them, petitioned Jupiter to be changed into birds. The skill (continued he,) consists in making them talk like

[10] To say that Goldsmith's style is primarily composed of main clauses is perhaps to labor the obvious. To be sure, many of his sentences are compound-complex, but Goldsmith's independent clauses far outnumber his dependent clauses.

[11] *From Script to Print* (Cambridge, 1950), p. 142.

little fishes." While he indulged himself in this fanciful reverie, he observed Johnson shaking his sides, and laughing. Upon which he smartly proceeded, "Why, Dr. Johnson, this is not so easy as you seem to think; for if you were to make little fishes talk, they would talk like WHALES." [12]

Johnson's complex sentence structure, so inseparably linked to written discourse, would indeed be inappropriate for "little fishes." Adaptability is, then, a distinctive trait of Goldsmith's prose, and this adaptability is partly explained by the correlation between main-clause sentence structure and oral discourse.

Main-clause sentence structure imposes certain restrictions on a writer's use of irony and satire. Though a major syntactical weapon of the prose satirist is the use of the dependent clause to undercut ironically the preceding independent clause, Goldsmith's sequences of main clauses set up a surface-level, fast-reading tempo that will often cause the subordinate ironic clause to be ignored. Because the use of the subordinate clause for irony is somewhat less effective in Goldsmith's main-clause style, more emphasis is placed on verbal irony, on the precise use of pejorative words, and on the repetition of these words at strategically chosen intervals. One of the virtues of Swift's "plain style" in terms of diction is that pejorative words are isolated, and hence stressed, because they are situated in a nonfigurative linguistic environment. It is a device used by Goldsmith, albeit with a considerably weaker effect than when used by Swift. The most obvious example of this is found in *The Good-Natured Man*. The central character, Honeywood, whose gullibility caused by his good nature is an object of satire throughout the play, is arrested by a bailiff, Mr. Twitch, and his follower Flan-

[12] Boswell, *Life*, II, 231.

igan.[13] When Mr. Twitch discovers Honeywood's weakness, he utters certain words which serve as stimuli to incite conditioned responses in a manner analogous to Pavlov's experiments:

Honeywood. Tenderness is a virtue, Mr. Twitch.

Bailiff. Ay, Sir, its a perfect treasure. I love to see a gentleman with a tender heart. I don't know, but I think I have a tender heart myself. If all that I have lost by my heart was put together, it would make a—but no matter for that.

Honeywood. Don't account it lost, Mr. Twitch. The ingratitude of the world can never deprive us of the conscious happiness of having acted with humanity ourselves.

Bailiff. Humanity, Sir, is a jewel. Its better than gold. I love humanity. People may say, that we, in our way, have no humanity; but I'll shew you my humanity this moment. There's my follower here, little Flanigan, with a wife and four children, a guinea or two would be more to him, than twice as much to another. Now, as I can't shew him any humanity myself, I must beg leave you'll do it for me.

Honeywood. I assure you, Mr. Twitch, your's is a most powerful recommendation (*giving money to the follower*).

(V, 46.)

The wordplay on "humanity" relies on the contrasting points of view of Honeywood and Mr. Twitch. Whereas Honeywood always considers humanity in the abstract, Mr. Twitch considers the word itself as a semantic signal to be used for material gain, as shown by his equation of "humanity" with a "jewel" and with "gold." The repetition of abstract words or words with multiple meanings, a device of exaggeration which calls the reader's attention

---

[13] In his little known but, to my mind, definitive discussion of this play, Robert B. Heilman refers to the bailiff's words as a "screaming parody." See "The Sentimentalism of Goldsmith's *Good-Natured Man*," in *Studies for William A. Read* (University, La., 1940), p. 245.

to the word, is an important device in Goldsmith's satire that goes hand in hand with his reliance on compound sentence structure. When such repetition takes place, as in the concluding portion of *The Vicar of Wakefield,* it should *not* be cavalierly dismissed as hasty or careless writing.

Skillful variation of sentence rhythms and sentence length is another characteristic of Goldsmith's prose. The first four paragraphs of "A City Night Piece" will repay a careful analysis.

> *Ille dolet vere qui sine teste dolet.* MART.

The clock has struck two, the expiring taper rises and sinks in the socket, the watchman forgets the hour in slumber, the laborious and the happy are at rest, and nothing now wakes but guilt, revelry and despair. The drunkard once more fills the destroying bowl, the robber walks his midnight round, and the suicide lifts his guilty arm against his own sacred person.

Let me no longer waste the night over the page of antiquity, or the sallies of cotemporary genius, but pursue the solitary walk, where vanity, ever changing, but a few hours past, walked before me, where she kept up the pageant, and now, like a froward child, seems hushed with her own importunities.

What a gloom hangs all around! the dying lamp feebly emits a yellow gleam, no sound is heard but of the chiming clock, or the distant watch-dog. All the bustle of human pride is forgotten, and this hour may well display the emptiness of human vanity.

There may come a time when this temporary solitude may be made continual, and the city itself, like its inhabitants, fade away, and leave a desart in its room.

(I, 430–31.)

The opening paragraph consists of two sentences and eight independent clauses, and has an aphoristic rhythm functional to the situation in which the essay is set. The narrator of the essay has apparently just completed a reading of an epigram by Martial, the last line of which sets the mood for the essay: "He truly sorrows who sorrows unseen." [14] He is then still thinking in the epigrammatic rhythms of Martial while reflecting on the lateness of the hour. The formal opening is also explained by the fact that most night pieces were poems; by this opening Goldsmith's essay would be immediately recognized as a prose rendering of a poetical genre.[15] In the second paragraph there is one long complex sentence in which the narrator alludes to himself in the first person and resolves to take a walk. The third paragraph shifts back to the compound sentence structure and to the aphoristic rhythm. Each aspect of the night is presented in a disjunctive manner so that the isolation of the walking narrator is paralleled by the relative isolation of each clause.[16] The fourth paragraph goes back to the single complex sentence and to the narrator's reflections on the vanity of human wishes. The two kinds of sentence structure are then merged throughout the rest of the essay after having served the function of presenting a vivid, colorful introduction. These first four paragraphs of "A City Night Piece" are also outstanding examples of Goldsmith's remarkable skill at paragraphing and bear out Sir Herbert Read's contention that the controlling unit of prose rhythm is not so much the sentence as the paragraph.[17]

[14] Martial *Epigrams* i. 33 (ed. Walter C. A. Ker, Loeb Classical Library, 2 vols.; London, 1919), I, 48–49.
[15] Compare, for example, the opening lines of Parnell's "A Night-Piece on Death," the poem that Austin Dobson believes "obviously suggested" Goldsmith's title to him. *Life of Oliver Goldsmith* (London, 1888), p. 70.
[16] I find the two opening stanzas of T. S. Eliot's "Rhapsody on a Windy Night" curiously reminiscent of these opening paragraphs of "A City Night Piece."
[17] As Herbert Read has observed, "A sentence must be isolated to stand secure in its rhythm, and this is one of the requisites of an aphorism—that it is complete in its own rhythm." *English Prose Style* (Boston, 1955), p. 48.

"A City Night Piece" is one of Goldsmith's most often anthologized essays, and an examination of its structure will throw further light on his artistic techniques. Ultimately, great prose depends not merely on the smaller units of diction, sentence structure, and paragraphing, but also on how well these units function in the total context in which they occur. Indeed, when we examine this essay as it first appeared in the *Bee*, we are struck with its apparently abrupt ending and its apparently loose structure. On a first reading, the thesis of the essay appears to be presented in the sixth paragraph, suggesting the causes for the decline of the great cities of the past: "They are fallen, for luxury and avarice first made them feeble. The rewards of state were conferred on amusing, and not on useful members of society. Thus true virtue languished, their riches and opulence invited the plunderer, who, though once repulsed, returned again, and at last swept the defendants into undistinguished destruction" (I, 431–32). "A City Night Piece" appears to be an attack on avarice and makes an appeal to the emotions in its description of the victims of avarice and luxury in paragraphs eight, nine, and ten. The effect of pathos is strengthened by the emotional plight of the narrator, who suffers because he is himself too poverty-stricken to give aid. It is here, however, that the essay begins to sound insincere, that the pathos reminds one of a Simon Legree melodrama. The narrator deplores the plight of these "poor shivering females" who have been "flattered into beauty," "prostituted to the gay luxurious villain," and "turned out to meet the severity of winter in the streets." Paul Fussell has complained of Gray's *Ode on a Distant Prospect of Eton College* that its image of ambush, in contrast to Johnson's similar image, is "theatrical and unconvincing," with "spatterings of exclamation points" that "seem to betray" Gray's "artistic discomfort and to confess that something

has failed badly." [18] The same criticism may be applied
to the conclusion of "A City Night Piece," in which the
narrator tells the world that his heart is formed with "so
much sensibility." John Forster uses this essay to conjecture that, like the narrator, Goldsmith was a "kindhearted
man" who "would wander through the streets at night,
to console and reassure the misery he could not otherwise give help to." [19] Such a biographical interpretation of
the essay would seem to vindicate the traditional portrayal
of a benevolent, smiling-through-tears Goldsmith. A rhetorical analysis of the conclusion, however, will show that
particular attention is paid to the plight of prostitutes and
that the last paragraph condemns the hypocritical liber-
tine:

> But let me turn from a scene of such distress to the
> sanctified hypocrite, *who has been talking of virtue till
> the time of bed,* and now steals out, to give a loose to
> his vices under the protection of midnight; vices more
> attrocious, because he attempts to conceal them. See how
> he pants down the dark alley, and, with hastening steps,
> fears an acquaintance in every face. He has passed the
> whole day in company he hates, and now goes to prolong
> the night among company that as heartily hate him. May
> his vices be detected; may the morning rise upon his
> shame: yet I wish to no purpose; villainy, when detected,
> never gives up, but boldly adds impudence to imposture.
>
> (I, 432–33.)

This last paragraph also appears to contribute to the seemingly loose structure of the essay, and perhaps this is why
Goldsmith omitted it when "A City Night Piece" was reprinted in *The Citizen of the World.* But this paragraph
can be best understood as a rhetorical device designed to

[18] Paul Fussell, *The Rhetorical World of Augustan Humanism* (New
York, 1965), p. 153.
[19] *The Life and Times of Oliver Goldsmith,* 2 vols. (London, 1854),
I, 213–14.

avoid overdoing the appeal to pity by appealing to indignation, thereby inciting the reader to constructive action.[20] The narrator's shift from pity to an attitude of extreme indignation is designed to convince the reader of the validity of the narrator's case and of the personal sincerity and moral goodness of the narrator himself.

What is the narrator's case? "A City Night Piece" goes beyond an attack on avarice and luxury and beyond an attack on the hypocrisy of society. The particular emphasis on prostitutes can only lead a reader familiar with eighteenth-century periodicals to suspect that in a clever and oblique manner Goldsmith was writing a piece of propaganda for a very worthwhile cause—the recently founded Magdalen Hospital for Reformed Prostitutes. When the narrator refers to "poor, houseless creatures," eighteenth-century readers would immediately think of the Magdalen Hospital. Why Goldsmith was using such an oblique approach is explained by two stories which appeared on the front page of the *Public Ledger* in March, 1760, both purportedly written by "a Grateful Magdalen," both presenting the life history of a prostitute finally redeemed by Magdalen Hospital, and both having the obvious appearance of propaganda designed to gain public support for the charity—and money.[21] Although the eighteenth-cen-

[20] In the *Institutio Oratoria* Quintilian observes that "appeals to pity should, however, always be brief, and there is good reason for the saying that nothing dries so quickly as tears." *Institutio Oratoria* vi. 1. 27 (ed. and trans. H. E. Butler, Loeb Classical Library, 4 vols.; London, 1921), II, 400. In its classical sense *pathos* refers to emotion, and it may appeal not only to pity, therefore, but to anger, dislike, fear, and hatred as well. See the *Institutio*, II, 429 (vi. 2. 20).

[21] *Public Ledger*, I (Mar. 19, 1760), 229; I (Mar. 29, 1760), 264. The second story occupied almost the entire front page, rather unusual for this periodical, in that most of the major stories, including Goldsmith's "Chinese Letters," rarely occupied more than two columns of print. Another propaganda piece disguised as a narrative for the Magdalen Hospital charity and entitled "A Letter from Mr. J. W. Lieutenant in ———'s Regiment, to his Brother in Cornwall" had appeared earlier in the *British Magazine*, I (1760), 26–30. For an interesting account of

tury is usually thought of as an age of benevolence, there was considerable opposition against the founding of Magdalen Hospital (August 19, 1758); it was therefore strategic that commercials be written in order to enlist public support.[22] Instead of using "A City Night Piece" as a *source* for biography, we discover that an examination of the *Public Ledger* explains why the essay ultimately fails: it is intentionally sentimental for the purpose of charity propaganda. Its failure also suggests Goldsmith's fundamental commitment to sense rather than sensibility.

"A City Night Piece" provides an excellent transition between an analysis of Goldsmith's prose rhythms and paragraphing and an analysis of his tone—the attitude which the writer takes toward his material and toward his audience. In the past, we have tended to take Goldsmith's work at face value without allowing for the existence of more complex attitudes. When we consider, however, that Goldsmith was writing for periodicals slanted to readers whose literary tastes may often have differed substantially from his own, we should not be too surprised to discover an oblique approach. It is just such a manner that is to be found in Goldsmith's review of Thomas Gray's *Odes* (1757). From remarks made in *An Enquiry* it is apparent that Goldsmith disliked this genre of poetry intensely. Instead of an outright assault, however, he pre-

the founding of this charity, see Betsy Rodgers, *Cloak of Charity: Studies in Eighteenth-Century Philanthropy* (London, 1949), pp. 42–61.

[22] Objections to a hospital for prostitutes fell under four headings: (1) Those who would seek shelter would only be those women no longer able to live by prostitution. (2) Such an institution might destroy prostitution as a profession, and some form of it should be legally tolerated to avoid worse evils. (3) Such an institution would encourage prostitution by making its consequences not so ruinous. (4) No provision could be made for these reformed women after they would leave the hospital, and they might suffer a relapse into prostitution. See "Some Account of the Magdalen Charity . . . by the Rev. Mr. Wm. Dodd . . . ," *Gentleman's Magazine and Historical Chronicle*, XXIX (1759), 279–80.

fers the pose of the detached, impartial critic, not condemning, but merely offering suggestions.

As this publication seems designed for those who have formed their taste by the models of antiquity, the generality of Readers cannot be supposed adequate Judges of its merit; nor will the Poet, it is presumed, be greatly disappointed if he finds them backward in commending a performance not entirely suited to their apprehensions. We cannot, however, without some regret behold those talents so capable of giving pleasure to all, exerted in efforts that, at best, can amuse only the few; we cannot behold this rising Poet seeking fame among the learned, without hinting to him the same advice that Isocrates used to give his Scholars, *Study the People*.

(I, 112.)

This introductory paragraph is a masterpiece of a pseudo-concessive attitude. Goldsmith immediately undermines Gray by suggesting (not asserting) that the poet is really writing only for the learned and that only the learned will understand and appreciate the odes. There follows a left-handed compliment to Gray's talents, after which the poet is rebuked for violating a fundamental English neoclassical dictum that poetry should be directed to the widest possible audience. There is a clever use of the editorial "we" in the second sentence that would tend to identify the critic with the "generality of readers" or at any rate to assimilate the attitude of the general reader with the point of view of the critic. By then citing Isocrates' dictum, "*Study the People*," and discussing the functionalism of Pindar's odes to the age in which they were written, the critic implies that he is one of those who have formed their taste by the models of antiquity and that even for the learned Gray's odes are inadequate. This oblique criticism is reinforced not by a direct attack upon Gray's odes but by a description of those past experiments with odes

THE CRAFT OF PERSUASION

in English literary history, experiments which for the critic were failures: "But, for us, several unsuccessful experiments seem to prove that the English cannot have Odes in blank Verse; while, on the other hand, a natural imperfection attends those which are composed in irregular rhymes:—the similar sound often recurring where it is not expected, and not being found where it is, creates no small confusion to the Reader,—who, as we have not seldom observed, beginning in all the solemnity of poetic elocution, is by frequent disappointments of the rhyme, at last obliged to drawl out the uncomplying numbers into disagreeable prose" (I, 113). By analogy, Gray's odes are equally unsuccessful. Such oblique criticism is a form of understatement, and it is not accidentally that the critic uses such litotes as "no small confusion to the reader" and "as we have not seldom observed." The ironical tone of pseudoconcession is intensified in the next paragraph:

> It is, by no means, our design to detract from the merit of our Author's present attempt: we would only intimate, that an English Poet,—one whom the Muse has *mark'd for her own,* could produce a more luxuriant bloom of flowers, by cultivating such as are natives of the soil, than by endeavouring to force the exotics of another climate: or, to speak without a metaphor, such a genius as Mr. Gray might give greater pleasure, and acquire a larger portion of fame, if, instead of being an imitator, he did justice to his talents, and ventured to be more an original.[23]

(I, 113–14.)

The assertion that the critic does not mean to detract from the merit of Gray's odes while he goes on to do so is ludicrous deadpan irony. Instead of calling the odes "florid"

---

[23] Friedman notes that the words in italics seem to be meant for, "And Melancholy marked him for her own," in Gray's "Elegy in a Country Church-yard."

(a pejorative word by neoclassical standards), the critic uses an expanded metaphorical statement which is itself a burlesque of floridity. This oblique use of burlesque in lieu of a direct attack is used again in the review when the critic discusses "The Bard": "The circumstances of grief and horror in which the Bard is represented, those of terror in the preparation of the votive web, and the mystic obscurity with which the prophecies are delivered, will give as much pleasure to those who relish this species of composition, as any thing that has hitherto appeared in our language, the Odes of Dryden himself not excepted" (I, 116). "Votive web" parodies such lines in "The Bard" as: "Weave the warp, and weave the woof"; "Weave we the woof. The thread is spun"; and "The web is wove. The work is done." [24] Readers of this review who would not see the sarcasm of "to those who relish this species of composition" would have failed to see the outright rejection of Gray's verse and Goldsmith's oblique irony in expressing these attitudes.

Goldsmith's real underlying attitude toward Gray's *Odes* remained constant. Five years later, in 1762, he could still complain that contemporary poetry was "nothing else but a mosaic of luxurious colours, cemented with a proper quantity of rash and inadequate epithets," and that "English Pindarics now also were made to over-top the obscurity of Pindar" (III, 190). In this same essay he parodies "The Bard" directly: *Perdition seize thee, shameless wight, / O blast thy eye-balls with eternal night; / May all the copper of thy forehead fail, / Thy bacon forehead smok'd in every jail"* (III, 190). Boswell records a discussion of Gray's poems in his first encounter with Goldsmith in 1762. Goldsmith recites another quatrain directly parodying the "rumbling thunder" of Gray's *Odes;*

---

[24] Thomas Gray, *The Poems of Gray and Collins,* ed. Austin L. Poole (London, 1937), pp. 58, 59, ll. 49, 98, 100.

Boswell replies that he admires Gray "prodigiously" and has read his odes until he "was almost mad"; Goldsmith complains that the odes are "terribly obscure" and require that readers be "historians and learned men" in order to understand them; Thomas Davies brings the argument to a close when he counters with, "And why not? He is not writing to porters or carmen. He is writing to men of knowledge." [25] (Needless to say, whenever he writes of Goldsmith, Boswell usually has the last word.)

It is distinctive of Goldsmith's prose style, when he is writing in his own voice, that he avoids direct assertions wherever possible, saving them for major emphasis, or that he surrounds such assertions with concessive qualifications. Goldsmith prefers in place of the outright assertion or direct imperative the use of the verb "let" as a weak imperative or a mild volitive. He also prefers in place of the assertion or statement of fact the use of "may" as a potential subjunctive. Not that Goldsmith doubts the validity of his assertions, but rather that he strives for the concessive attitude toward his reader as a valuable device for persuasion. [26] It is this attitude toward his readers that explains the frequent use of "seems" instead of "is" and the frequent use of such adverbial qualifiers as "perhaps" and "probably." All of these verbal and syntactic mannerisms characterizing Goldsmith's concessive attitude can be demonstrated by two passages from *An Enquiry into the Present State of Polite Learning in Europe,* with the relevant words placed in italics.

> As in the best regulated societies, the very laws which at first give the government solidity, *may* in the end con-

[25] James Boswell, *London Journal, 1762–63,* ed. Frederick A. Pottle (London, 1950), pp. 105–6.
[26] Stronger alternatives in place of *let* would be *must, have to,* or the direct imperative form. See George O. Curme, *Syntax* (Boston, 1931), pp. 393–94. For the use of *may* as the potential subjunctive, see *ibid.,* p. 391.

tribute to its dissolution, so the efforts which *might* have promoted learning in its feeble commencement *may, if* continued, retard its progress. The paths of science which were at first intricate because untrodden, may at last grow toilsome because too much frequented. As learning advances, the candidates for its honours *may* become more numerous, and the acquisition of fame more uncertain; the modest *may* despair of attaining it, and the opulent think it too precarious to pursue; thus the task of supporting the honour of the times *may* at last devolve on indigence and effrontery, and learning partake the contempt of its professors.

(I, 260.)

Not only is "may" used instead of a stronger form, but it is also the primary means of achieving parallel structure:

Common sense *would be apt to suggest,* that the art *might* be studied to more advantage, rather by imitation than precept. *It might suggest,* that those rules were collected, not from nature, but a copy of nature, and would consequently give us still fainter resemblances of original beauty. *It might* still suggest, that explained wit, makes but a feeble impression, that the observations of others, are soon forgotten, those, made by ourselves, are permanent and useful. But, *it seems,* understandings of every size were to be mechanically instructed in poetry.

(I, 266.)

By personifying "common sense" and making it the subject of the first sentence, Goldsmith very cleverly makes value judgments without appearing to be personally involved. If one were to encircle every word and phrase of *An Enquiry* that contributes to the concessive and pseudoconcessive tone of the work, a remarkably consistent pattern would emerge that would explain in large part the amiability which has generally been considered to be a major characteristic of Goldsmith's work.[27] Whether he is writing serious exposition or subtle satire, Goldsmith concedes whenever possible—in exposition as an aid to persuasion and in satire as a means of irony enabling him to express private attitudes under the guise of catering to public taste.

While recognizing his amiability, one must avoid viewing Goldsmith as a mere amuser. In his review of the *Connoisseur* in 1757, Goldsmith praises the writer for being "the *Friend* of Society," for conversing rather than dictating, for being "perfectly satyrical, yet perfectly good-natured," and for having the "solidity to please the grave, and humour and wit to allure the gay . . ." (I, 14). There need be no contradiction between the amiable attitude toward one's fellow man and the belief that the writer is also a moral reformer. As Goldsmith wrote in the *Enquiry*, "new fashions, follies, and vices, make new monitors necessary in every age," and the author "may be considered as a merciful substitute to the legislature" (I, 314–15). Amiable satire can attack the foible or affectation and yet forgive the offender; hate the sin and yet forgive the sinner. Goldsmith's own words may seem to distinguish his humor from the more corrosive kind that we associate with Juvenal and Swift. Nonetheless, he still retains the word "satyrical," and unless we understand the moral function of many of his character creations as criticisms of the affectations of his age, we shall fail to

---

[27] This approach is based on Leo Spitzer's "philological circle" as summarized by Stephen Ullmann: "The philological circle is an operation with three distinct phases. In the first phase, the student will merely read and reread the text and allow it to act on him until he is struck by some persistently recurrent peculiarity: a type of imagery, a syntactical construction, a rhythmic pattern or any other feature. Next, he will try to relate this stylistic trait to some element in the author's psyche. In the third phase, he will make the return journey from the centre to the periphery and will look for further manifestations, linguistic or otherwise, of the same mental feature." See his *Style in the French Novel*, p. 27.

understand his true artistry and shall continue to label him merely an amuser and entertainer with very little relevance for the modern reader.

As a prose stylist Goldsmith was not unappreciated in his own lifetime. As early as 1762, William Rider praised him for having "happily found out the Secret to unite Elevation with Ease, a Perfection in Language, which few Writers of our Nation have attained to, as most of those who aim at Sublimity swell their Expressions with Fustian and Bombast, whilst those who affect Ease, degenerate into Familiarity and Flatness." [28] And, it is natural that Goldsmith's prose style is often compared to Samuel Johnson's. Such a comparison has been overstated, I think, by Chauncey Tinker:

> Consider, in particular, Johnson's influence upon Goldsmith. Who can doubt that the style of Doctor Minor, superior as it is to that of Doctor Major, would yet have been a very different thing if Goldsmith had never read the *Rambler?* Both Boswell and Dr. Warton noted the influence of Johnson upon Goldsmith's conversation, particularly in his attempt to employ difficult words, but they might have discovered even subtler evidences of it in his writings. The particular power of Johnson that Goldsmith longed for was the older man's ability to sum up a whole department of things in one telling sentence. It was a power that Goldsmith never attained, but his attempts were numerous. Hear, for example, the voice of Johnson speaking through these words of Goldsmith at the opening of the latter's *Life of Nash*: "History owes its excellence more to the writer's manner than to the materials of which it is composed," or this from the *Life of Voltaire*, "That life which has been wholly employed in the study is properly seen only in the author's writings; there is no variety to entertain, nor adventure to interest us in the calm suc-

[28] *Historical and Critical Account of the Lives and Writings of the Living Authors of Great Britain* (London, 1762), p. 14.

cession of such ancedotes." It is only an echo, to be sure, but we know whence issued the original sound.[29]

Tinker's assertion cannot be substantiated. We now know that the examples which he cites represent not Goldsmith imitating Johnson's style, but rather Goldsmith borrowing outright Johnson's theory of biography.[30] Nor were long, involved periodic sentences necessarily equated entirely with Samuel Johnson, as Wimsatt has pointed out.[31] In fact, on the one occasion when Goldsmith was consciously trying to imitate Johnson's prose style, he was so successful that even Boswell was fooled, as he testifies in his *Life of Johnson*:

> On Saturday, April 3, the day after my arrival in London this year, I went to his house late in the evening, and sat with Mrs. Williams till he came home. I found in the London Chronicle, Dr. Goldsmith's apology to the publick for beating Evans, a bookseller, on account of a paragraph in a news-paper published by him, which Goldsmith thought impertinent to him and to a lady of his acquaintance. The apology was written so much in Dr. Johnson's manner, that both Mrs. Williams and I supposed it to be his; but when he came home, he soon undeceived us. When he said to Mrs. Williams, 'Well, Dr. Goldsmith's *manifesto* has got into your paper;' I asked him if Dr. Goldsmith had written it, with an air that made him see I suspected it was his, though subscribed by Goldsmith. JOHNSON. 'Sir, Dr. Goldsmith would no more have asked me to write such a thing as that for him, than he would have asked me to feed him with a spoon, or to do any thing else that denoted his imbecility. I as much believe that he wrote it, as if I had seen him do it. Sir, had he shewn it to any one

---

[29] *Dr. Johnson and Fanny Burney* (New York, 1911), xxxiii–xxxiv.
[30] See Joseph E. Brown, "Goldsmith and Johnson on Biography," *Modern Language Notes*, XLII (1927), 168–71.
[31] William K. Wimsatt, Jr., *The Prose Style of Samuel Johnson* (New Haven, 1941), pp. 168–71.

friend, he would not have been allowed to publish it. He has, indeed, done it very well; but it is a foolish thing well done.[32]

Goldsmith's idiom was his most original attribute, and the nebulous conjecture that Goldsmith was constantly trying to imitate Johnson and failed is grossly unfair to his creative craft. Such a conjecture obscures the differences between their idioms, and literary history will not be served best by praise of one at the expense of the other. Both men wrote prose functional to their needs, each prose idiom having its own aesthetic value. The proper attitude was stated unforgettably by Johnson himself when once he was asked to judge whether the plain style of Swift or a more eloquent style was better: "'Sir, you must define what you mean by style, before you can judge who has a good taste in style, and who has a bad. The two classes of persons whom you have mentioned don't differ as to good and bad. They both agree that Swift has a good neat style; but one loves a neat style, another loves a style of more splendour. In like manner, one loves a plain coat, another loves a laced coat; but neither will deny that each is good in its kind.'"[33]

The Persuasive Strain in Verse

One biographer claims that if Goldsmith "had had full confidence in his convictions and had had the leisure to develop them, he might well have been a leader in the Romantic Revival in English literature."[34] Such a belief demonstrates an untenable adherence to an interpreta-

---

[32] Boswell, *Life,* II, 209–10.
[33] *Ibid.,* 191–92.
[34] Ralph Wardle, *Oliver Goldsmith* (Lawrence, Kan., 1957), p. 296. The *Johnsonian News Letter* objected to Wardle's "constantly looking for Romantic qualities in the principal works" (XVII [October, 1957], 6–7).

tion of Goldsmith as a "pre-Romantic." [35] Such a belief also demonstrates a profound misunderstanding of the rhetorical function of Goldsmith's *The Traveller* and *The Deserted Village*. Implicit in this approach to Goldsmith as a "pre-Romantic" is the assumption that *The Deserted Village* is his best work and and that *The Vicar of Wakefield* is a prose version of the poem. Samuel Johnson, however, preferred *The Traveller*: "Take him as a poet, his 'Traveller' is a very fine performance; ay, and so is his 'Deserted Village', were it not sometimes too much the echo of his 'Traveller.' " [36] If we compare the two poems we can understand Johnson's point of view. Because the two works echo each other, modern critics looking back at Goldsmith through the eyes of nineteenth-century critics tend to read *The Deserted Village* first, so that *The Traveller* appears to be the repetitive poem. It is therefore difficult to recreate the feeling of originality gained from reading *The Traveller* first, which was possible to Johnson's circle before the publication of *The Deserted Village*.

Frederick Hilles sees the poem as "an ideal example of the neoclassic ethic poem" with a "balanced structure" supporting "the statement which the poem as a whole is making": "Its balanced discussion (the friendliness or hostility of nature versus the follies or virtues of the natives) reenforces the theme of moderation." [37] On the other hand, Hilles' praise of balanced structure would seem difficult to reconcile with F. L. Lucas' belief that as political argument *The Traveller* "rambles too much." [38] The poem by no means rambles, however, if we read the

[35] The inadequacy of the term is shown by Bertrand H. Bronson, in "The Pre-Romantic or Post-Augustan Mode," *ELH*, XX (1953), 15–16.
[36] Boswell, *Life*, II, 236.
[37] *The Vicar of Wakefield and Other Writings*, ed. F. W. Hilles (New York, 1955), xxi.
[38] *The Search for Good Sense* (London, 1958), p. 326.

first edition (416 lines) rather than the sixth edition (438 lines). Seventeen of the additional 22 lines in the later editions occur in one verse paragraph attacking freedom (lines 363–80). Coming at a heightened moment in the poem, this passage does not add emotional intensity to the context but instead actually weakens such intensity by unnecessary expansion. When read in the first edition, *The Traveller* does not ramble and possesses more of a poetic structure than *The Deserted Village*. That all of the best-known editions of Goldsmith's collected works and poetry print the later editions of *The Traveller* is another reason critics consider *The Deserted Village* the better poem. The text used for the critical analysis of *The Traveller* in this chapter will therefore be the 416-line first edition—the version which originally established Goldsmith's reputation as a major poet of his day.[39]

It would be difficult to assign *The Traveller* to a particular genre. Hilles refers to it as a "neoclassic ethic poem." Geoffrey Tillotson refers to the poem as "pastoral" and "georgic."[40] Ralph Cohen has brilliantly analyzed the complexities of the "prospect" poem as a primary poetic form of the Augustan mode. If the poetic universe of the prospect poem, in Cohen's words, connects "patriotism with peace, plenty, and property," and provides the "organizing procedure" for a "harmony of particulars," for "recognizing God's presence through his spatial diversity," Goldsmith's poem uses the prospect form to reverse the procedure, to show that the traditional form is no longer supported by an adequate social and political structure.[41] The prospect movement seen by Cohen to

[39] Hilles' Modern Library Edition prints a version of the poem which comes close to the first edition but which contains in brackets some of the best lines Goldsmith added to later editions.

[40] *Essays in Criticism and Research* (Cambridge, 1942), p. 68.

[41] "The Augustan Mode in English Poetry," *Eighteenth-Century Studies,* I (1967), 9–13.

"progress from physical space to infinite space" is reversed in *The Traveller* so that there is ultimately a melancholic retreat back into the individual self. In its melancholy tone *The Traveller,* particularly in the conclusion, shares a likeness with Johnson's *The Vanity of Human Wishes* —a likeness with what Ian Jack has called the "primary rhetorical function of 'diminishing' human life." [42] In dealing with the theme of happiness and in the use of synonyms for happiness repeated as control words, *The Traveller* resembles Epistle IV of Pope's *Essay on Man.* To approach Goldsmith's poem in terms of a genre would be inadequate, for, as George Sherburn remarks, "A poet like Goldsmith, conservative in many of his sympathies, could sit down to write poems like *The Traveller* and *The Deserted Village* without asking himself whether he was writing a Georgic, an elegy, or a pastoral." [43]

The verse paragraph in *The Traveller* (and in *The Deserted Village*) is the basic unit of composition. Goldsmith's tendency to express themes and ideas first in his prose essays and then later to reiterate them in verse would be ideally aided by his reliance on the verse paragraph as the basic unit. Furthermore, by treating a poem as a sequence of paragraphs, a brilliant essayist like Goldsmith would have very little difficulty with over-all structure and transitions, virtues which T. S. Eliot praised so highly in *The Deserted Village.* The central unity of *The Traveller* is found in the narrator of the poem, in the "I" (not to be equated with Goldsmith) who is described objectively in the title. As a philosophical poem *The Traveller* presents certain themes through concrete ex-

[42] *Augustan Satire: Intention and Idiom in English Poetry, 1660–1750* (Oxford, 1952), p. 135. The retreat into self is another variation of the "prospect" convention, as both Jack and Cohen clearly recognize. This retreat is not the same, it seems to me, as that in certain Romantic poems, which involves a profoundly different epistemological transformation.

[43] *A Literary History of England,* p. 973.

amples so that the reader will feel their validity. The emotional mood of the narrator that determines the tone of the poem is an important structural device in directing the feeling and responses of the reader. In other words, the pursuit of happiness which is a major theme of *The Traveller* is rendered complex by an unhappy pursuer narrating his own quest. The attempt to define happiness is traditionally not only philosophical but rhetorical, and we cannot really understand Goldsmith's poetic technique unless we are prepared to analyze *The Traveller* in terms of both a rhetorical and a poetical structure.[44] Goldsmith is not above writing propaganda in his two major poems, and when in *The Deserted Village* "sweet Poetry" is invoked to "Aid slighted truth, with thy persuasive strain" (IV, 303), this definition of poetry is synonymous with the classic definition of rhetoric as the art of persuasion. An increased appreciation of *The Traveller* comes with a better understanding, then, of the art of persuasion as practiced in the poem.[45] This approach not only enables us to understand Goldsmith's artistry but also concentrates on the presentation of theses rather than on value judgments of the theses themselves.

Goldsmith's treatment of the narrator in *The Traveller* is analogous to the rhetorician's treatment of the orator: the personal character of the speaker is an extremely important means of persuasion.[46] The first verse paragraph

[44] In Book One, Chapter Five, of his *Rhetoric*, Aristotle discusses the various definitions of happiness because, in urging his hearers to take or avoid a course of action, the orator must show that he has an eye to their happiness. *Aristotle's Rhetoric and Poetics*, trans. W. Rhys Roberts and Ingram Bywater, introduction by Friedrich Solmsen (New York, 1954), pp. 37–42.

[45] Ronald S. Crane suggests that Aristotle would have been more apt to have dealt with eighteenth-century didactic poetry in terms of rhetoric rather than in terms of his poetic. See *The Languages of Criticism and the Structure of Poetry* (Toronto, 1953), p. 197, n. 57.

[46] Aristotle asserts that a speaker's character "may almost be called the most effective means of persuasion he possesses." See *Aristotle's Rhetoric and Poetics*, p. 25.

is designed to win the reader's pity by portraying the spiritual exhaustion of the traveler:

> Remote, unfriended, melancholy, slow,
> Or by the lazy Scheld, or wandering Po;
> Or onward, where the rude Carinthian boor
> Against the houseless stranger shuts the door;
> Or where Campania's plain forsaken lies,
> A weary waste expanded to the skies.
> Where'er I roam, whatever realms to see,
> My heart untravell'd fondly turns to thee;
> Still to my brother turns, with ceaseless pain,
> And drags at each remove a lengthening chain.
>
> (ll. 1–10)

The sound pattern in conjunction with the reliance on adjectives strikes the dominant tone of the poem at the very beginning. The end rhyme of the first couplet shows Goldsmith's craftsmanship. "Slow" not only suggests a slow manner of walking *and* the "sluggishness of mind which comes upon a man in solitude," but by rhyming with "Po" it tends to modify the noun, while linking the name of the river to the narrator through its syntactical and adjectival modifying of "I" in line seven. In turn "lazy" and "wandering," when applied to rivers, personify these rivers by endowing them with human traits. The over-all effect is to portray the internal spiritual weariness of the narrator by associating it with the external pictorial image of the rivers. The slow rhythm of the paragraph is achieved by the heavy use of word repetition ("or" and "where"), repetition of initial consonants (*w,c*), consonance (*r*), and the repetition of sonorous back vowels in stressed positions lengthened by the following continuant consonants, Syntactically, the slow rhythm is created by the piling up of adjectives, co-ordinate phrases, and co-ordinate clauses before the main clause is sprung in line eight. These excesses of sound and syntax contribute to the initial impression that the narrator will make of a weary wanderer in a spiritual wasteland. This initial impression is even more important because the spiritual melancholy of the narrator remains static throughout the poem. By winning the reader's pity and sympathy at the beginning of the poem, the narrator can get a sympathetic hearing for the controversial ideas he will express later in the poem.

In abrupt contrast to the personal plight of the narrator, we are presented in the second verse paragraph with:

> Eternal blessings *crown* my earliest friend,
> And *round* his dwelling guardian saints attend;
> Blest be that spot, where chearful guests retire
> To pause from toil, and trim their evening fire;
> Blest that abode, where want and pain repair,
> And every stranger finds a ready chair;
> Blest be those feasts where mirth and peace abound,
> Where all the ruddy family *around*
> Laugh at the jests or pranks that never fail,
> Or sigh with pity at some mournful tale,
> Or press the bashful stranger to his food,
> And learn the luxury of doing good.
>
> (ll. 11–22)

The use of religious diction—"eternal blessings," "guardian saints," and "blest"—endows this circle of domestic felicity with an aura of virtue, and the narrator's use of such diction reveals that he is a virtuous man.[47] The center of this family circle, the narrator's "earliest friend," is comparable to the monarch of a country. "Round" and "around" are extremely important in this paragraph:

---

[47] According to Aristotle, the three traits that inspire confidence in the orator's own character are good sense, good moral character, and good will. See *Aristotle's Rhetoric and Poetics*, p. 91. These attributes of the narrator's character in *The Traveller* are implied by what he praises in others.

"round" is stressed by the internal rhyme with "crown,"
and "around" is stressed by the end rhyme with "abound."
Throughout the poem these prepositions are used at strategic positions as control words to define parallel circles
of spiritual cohesion—in the domestic domain (home and
family), in the national domain (the middle class and a
benevolent monarch), and in the domain of the individual
human soul. These parallel circles of spiritual cohesion
reflect the thesis of centripetal spiritual force as the prime
value, and it is this thesis which constitutes the genuine
poetic structure of *The Traveller*. Also of extreme importance in the second verse paragraph is the repetition of
"blest," with the added syntactical stress of parallel structure. The four synonyms for *felicity* listed in Johnson's
Dictionary are "happiness," "prosperity," "blissfulness,"
and "blessedness." All of these synonyms share one sound
in common, the unvoiced fricative consonant (s); and by
repeating these synonyms for felicity frequently throughout the poem, Goldsmith has so conditioned the reader's
responses that the unvoiced fricative sound patterns in
the poem are unconsciously associated with the semantic
verbal pattern dealing with the theme of happiness. This
technique, too, is poetic rather than rhetorical and contributes to the poetical coherence of *The Traveller*. The
technique is found in Epistle IV of Pope's *Essay on Man*,
in which "bliss" is used thirteen times, "blessing" six times,
and "blessed" (or "blest") six times. We may conjecture
that Goldsmith had Pope's poem in mind when he composed *The Traveller*, even to the extent, as we shall see,
of concluding with the same thesis, "That VIRTUE only
makes our Bliss below." [48] The sound pattern is especially
evident in line seventeen: "Ble*st* be those fea*st*s where
mirth and pea*ce* abound."

[48] Alexander Pope, *Essay on Man*, Ep. iv, l. 397, *The Poems of Alexander Pope*, gen. ed. John Butt, The Twickenham Edition, 10 vols.
(London, 1939–67), III, i, 166.

The ideal of domestic bliss presented in the second verse paragraph is linked with virtue not only by the religious diction but by the description of practical benevolence—"the luxury of doing good." The professed intention of *The Traveller*, expressed in the "Dedication," must be kept in mind: "I have endeavoured to shew, that there may be equal happiness in other states, though differently governed from our own; that each state has a peculiar principle of happiness, and that this principle in each state, and in our own in particular, may be carried to a mischievous excess" (p. iv). It is an ironic comment on the world outside this center of domestic cohesion that the only excess within is the "luxury of doing good." This is obviously *not* a "mischievous excess" and is the only principle of happiness presented in the poem in which there is no real excess. By its position in the poem the second verse paragraph presents an ideal embodiment of happiness by which the reader can evaluate other states of happiness.

The next verse paragraph returns to the narrator-traveler's personal pursuit of happiness:

> But me, not destin'd such delights to share,
> My prime of life in wand'ring spent and care:
> Impell'd with steps, unceasing to pursue
> Some fleeting good, that mocks me with the view;
> That, like the *circle* bounding earth and skies,
> Allures from far, yet, as I follow, flies;
> My fortune leads to traverse realms alone,
> And find no spot of all the world my own.
>   (ll. 23–30)

What is the "fleeting good" pursued by the traveler? It is the pursuit of happiness, as we learn later from lines 59–60: "And oft I wish, amidst the scene, to find / Some spot to real happiness consign'd." In one of the most important metaphors in the poem, happiness as an abstraction is compared to the ever expanding horizon, and the narrator becomes the victim of his own mental mirages— the victim of centrifugal force that threatens at worst spiritual disintegration and at best spiritual exhaustion. The ultimate isolation of the traveler after his pursuit is summed up perfectly in the end rhymes of the paragraph: "share: care; pursue: view; skies: flies; alone: own."

In the next verse paragraph (lines 31–36) the narrator meditates on top of a mountain in the Alps. The panoramic physical view inspires him to reflect on the universal spiritual view of mankind, and his position, "plac'd on high above the storm's career," serves the rhetorical function of making the narrator appear to be detached and thus impartial. Perhaps the central device of persuasion in *The Traveller* is the increasing emotional involvement of the narrator with his meditation, parallel to the change of setting as it shifts northward to Britain. Thus, if the reader at the beginning of the poem is sympathetic to the seemingly detached and impartial traveler, later the reader will become unconsciously more sympathetic to the narrator's argument and more likely to accept his thesis. To the traveler taking a universal view of mankind, "The pomp of kings, the shepherd's humbler pride" (l. 36) are of equal value: "And wiser he, whose sympathetic mind / Exults in all the good of all mankind" (ll. 43–44).

Then follows what appears to be a conventional apostrophe:

> Ye glittering towns, with wealth and splendour crown'd,
> Ye fields, where summer spreads profusion round,
> Ye lakes, whose vessels catch the busy gale,
> Ye bending swains, that dress the flow'ry vale,
> For me your tributary stores combine;
> Creation's heir, the world, the world is mine.
>
> (ll. 45–50)

Austin Dobson believed that both *The Traveller* and *The Deserted Village* were jeopardized as great poetry because of their diction, which to Dobson represented a compromise between the direct, plain diction of Wordsworth and the "gradus epithet" of Pope.[49] The use of the archaic vocative "Ye" with such stock epithets as "bending swains" and "flow'ry vale" would appear to bear out Dobson's contention. In spite of the Virgilian connotations that many of these words had for eighteenth-century readers, this passage would appear stilted—stilted, however, because Goldsmith meant it to be so. Lines 45–50 are not a continuation of the narrator's discourse directed to the reader, but represent rather a poem within a poem whereby the narrator expresses his "sympathetic mind" exulting as he temporarily ceases to "repine." But what happens to this exultation in the next verse paragraph? The tone shifts back to a melancholy realization of the here and now, back to reality. The artificial diction of the short poem within the poem reflects the artificial nature of the exultation of the narrator; conversely, the diction in the rest of the poem seems even more natural by comparison.

The foreshadowing of an indictment of laissez faire political economy is presented in the hoarding miser simile of the next verse paragraph:

> As some lone miser visiting his store,
> Bends at his treasure, counts, recounts it o'er;
> Hoards after hoards his rising raptures fill,
> Yet still he sighs, for hoards are wanting still:
> (ll. 51–54)

"Hoards" would undoubtedly have economic connotations for the many eighteenth-century intellectuals who were well read in the literature of political economy. Jacob

[49] *Miscellanies* (New York, 1898), p. 32.

Viner cites Malachy Postlethwayt, who in his *Great-Britain's True System* (1757) attacks hoarding not only because it is immoral by Christian standards but also because it is detrimental to trade:

> Postlethwayt, in a curious argument, claimed that lending of money at interest involved hoarding, and therefore on circulation grounds was to be condemned. If some money is hoarded, the volume of trade will fall. In order to bring the hoarded money back into trade, those in great need of it will offer interest ("profit") for its loan. The result will be that other monied men, instead of "circulating their money" in trade, will "lock it up," while awaiting the opportunity to lend it, preferring to get their income by usury instead of by trade. Eventually the money so withdrawn from trade would be lent and would thus return to trade, but bearing an interest charge which would act as a restraint on trade.[50]

Rhetorically the hoarding miser simile subtly conditions the reader by putting him into a frame of mind more favorable to the specific politico-economic thesis presented later in the poem.

The narrator shifts now to the problem of where happiness is to be found geographically, only to discover: "Nor less the patriot's boast, where'er we roam, / His first best country ever is at home" (ll. 73–74). The experienced traveler rejects the parochial view of happiness:

> And yet, perhaps, if states with states we scan,
> Or estimate their bliss on Reason's plan,
> Though patriots flatter, and though fools contend,
> We still shall find uncertainty suspend,
> Find that each good, by Art or Nature given,
> To these or those, but makes the balance even:

[50] Jacob Viner, "English Theories of Foreign Trade Before Adam Smith," *Journal of Political Economy*, XXXVIII (1930), 295.

Find that the bliss of all is much the same,
And patriotic boasting reason's shame.

(ll. 75–82)

The "patriot" allusions can be understood most plausibly
if we accept the theory that Goldsmith wrote *The Traveller* in part as an answer to his contemporary, Charles
Churchill.[51] In his "Dedication" Goldsmith attacks the use
of poetry for partisan purposes:

> Party entirely distorts the judgment, and destroys the
> taste. A mind capable of relishing general beauty, when
> once infected with this disease, can only find pleasure in
> what contributes to encrease the distemper. Like the tyger,
> that seldom desists from pursuing man after having once
> preyed upon human flesh, the reader, who has once grat-
> ified his appetite with calumny, makes, ever after, the
> most agreeable feast upon murdered reputation. Such
> readers generally admire some half-witted thing, who
> wants to be thought a bold man, having lost the character
> of a wise one. Him they dignify with the name of poet; his
> lampoons are called satires, his turbulence is said to be
> force, and his phrenzy fire.
>
> (pp. iii–iv.)

Churchill had enlisted his poetry in support of John Wilkes
as early as January, 1763, in "The Prophecy of Famine,"
and before his death late in 1764 his reputation as a poet
had diminished considerably, largely because of reviews
hostile to his commitment of verse to politics. Churchill's
verse satire offers another explanation for why Johnson,
Goldsmith, and the other great conservative writers of
this period did not write comic verse satire in the tradi-

[51] Ronald S. Crane believes that "one impetus toward the publication
(though not the writing) of the poem was a desire to answer Churchill."
See *A Collection of English Poems 1660–1800*, ed. Ronald S. Crane
(New York, 1932), p. 1245.

tion of Swift and Pope. The radicals working for social and political change had appropriated aggressive verse satire as a weapon for their cause. The conservatives pretended to be above the compromising of poetry for political purposes (they could still use prose and did), and by this pretense they could through reviews deprive the radicals of one of their chief propaganda weapons—verse satire. This strategy explains Goldsmith's scorn of party in the "Dedication" to *The Traveller*, while the actual poem itself does have a conservative political thesis on one level. If any contemporary should attack *The Traveller* as a political poem, the attacker himself would be open to the accusation of corrupting taste by promoting faction and party. For the most part, Goldsmith reserved satire for prose and his poetry for rhetorical persuasion.[52]

The doctrine of compensation presented in lines 75–96 is essentially a doctrine of the golden mean: Nature provides the necessary material for man's survival, but Art sends other blessings: "From Art more various are the blessings sent; / Wealth, splendours, honor, liberty, content: / Yet these each other's power so strong contest, / That either seems destructive of the rest" (ll. 87–90). Concentration on any one of these "blessings" is an excess that "begets peculiar pain," so that consequently "blessing" ironically turns out to be a curse.

Lines 97–102 return to the melancholy mood of the narrator and propose to demonstrate the doctrine of compensation by more concrete examples. Up to this point the narrator-traveler has been uttering general truths in the form of maxims, and it is appropriate that he speaks like an older, experienced man—"My prime of life in

---

[52] The traditional poets were also conscious of Pope's greatness and would hesitate to imitate or compete with him. See Johnson's *Rambler*, no. 86 ("The danger of succeeding a great author . . .").

wand'ring spent and care" (l. 24)—for whom such an expression of maxims is effective rhetorically.[53] The narrator's own inner state is projected into another external image: "Here let me sit in sorrow for mankind, / Like yon neglected shrub, at random cast, / That shades the steep, and sighs at every blast" (ll. 100–2). Though this pathetic fallacy may be bad poetry by twentieth-century standards, rhetorically it reminds the reader again of the tone that the narrator holds toward the argument which he presents.

The structural pattern in presenting the concrete examples (the various nations) has been described by Hilles: (1) the state of external nature, i.e., environment; (2) the particular "blessing" of the nation; and (3) the excess or vice that results from exclusive concentration on that "blessing." As we have seen earlier, Goldsmith was fully aware of the importance of environment in influencing culture.[54] The state of Nature in Italy is extraordinarily suitable for man—Nature is in fact luxurious. Goldsmith's poetic diction in lines 109–20 is functionally Virgilian, and his use of heavy alliteration and consonance reinforces the semantic theme of the luxury of Nature.[55] This luxury of Nature leads to sensuality ("sensual bliss is all this nation knows" [l. 122]), and sensuality in turn leads to extremes in the "blessing" of Art:

[53] Aristotle writes: "The use of Maxims is appropriate only to elderly men. . . ." He also observes: "There is moral character in every speech in which the moral purpose is conspicuous: and maxims always produce this effect, because the utterance of them amounts to a general declaration of moral principles: so that if the maxims are sound, they display the speaker as a man of sound moral character." *Aristotle's Rhetoric and Poetics*, pp. 137, 139.

[54] See also Goldsmith's "The Effect Which Climates Have Upon Men and Other Animals" (III, 112–14).

[55] Tillotson points out that "gelid" (l. 119) is used by Goldsmith with the Virgilian connotation of "cool" rather than icy cold and that "smiling" (l. 120) is the English equivalent of *laetus*, which Virgil uses so often in his pastoral poetry. See his *Essays in Criticism and Research*, p. 77.

> *All evils* here contaminate the mind,
> That *opulence* departed, leaves behind;
> For *wealth* was theirs, not far remov'd the date,
> When *commerce* proudly flourish'd through the state;
>
> (ll. 129–32)

The rhetorical effectiveness of these lines depends on the pattern working from the pejorative noun "evils" to the honorific word "commerce." The increasing length of each line reinforces the noun pattern, and the movement from the present tense of "contaminate" to the past tense of "proudly flourish'd" builds up to a climax in which commerce has so declined, in spite of the friendliness of natural environment, that Italy's "former strength was now plethoric ill" (l. 140). Commerce per se is not the villain, however, for commerce is a healthy, functional use of wealth. It is wealth for wealth's sake or "opulence" that brings about the decline of commerce. A reflection of the eighteenth-century delight in controlling the connotation of words by using scientific words that are primarily denotative, "plethoric" is the perfect adjective to depict the pathological reality of commercial stagnation in the body politic. The alliterative pattern of the *p*'s in lines 141–47 reveals Goldsmith's minute attention to texture. The pattern begun by "plethoric" in line 140 falls on key nouns pejorative in their context:

> Yet, though to fortune lost, here still abide
> Some splendid arts, the wrecks of former *pride*;
> From which the feeble heart and long fall'n mind
> An easy compensation seem to find.
> Here may be seen, in bloodless *pomp* array'd,
> The *paste-board* triumph and the cavalcade;
> *Processions* form'd for *piety* and love,
> A mistress or a saint in every grove.
>
> (ll. 141–47)

The seemingly natural syntax of Goldsmith's verse should not blind us to the complex rhetoric in some of his couplets: the chiastic construction of "*b*loodless *p*omp"–"*p*asteboard triumph" is every bit as brilliant as similar constructions by Pope. Again, as in lines 129–32, the use of pejorative words to begin a verbal pattern undercuts the honorific or neutral quality of parallel words at the end of the pattern: "Processions" and "piety" are made to appear the opposite of what they mean in their normal context. The narrator's examination of Italy gives us a case history of social failure due to excess; he gives us a vignette echoing the decline and fall of the Roman Empire in the modern-day fall of eighteenth-century Italy from the glorious Italy of the High Renaissance.

In contrast to the luxurious natural environment of Italy, Switzerland's natural environment is barren and hostile to man. The semantic pattern is reinforced by the blunt alliteration of *b*'s and the hostile hissing of the *s*'s.[56]

> Where the *bleak* Swiss their stormy mansions tread,
> And force a churlish soil for scanty *bread*;
> No product here the *barren* hills afford,
> But man and steel, the soldier and his sword.
> (ll. 165–68)

Because Nature is hostile to man and because there is little wealth, and consequently no desire to accumulate excessive wealth, the Swiss live in a pattern congenial to centripetal force: "Each wish *contracting*, fits him to the soil" (l. 182). As in the portrayal of cohesive domestic

---

[56] In 1760 Goldsmith had complained of the current fad for alliteration (III, 53), and in the dedication to *The Traveller* he complained again of the zeal for "alliterative care." It is possible that Goldsmith does cater here to the taste of his readers for purposes of persuasion. I believe that such artistic weaknesses in the persuasive strain show Goldsmith's fundamental commitment to be to sense rather than sensibility.

happiness (ll. 11–22) where the narrator wished, "Eternal blessings crown my earliest friend" (l. 11), the Swiss peasant is also compared to a king:

> At night returning, every labour sped,
> He sits him down the *monarch* of a shed;
> Smiles by his chearful fire, and *round* surveys
> His childrens looks, that brighten at the blaze:
>
> (ll. 189–92)

The ideal of centripetal force is intensified in the Swiss peasant's circle of cohesion by ominous storm forces outside, "the loud torrent, and the whirlwind's roar" (l. 203). The "monarch of a shed" surveying "round" is in antithesis to the narrator-traveler's past pursuit of the "circle bounding earth and skies." Similarly, the peasant's wife, "boastful of her hoard," i.e., food, is in antithesis to the far more serious kind of hoarding (wealth) of the miser. But even in Switzerland bliss is sensual and temporal, and "morals, like their pleasures, are but low" (l. 224). Swiss culture lacks idealism and sensitivity, and "sterner virtues o'er the mountain's breast" (l. 229), surely a reference to Calvinism, reflect the sternness of the Swiss natural environment.

Nature in France, "Gay sprightly land of mirth and social ease" (l. 237), is pleasant, but France's principle of happiness is based on Art rather than Nature:

> So blest a life these thoughtless realms display,
> Thus idly busy rolls their world away:
> Theirs are those arts that mind to mind endear,
> For honour forms the social temper here.
> Honour, that praise which real merit gains,
> Or even imaginary worth obtains,
> Here passes current; paid from hand to hand,
> It shifts in splendid traffic round the land:
> From courts to camps, to cottages it strays,
> And all are taught an avarice of praise;

> They please, are pleas'd, they give to get esteem,
> Till, seeming blest, they grow to what they seem.
>
> (ll. 251–62)

Such bias words as "thoughtless," "idly busy," and "imaginary worth" undermine "blest," a control synonym for happiness. The comparison of honor to the exchange of money is summed up in "avarice of praise," which, like the earlier hoarding miser simile, is designed to condition the reader for the worse practice of material avarice that occurs later in the poem. The relativity of all cultural values results in the enfeebling of "all internal strength of thought" (l. 266), and, like the bliss of the Italians, the bliss of the French is morally hollow. It is appropriate that as the French place an undue importance on social virtues, so should their social vices be described in the concrete mode of personification:

> Hence ostentation here, with tawdry art,
> Pants for the vulgar praise which fools impart;
> Here vanity assumes her pert grimace,
> And trims her robes of frize with copper lace,
> Here beggar pride defrauds her daily cheer,
> To boast one splendid banquet once a year;
> The mind still turns where shifting fashion draws,
> Nor weighs the solid worth of self applause.
>
> (ll. 269–76)

Nature is even more hostile to man in Holland than in Switzerland. Man has transformed his environment to cope with the constant threat of the ocean. This artificiality of the landscape is reflected in the artificiality of Holland's bliss:

> Thus, while *around*, the wave-subjected soil
> Impels the native to repeated toil,
> Industrious habits in each breast obtain
> And industry begets a love of gain.
> Hence all the good from opulence that springs,

With all those ills superfluous treasure brings,
Are here display'd. Their much-lov'd wealth imparts
Convenience, plenty, elegance, and arts;
But view them closer, craft and fraud appear,
Even liberty itself is barter'd here.
At gold's superior charms all freedom flies,
The needy sell it, and the rich man buys:
A land of tyrants, and a den of slaves,
Here wretches seek dishonourable graves,
                                    (ll. 293–306)

Holland, too, is a circle threatened from the outside by the natural force of the ocean, but within the circumference, instead of human community, there is "craft and fraud." Goldsmith's description of the development of Dutch commerce reads like a poetic condensation of Tawney's *Religion and the Rise of Capitalism,* and the theory of conspicuous consumption as a means of achieving status is clearly portrayed in this verse paragraph. Whereas in France honor was traded like money, in Holland liberty itself is treated as a commodity. The corrupting influence of wealth for wealth's sake associated with Holland is in reality a deliberate attempt to prejudice the reader against a similar vice when Britain is described.

The argument has now been prepared for the main concern of the poem, Britain, and the transitional verse paragraph begins and ends with an exclamation, a sign of the narrator-traveler's increasing emotional involvement with his thesis as the poem moves closer toward Britain:

Heavens! how unlike their Belgic sires of old!
Rough, poor, content, ungovernably bold;
War in each breast, and freedom on each brow;
How much unlike the sons of Britain now!
                                    (ll. 309–12)

These structural contrasts of Nature are cleverly contrived; Nature in Italy is luxurious, in Switzerland barren, in France friendly, and in Holland threatening. This balanced alternation of varying states of Nature culminates with Britain, in which Nature is the golden mean: "Creation's mildest charms are there combin'd, / Extremes are only in the master's mind" (ll. 319–20). The rhetorical importance of Nature as the golden mean is that there is no good reason not to have a golden mean in British culture: human extremes cannot be blamed on environmental influences:

> Stern o'er each bosom reason holds her state.
> With daring aims, irregularly great,
> I see the lords of human kind pass by
> Pride in their port, defiance in their eye,
> Intent on high designs, a thoughtful band,
> By forms unfashion'd, fresh from Nature's hand;
> Fierce in a native hardiness of soul,
> True to imagin'd right above controul,
> While even the peasant boasts these rights to scan,
> And learns to venerate himself as man.
>   (ll. 321–30)

The return to the "I" of line 323 also marks the growing involvement of the narrator, and the subtle bias words, "imagin'd right above controul," prepare the reader for the attack on freedom in lines 335–42:

> That independence Britons prize too high,
> Keeps man from man, and breaks the social tie;
> See, though by *circling* deeps together held,
> Minds combat minds, repelling and repell'd;
> Ferments arise, imprison'd factions roar,
> Represt ambition struggles *round* her shore,
> Whilst over-wrought, the general system feels
> Its motions stopt, *or phrenzy fires the wheels.*
>   (ll. 335–42)

Internal cohesion is a desired virtue favored by Britain's

insularity and the threatening forces of Nature outside the island symbolized by the ocean. The "phrenzy-fired wheels" metaphor depicts centrifugal forces in the political and social realms that threaten to destroy internal cohesion. Excessive accumulation of wealth, using law as a weapon, threatens to destroy the traditional British social structure as it exists in the mid-eighteenth century.

> Till Time may come, when, stript of all her charms,
> That land of scholars, and that nurse of arms;
> Where noble stems transmit the patriot flame,
> And monarchs toil, and poets pant for fame;
> One sink of level avarice shall lie,
> And scholars, soldiers, kings unhonour'd die.
>
> (ll. 349–54)

The impact of line 353 depends upon the pejorative overtones of "sink." Not only does "sink" refer to a bog or a level piece of land where water collects and then is absorbed or drained off, but it also has the connotation of a sewer. Thus earlier in *The Traveller,* in the description of Italy, "All evils here *contaminate* the mind" (l. 129); later in lines 372–74, ambition strikes "at legal power" and, "*polluting* honour in its source, / Gave wealth to sway the mind with double force."

In the next verse paragraph the narrator-traveler uses the rhetorical device of pseudoconcession:

> Yet think not thus, when Freedom's ills I state,
> I mean to flatter kings, or court the great;
> Perish the wish; for, inly satisfy'd,
> Above their pomps I hold my ragged pride.
>
> (ll. 355–58)

In line 358 the narrator shows his sympathy to be with the poorer classes and drops the guise of detachment shown in line 36, "The pomp of kings, the shepherd's humbler pride." Paradoxically, at the very moment when

[87]

he appears to be bending backward in order to appear impartial, his emotional involvement and personal commitment to the argument of the poem are shown in the frequent use of the first-person pronoun (five times). The thesis of this verse paragraph is that the throne provides the center of centripetal force and internal cohesion. When the monarchy is undercut by "contending chiefs" who "blockade the throne, / *contracting* regal power to stretch their own" (ll. 359–60), national disintegration takes place. Then occurs the most terrifying avarice of all:

> Have we not seen, *round* Britain's peopled shore,
> Her useful sons exchang'd for useless ore?
> Seen all her triumphs but destruction haste,
> Like flaring tapers brightening as they waste;
> Seen opulence, her grandeur to maintain,
> Lead stern depopulation in her train,
>
> (ll. 375–80)

Here the poetic imagery based on the conflict between centripetal and centrifugal force blends with the political thesis of the poem: the departure of Englishmen for America is centrifugal, the result of phrenzy-fired wheels.

The strategy in the poem up to this point has been to make domestic cohesion a positive value that remains relatively untouched by historical change. Now domestic cohesion, equated with the poorer classes, is threatened by wealth and commerce so that these classes are forced to migrate. Here *The Traveller* depicts what to an eighteenth-century reader fresh from newspaper accounts of Indian raids against American settlers would not seem half so exaggerated as it does to a twentieth-century reader:

> Even now, perhaps, as there some pilgrim strays
> Through tangled forests, and through dangerous ways;
> Where beasts with man divided empire claim,

And the brown Indian takes a deadly aim;
There, while above the giddy tempest flies,
And all *around* distressful yells arise,
The pensive exile, bending with his woe,
To stop too fearful, and too faint to go,
Casts a fond look where England's glories shine,
And bids his bosom sympathize with mine.

(ll. 391–400)

The narrator's personal plight is paralleled by the plight of the pilgrims. Whereas he went "to traverse realms alone" (l. 29), the villagers are forced to "traverse climes beyond the western main" (l. 388). It is this verse paragraph that seems vulnerable to the charge of sentimentality as defined by Cleanth Brooks: "The sentimentalist takes a short cut to intensity by removing all the elements of the experience which might conceivably militate against the intensity. . . . the sentimental poet makes us feel that he is sacrificing the totality of his vision in favour of a particular interpretation. Hence the feeling on reading a sentimental poem that the intensity is the result of a trick." [57] To be sure, the sentimentality of this passage need not be attributed to Goldsmith's personality as reflected in his writing, for by traditional standards of rhetoric the orator in his conclusion was expected to "magnify or minimize the leading facts" and to "excite the required state of emotion" in his hearers.[58] Goldsmith deliberately magnifies the plight of the settlers to incite in his readers the emotions both of pity and of indignation. Such deliberate magnification is a blemish, however, and this passage is the weakest in the poem.

The narrator now returns to his own problem—the pursuit of happiness:

Vain, very vain, my weary search to find
That bliss which only centers in the mind:

[57] *Modern Poetry and the Tradition* (London, 1948), p. 46.
[58] *Aristotle's Rhetoric and Poetics*, p. 217.

[89]

Why have I stray'd, from pleasure and repose,
To seek a good each government bestows?
In every government, though terrors reign,
Though tyrant kings, or tyrant laws restrain,
How small, of all that human hearts endure,
That part which laws or kings can cause or cure.
Still to ourselves in every place consign'd,
Our own felicity we make or find:
With secret course, which no loud storms annoy,
Glides the smooth current of domestic joy.
The lifted ax, the agonizing wheel,
Luke's iron crown, and Damien's bed of steel,
To men remote from power but rarely known,
Leave reason, faith and conscience all our own.

(ll. 401–16)

It is important to recognize that here the narrator has left his political thesis and shifted back to the philosophical problem of what constitutes felicity. The symbols of excruciating torture applied to individuals who revolted against "tyrant kings" or "tyrant laws" again reinforce the value of centripetal force. The individual is driven inward, into the self, into the virtues of "reason, faith and conscience." The melancholy narrator-traveler finds his happiness in virtue. This virtue need not be Stoic and has a distinctly Christian cast. In Johnson's *Dictionary* (1750), "reason" is defined as a rational power or faculty and is illustrated by at least one quotation (from Swift) which is theologically Augustinian; "Faith" is defined first as the "belief of the revealed truths of religion" and second as the "system of revealed truths held by the Christian church": "Conscience" is defined as self-knowledge of our goodness or wickedness and is illustrated by a quotation from Swift in which a man's actions are judged by "comparing them with the law of God." [59]

[59] My colleague Arthur McGuinness has in hand an interesting interpretation of the theological dimension in *The Traveller*.

Macaulay interprets the conclusion as follows: "An English wanderer, seated on a crag among the Alps, near the point where the three great countries meet, looks down on the boundless prospect, reviews his long pilgrimage, recalls the varieties of scenery, of climate, of government, of religion, of national character, which he has observed, and comes to the conclusion, just or unjust, that our happiness depends little on political institutions, and much on the temper and regulation of our own minds." [60] Macaulay's summary not only vastly oversimplifies the poem but raises the question of why, if Goldsmith is writing a political poem, he concludes with an antipolitical thesis. The problem is not solved merely by accepting Boswell's assertion that Johnson wrote the concluding ten lines, with the exception of the penultimate couplet; we would still have an apparent structural inconsistency that would reflect as much on Johnson's bad artistry as on Goldsmith's. One solution is to realize that there are several levels of happiness being examined—national, domestic, and individual—and that the unifying element of these levels is spiritual centripetal force. This force on a national level will be best realized by a cohesive government centered around a benevolent but strong monarchy protecting the lower classes against a potential plutocracy. The domestic level of happiness centers around the head of a family, who is analogous to a king. The social bonds of love, duty, and honor supply the cohesive force both on the national and on the domestic levels of happiness. When cohesion ceases on a national level and centrifugal force becomes the prime motivation, then domestic happiness too is threatened. When both national and domestic happiness are no longer possible, the individual as a last resort may always find an imperfect happiness by living

[60] "Oliver Goldsmith," *Encyclopaedia Britannica*, 11th ed. (New York, 1910–11), p. 216.

a life of virtue. Virtue as happiness does not imply, however, that the individual will be cheerful, and there is a considerable difference between the optimistic tone of Epistle IV of Pope's *Essay on Man* and the melancholy tone of *The Traveller*. In a lighter vein Goldsmith once coined the phrase "gloom of solid felicity" (not to be mistaken for melancholy and spleen as they were used in the medical sense), a phrase which he used to describe the national characteristic of Englishmen because of their concern with, and responsible participation in, British government (III, 85). Johnson held a similar view of happiness that has been beautifully summarized by James Clifford:

> The important thing, he stresses over and over again, is to be realistic, never to fool oneself. One should see clearly the inevitable tragedy of mankind as well as its nobility. A sensible person must realize the hopelessness of most human aspirations—man cannot by himself create a brave new world—and yet keep them as goals. Though the best that can be done is to palliate suffering, not remove it altogether, men must not sink back into supine inaction. Retirement from society is not the answer, nor is a blind refusal to recognize evil. It is necessary, he felt, to accept the improbability of major improvement and yet try continually to better the conditions of individual men and women.[61]

The Traveller describes the failure of the British nation to promote national cohesion. In the full context of the poem the final verse paragraph is not antigovernmental but rather asserts that, when cohesive government fails, the last resort of individual happiness is to be found in individual virtue. The inversion of word order in the

[61] *Young Sam Johnson* (New York, 1955), p. 322.

last line, which concludes with "all our own," admirably reinforces the semantic statement.[62]

To place the poem's antithesis of centripetal and centrifugal patterns in a more meaningful framework, we may view it more precisely as a conflict between centripetal *action* and centrifugal *motion*. *Action*, as Kenneth Burke observes, "involves *character*, which involves choice; and the *form* of choice attains its perfection in the distinction between Yes and No (between *thou shalt* and *thou shalt not*)," whereas *motion* is "non-ethical." [63] If we remember Locke's distinction between *Physica* (natural philosophy), the end of which is "bare speculative truth," and *Practica* (ethics), the end of which is "not bare speculation and the knowledge of truth" but "right, and a conduct suitable to it" (*An Essay*, Bk. IV, Ch. XXI), we might identify centripetal *action* with *Practica* and centrifugal *motion* with *Physica*. We might then suggest that one aspect of literary change in eighteenth-century culture is a shift from assuming poetry as a species of virtue to assuming poetry as a species of knowing ("bare speculative truth"). We might further suggest that this shift is from an Augustan mode representing poetry honorifically as virtue by centripetal image

[62] This last line echoes line 30: "And find no spot of all the world my own." The centripetal imagery of *The Traveller* as opposed to the centrifugal imagery (the dialectic poetic structure of the poem) ought to show the weakness in Wallace C. Brown's statement that in "total structure *The Deserted Village* is *less obviously and mechanically* put together than *The Traveller* (italics mine). . . ." See his *The Triumph of Form* (Chapel Hill, N. C., 1948), p. 154. The centripetal thesis of this poem is identical with the centripetal character that Walter Jackson Bate finds in Johnson's thought. See his *The Achievement of Samuel Johnson* (New York, 1955), p. 166.

[63] *The Rhetoric of Religion: Studies in Logology* (Boston, 1961), p. 41. See also Norman Maclean, "From Action to Image: Theories of the Lyric in the Eighteenth Century," in *Critics and Criticism*, ed. R. S. Crane (Chicago, 1952), pp. 408–60; and Irene Chayes, "Rhetoric as Drama: An Approach to the Romantic Ode," *PMLA*, LXXIX (1964), 67–79.

patterns of *action* to another mode (the "Romantic Odes") representing poetry honorifically as epistemological speculation by centrifugal image patterns of motion. In *The Traveller* the poetic figure torn spiritually apart centrifugally ("the agonizing wheel") is in a passive state of drift and capable only of being acted *upon* by nature; the poetic figure at the end of the poem has resolved to be centripetally inner-directed and to be capable in the future of ethical choice and of acting *on* nature. We have already seen Goldsmith's own commitment to literature as a species of virtue (Chapter One); this commitment is expressed in the resolution of the conflict facing the poetic figure in the poem.

That the various circles of happiness can be found only in centripetal patterns of virtue is a comprehensive proposition that raises in question any reduction of the poem to a merely political thesis and subsequent criticism of the structure of the poem for rambling too much in proportion to its thesis. For many twentieth-century readers *The Traveller* should be a considerably more interesting poem than *The Deserted Village* in that the rhetoric supporting a political thesis is ultimately subordinated to a poetic structure that explores philosophically the pursuit of happiness. The concept of happiness as virtue practiced by a saddened individual is a more tough-minded attitude than many of our modern solutions predicated on trite concepts of happiness. Howard Mumford Jones has defended this eighteenth-century attitude toward happiness:

> Perhaps the very word is unfortunate. Obviously the eighteenth-century men did not mean by happiness that wholly emotional and transient euphoria connoted by wedding parties, love affairs, skiing, and the endless pursuit of thrills. They had in mind not so much happiness as contentment; and if their concept of content was to our taste overly colored with a melancholy resignation, there

is no essential logic whereby the doctrine of contentment has to be gray. It may be that Jefferson was wiser than are we, and that to rest content with limited, yet not unsatisfactory, opportunities and powers is the highest felicity an individual or a nation can achieve in an indifferent universe.[64]

That Goldsmith should tackle such a complex problem in poetry and succeed proves once again that we cannot easily ignore Johnson's critical judgment. If the interpretation presented here is at all valid, it should suggest that neither *The Traveller* nor *The Deserted Village* can legitimately be read as an autobiographical statement. Rather, like "A City Night Piece," these poems must be viewed in the objective context of rhetoric. Even when Goldsmith seems most sentimental, more often than not he is working in a craft of persuasion. If we use *sentimental* to mean a falsified appeal to sentiment and not to apply to a confusion between Goldsmith and his *personae*, and if we then object on aesthetic grounds to the use of imaginative literature for persuasive or didactic functions, our objections to Goldsmith's persuasive craft will be sounder and far more intelligible than the past praise of his persuasive craft for the wrong reasons or the distortion of his persuasive craft for journalistic biography. If, however, we use *sentimental* to mean a simplistic view of experience, the artistic complexity of *The Traveller*, analogous to the complexity of experience, is for the most part strikingly unsentimental and an enduring poetic statement.

[64] *The Pursuit of Happiness* (Cambridge, Mass., 1953), pp. 164–65.

Chapter Three

THE CRAFT OF SATIRE
(*THE CITIZEN OF THE WORLD*)

If the *Enquiry* failed to make Goldsmith's reputation as a man of letters, his subsequent work for the magazines and periodicals established his reputation, among the publishers at least, as a productive and graceful essayist. In his book *The English Novel in the Magazines 1740–1815*, Robert Mayo is the first modern critic who seems *not* to be disturbed by the fact that about half of the *Bee* is made up of translations, many unacknowledged.[1] In their discoveries of new borrowings in the *Bee* from French works, scholars have not indicated whether such translations were more common than realized in other miscellanies of the era. One could also consider the value of these translations and of Goldsmith as a literary middleman transfusing into bourgeois culture some of the refined elegance of the French Enlightenment. The very title of the *Bee* should have warned readers as to its borrowed contents. The following quotation and translation with a comment comes from a 1758 review of Lawson's *Lectures concerning oratory*, with which Goldsmith was almost certainly familiar: "*Floriferis ut apes en saltibus omnia libant.* You should, like bees, fly from flower to flower, extracting the juices fittest to be turned into honey. The severest

---

[1] (Evanston, Ill., 1962), pp. 292–98.

critics allow such amiable plundering." [2] This line from Lucretius' *De Rerum Natura* (iii. 11) turns up as the epigraph on the title page of the *Bee,* and it should have reminded readers that the bee was the symbol of "sweetness and light" and that in the tradition of Swift's *Battle of the Books* the obsession for originality was associated with excrement and with the spider.

Mayo writes that of the three or four hundred miscellanies patterned on the mode of the *Bee* only Goldsmith's is still worth reading today "in its entirety." [3] Most important, however, is Mayo's recognition that Goldsmith was writing satire and that even the seemingly sentimental pieces in the *Bee* and the *British Magazine* may be interpreted as antisentimental and as tongue-in-cheek satire. Mayo's most perceptive suggestion, hidden in a footnote, is that "The History of Miss Stanton" (which contains the germ of *The Vicar of Wakefield*) is not a puerile story written under pressure but "a sly joke upon magazine readers, a kind of mock-sentimental romance wittily undercutting some of their most cherished clichés." [4] Because this story has been used in support of an interpretation of *The Vicar of Wakefield* as a sentimental novel, a brief analysis of "The History of Miss Stanton" in the light of Mayo's suggestion is very much in order.

The internal clue to ironical intention occurs in the first paragraph of the epistolary story, when the correspondent complains of previous correspondents imposing on the *British Magazine* "with fictitious stories of distress" (III, 128). The correspondent does admit (with a pun)

[2] *Critical Review,* VI (November, 1758), 398. In rejecting Goldsmith's authorship of this review, Arthur Friedman is forced to admit that Goldsmith was probably familiar with it. See "Goldsmith's Contributions to the *Critical Review,*" *Modern Philology,* XLIV (1946–47), 44–45.
[3] Mayo, *English Novel,* p. 293.
[4] *Ibid.,* pp. 414–15, n. 23.

that such stories may have "real merit" in their design to promote "tenderness and benevolent love" (III, 128). In the next paragraph the writer promises (again with the same pun) that "if" his story is found to have any "real merit," it must be "wholly ascribed to that sincerity which guides the pen." The conditional mood of "if" opens up a dual interpretation depending on the reader's orientation. When the writer refers in the next sentence to his tale as "true though artless," the trap has been set. The plot is characterized by its blatant improbability. Mr. Dawson, a rake, compromises the reputation of Fanny, the daughter of Mr. Stanton, a clergyman. Mr. Stanton challenges Mr. Dawson to a duel; Mr. Dawson believes he has killed the father and vows to reform and marry Fanny; then, in a reversal, Mr. Stanton jumps up alive, having only pretended to be dead, and the couple marry honorably. As Mayo suggests, all of the bourgeois romance clichés in which virtue and sexual virginity and material success become synonymous are played upon in this satire. Mr. Stanton's "continued perseverance in benevolence" (III, 128) disappears when he discovers that his daughter is "now *contaminated* for ever" (III, 131; italics mine). Only the puerile reader would pass over the incongruity of a clergyman fighting a duel, and, even worse, of a gentleman accepting such a duel. Mayo's suggested interpretation has long been overdue. A new look at Goldsmith's next major journalistic effort, the "Chinese Letters," is also long overdue.

In May, 1759, Goldsmith's contemptuous attitude toward the taste for Oriental culture was expressed unmistakably in his review of Arthur Murphy's *Orphan of China*. Goldsmith referred to the fad as a "recourse even to absurdity for redress," as motivated by a pursuit of novelty, and as a "perversion of taste" (I, 170). When in this same review he termed Chinese literary productions "the most phlegmatic that can be imagined" and "very improper models for imitation," there would appear to be a most remarkable inconsistency in his publication of his Chinese letters only eight months later in the *Public Ledger*. One interpretation would have it that Goldsmith was sacrificing his critical principles in order to reap the hack writer's rewards by catering to popular taste.[5] A more plausible interpretation, originally suggested by Frank F. Moore and supported by Arthur Lytton Sells, views Goldsmith's publication of the Chinese letters as only pretending to cater to the popular taste for pseudo-oriental culture while in reality mocking such taste by means of burlesque. Once these letters were acclaimed by the public, Goldsmith wrote more letters and expanded the range of his satire, thus going beyond his original intention.[6] This latter interpretation is supported by a careful reading of the preface to the first edition of *The Citizen of the World*. Goldsmith reveals the same contemptuous attitude toward the oriental fad that he had expressed several years before in his review of Murphy's play. The "Editor" writes: "Were I to estimate the merits of our Chinese Philosopher . . . I would not hesitate to state his genius still higher; but as to his learning and gravity, these I think might safely be marked as nine hundred and ninety nine, within one degree of absolute frigidity" (II, 13). Goldsmith then reiterates through the "Editor" the position which he had earlier taken in *An Enquiry:* "The truth is, the Chinese and we are pretty much alike. Different degrees of refinement, and not of distance, mark the distinctions among mankind. Savages of the most opposite climates, have all but one character of improvidence and rapacity; and tutored nations, how-

[5] Hamilton Jewett Smith, *Oliver Goldsmith's The Citizen of the World,* Yale Studies in English, LXXI (New Haven, 1926), p. 11.

[6] Frank F. Moore, *The Life of Oliver Goldsmith* (New York, 1911), p. 201; Sells, *Les Sources Françaises,* p. 90.

ever separate, make use of the very same methods to procure refined enjoyment" (II, 14).

In spite of this similarity, the current fad for pseudo-oriental literature as a form of novelty mushrooms. The "Editor" warns of a dialectical comic play between Lien Chi Altangi's "Eastern sublimity" and his own "colloquial ease" (II, 14). Like Swift, Goldsmith will intrude through a plain style without violating technically the formal narrative structure. Then follows a dream vision of "FASHION FAIR," in which the "Editor" resolves to join his acquaintances in exploiting current fashions: "I am resolved to make a new adventure. The furniture, frippery and fireworks of China, have long been fashionably bought up. I'll try the fair with a small cargoe of Chinese morality. If the Chinese have contributed to vitiate our taste, I'll try how far they can to help to improve our understanding. But as others have driven into the market in waggons, I'll cautiously begin by venturing with a wheel-barrow" (II, 15). Upon awakening from his reverie, the "Editor" portrays himself as the alienated artist belonging "to no particular class" and resembling "one of those solitary animals, that has been forced from its forest to gratify human curiosity" and "set up for halfpence, to fret and scamper at the end" of his "chain" (II, 15). This is the closest Goldsmith comes to portraying the real ambivalences of the writer forced to make artistic compromises in catering to his readers. Irony becomes a necessary defense and complexity a central value in fighting against the reductionisms of foppish literary fashions. To recognize that *The Citizen of the World* parodies pseudo-oriental literature suggests in turn that Goldsmith's treatment of his central oriental character, Lien Chi Altangi, is perhaps more complex than has often been stated. George Sherburn focuses on the French radical tradition of the Chinese traveler who embodies "the pure light of reason," who is a relativist for whom "nothing established had an absolute validity," and who represents the emancipated mind of the *philosophe*. He finds Goldsmith's work less "brilliantly trenchant than the best of his French models" (because England, unlike France, had more freedom), and he finds Goldsmith "more of the literary man, less of the revolutionary." [7] This judgment tends to blur the sharp differences between the ideologies of French and English satirists by trying to find similarities. Goldsmith is not less of a *philosophe:* he is, perhaps, compared to Swift, less of a conservative realist. Goldsmith uses the radical genre of the travelogue just as Swift had used it: to burlesque the very genre itself and to use it as a weapon launched from an ethical position in order to attack human folly. Goldsmith was a citizen of the world who deplored the excessive glorification of either oriental or European culture and who, while recognizing the external differences between civilizations, would find human nature in all ages and all cultures very much the same. It is this attitude which underlies his parody of the oriental fad, and as a part of this parody Lien Chi Altangi is himself occasionally an object of satire.[8]

And yet Goldsmith need only to have turned to Montesquieu's *Lettres Persanes* for a model, as has been shown by Geoffrey Tillotson, who refers to "the use made by Montesquieu and Goldsmith, to name only the great, of the instance of the Persian visiting Europe and drawing his comically false conclusions," and who refers to the neoclassical belief that "what mattered most to the theorists about Nature was the evidence gathered from human nature near home." [9] It is this approach to *The*

---

[7] *A Literary History of England,* p. 1059.
[8] Franklyn C. Nelick has recognized this in his "Oliver Goldsmith—Traveller" (Ph.D. diss., University of Wisconsin, 1952).
[9] *Pope and Human Nature* (Oxford, 1958), p. 17.

Citizen of the World that will be used here in examining Goldsmith's prose satire.

Lien Chi Altangi and the Pride of Fortitude

Narrative continuity in *The Citizen of the World* is provided by means of a frame tale that relates Altangi's misfortunes in leaving China, the adventures of his son Hingpo, who flees from China to seek his father, and finally the marriage of Hingpo and the beautiful Christian Zelis, who turns out to be the niece of the Man in Black.[10] Within this frame tale there is a thematic continuity which reveals all the subtlety and artistry of Goldsmith's satire. The thematic pattern is initiated in Letter VI—"Happiness lost, by seeking after refinement. The Chinese philosopher's disgraces"—addressed to Lien Chi Altangi, *"the discontented wanderer,"* and written by Fum Hoam, whose point of view undermines Altangi's quest for wisdom. Fum Hoam asks how long Altangi will continue to seek for knowledge and then in a key paragraph attacks the traveler's philosophic position:

> I know you will reply, that the refined pleasure of growing every day wiser is a sufficient recompence for every inconvenience. I know you will talk of the vulgar satisfaction of soliciting happiness from sensual enjoyment only; and probably enlarge upon the exquisite raptures of sentimental bliss [i.e., rational bliss]. Yet, believe me, friend, you are deceived; all our pleasures, though seemingly never so remote from sense, derive their origin from some one of the senses. The most exquisite demonstration in mathematics, or the most pleasing disquisition in metaphysics, if it does not ultimately tend to increase some sensual satisfaction, is delightful only to fools, or to

[10] Hamilton Jewett Smith discusses this frame tale and shows it occurring in Letters VI, XXII, XXXV, XXXVI, XXXVII, XLVII, LIX, LX, LXI, XCIV, and CXXIII. See his *Goldsmith's Citizen*, p. 22.

men who have by long habit contracted a false idea of pleasure; and he who separates sensual and sentimental enjoyments, seeking happiness from mind alone, is in fact as wretched as the naked inhabitant of the forest, who places all happiness in the first, regardless of the latter.

(II, 37.)

Altangi is accused of having a lopsided view of life, of placing an undue emphasis on reason, and of thereby ignoring the rational-empirical golden mean that rejects both the hedonistic, excessive indulgence of the senses and excessive reliance on reason. Fum Hoam proceeds to inform Altangi that because he has left China, the emperor has made slaves of his family and appropriated his property; only his son Hingpo has escaped. The situation most assuredly undercuts Altangi's role as the philosophic traveler, for it would have been easy for Goldsmith to have made his traveler a bachelor. The point is that Altangi's pursuit of knowledge which will in turn lead to happiness is rendered absurd by the plight of his family. This interpretation of Fum Hoam's letter is reinforced by Altangi's reply in Letter VII—"The tye of wisdom, only to make us happy. The benefits of travelling upon the morals of a philosopher." In order to highlight beyond doubt the irony in the deadpan presentation of Altangi's "maxim morality," Goldsmith inserts an editorial comment at the beginning of the letter: *The Editor thinks proper to acquaint the reader, that the greatest part of the following letter, seems to him to be little more than a rhapsody of sentences borrowed from Confucius, the Chinese philosopher.*" Needless to say, no alert eighteenth-century reader would miss the irony contained in the word "rhapsody," a traditionally pejorative word by 1760.[11] Altangi begins with sorrow over his family's plight:

[11] Smith does not discuss the ironical function of the "rhapsody" footnotes and the subheadings.

A Wife, a daughter carried into captivity to expiate my offence, a son scarce yet arrived at maturity, resolving to encounter every danger in the pious pursuit of one who has undone him, these indeed are circumstances of distress; tho' my tears were more precious than the gem of Golconda, yet would they fall upon such an occasion.

But I submit to the stroke of heaven, I hold the volume of Confucius in my hand, and as I read grow humble and patient, and wise. We should feel sorrow, says he, but not sink under its oppression, the heart of a wise man should resemble a mirrour, which reflects every object without being sullied by any. The wheel of fortune turns incessantly round, and who can say within himself I shall today be uppermost. We should hold the immutable mean that lies between insensibility and anguish; our attempts should be not to extinguish nature, but to repress it; not to stand unmoved at distress, but endeavour to turn every disaster to our own advantage. Our greatest glory is, not in never falling, but in rising every time we fall.

(II, 39.)

The letter continues in a similar vein; Altangi's insistence on turning his "misery" to his "greatest glory" indicates not only excessive pride but also an optimism analogous to that of Soame Jenyns, which explains away evil by making it a positive good. Ultimately, Altangi's pursuit of wisdom is motivated by a pursuit of happiness, as indicated by the title of the letter; it would be incredible that the intelligent readers of this letter in 1760 would not recognize the satire of the pursuit of happiness in an oriental framework, especially in view of the fame already achieved by the publication in 1759 of *Candide* and *Rasselas,* both of which present a double-barreled blast against eighteenth-century optimism. Altangi's foible is pride, and the way in which eighteenth-century con-

servatives reacted to pride has been beautifully summarized by Arthur O. Lovejoy:

> Man must not attempt to transcend the limitations of his
> "nature"; and his nature, though not the same as that of
> the animals below him in the scale, is close to it. "Reason"
> has a part in the conduct of human life, but it is an
> ancillary part. Pope devotes many lines of versified argu-
> mentation to showing that the motive-power and the prin-
> cipal directive force in man's life is—and should be—not
> reason, but the complex of instincts and passions which
> make up our "natural" constitution. "Pride," then, in an
> especially important sense, meant a sort of moral over-
> strain, the attempt to be unnaturally good and immoder-
> ately virtuous, to live by reason alone. Erasmus and Mon-
> taigne had come to have an antipathy to this lofty and
> strenuous moral temper through a direct revulsion against
> the revived Stoicism in fashion in the late Renaissance;
> and the Stoics passed in the eighteenth century for the
> proverbial embodiments of "pride" in this sense.[12]

Altangi's pride of fortitude is demonstrated in Letter
XXII (the second in the frame tale), which describes his
emotions on hearing that his son Hingpo is now a slave
in Persia:

> Every account I receive from the east seems to come
> loaded with some new affliction. My wife and daughter
> were taken from me, and yet I sustained the loss with
> intrepidity; my son is made a slave among barbarians,
> which was the only blow that could have reached my
> heart: yes, I will indulge the transports of nature for a
> little, in order to shew I can overcome them in the end.

[12] *Essays in the History of Ideas* (Baltimore, 1948), pp. 67–68. Lovejoy
here buttresses Donald Greene's warning against equating Augustan
rationalism with Stoicism. "Augustinianism and Empiricism," 64–66. See
also John Dussinger, "Oliver Goldsmith, citizen of the world," *Studies
on Voltaire and the Eighteenth Century*, LV (1967), 445–61.

True magnanimity consists not in NEVER *falling, but in*
RISING *every time we fall.*

(II, 94–95.)

This last maxim, repeating a passage in Letter VII, the-
matically links the two letters. While boasting of his intrepidity, Altangi is again demonstrating his phlegmatic
nature. He seems, in fact, to welcome misfortune for the
opportunity it provides to indulge in rhetorical bombast
in order to prove his courage. In the last three paragraphs,
however, Altangi's intrepidity breaks down completely,
as he plunges into despair. He even admits that the "Reason cannot resolve" and then declaims the inadequacy of
the world's religions: "How am I surprized at the inconsistency of the Magi; their two principles of good and
evil affright me. The Indian who bathes his visage in
urine, and calls it piety, strikes me with astonishment.
The christian who believes in three gods is highly absurd.
The Jews who pretend that deity is pleased with the
effusions of blood, are not less displeasing. I am equally
surprized that rational beings can come from the ex-
tremities of the earth, in order to kiss a stone, or scatter
pebbles. How contrary to reason are those; and yet all
pretend to teach me to be happy" (II, 96). This passage
is an excellent example of what Geoffrey Tillotson has
called "comically false conclusions": Altangi, the traveler,
measures religions by their outward forms and not by
their corresponding inward spirit. Goldsmith's satirical intention is made even more emphatic by another editorial
footnote: "This whole apostrophe seems almost literally
translated from Ambulaaohamed, the Arabian poet." To
a twentieth-century reader, living in an age of religious
skepticism, the irony of this essay might not be evident;
but an eighteenth-century English reading audience, holding a community belief in the absolute validity of Christianity, would immediately brand Altangi as a fool—

especially when, in the final paragraph, he pleads for "a revelation of himself, for a plan of his universal system." The subtlest of the ironic nuances of this passage is not capitalizing "christian," "himself," and "his."

Letters XXXV, XXXVI, and XXXVII introduce into the narrative the point of view of Hingpo, a prisoner in Persia. Throughout these letters there are bits of criticism that reveal the futility of Altangi's "maxim morality" when it is actually confronted with experience. In Letter XXXV, Hingpo, who is falling in love with Zelis, tries to reassure his father that he is still the phlegmatic philosopher who could not "stoop to so degrading a passion" as love (II, 154). In Letter XXXVI it becomes apparent that Hingpo is fighting a losing battle by trying to suppress his passions, and he begins to doubt Altangi's assumption that wisdom leads to happiness.

> Mostadad, O my father is no philosopher; and yet he seems perfectly contented with his ignorance. Possessed of numberless slaves, camels, and women, he desires no greater possession. He has never opened the page of Mentius, and yet all the slaves tell me that he is happy.
>
> Forgive the weakness of my nature, if I some times feel my heart rebellious to the dictates of wisdom, and eager for happiness like his. Yet why wish for his wealth with his ignorance; to be like him, incapable of sentimental pleasures; incapable of feeling the happiness of making others happy, incapable of teaching the beautiful Zelis philosophy.
>
> (II, 155–56.)

A comic contrast exists here between what Hingpo professes and what he actually feels; in trying to persuade Altangi that he has not changed, Hingpo is trying to convince himself. The disparity between Altangi's rationalism and Hingpo's experience reminds us of the advice which Imlac gives to Rasselas: "Be not too hasty . . . to trust, or to admire, the teachers of morality: they discourse like angels, but they live like men." In Letter XXXVII, by means of an allegory that is an obvious parallel to *Rasselas,* Hingpo rejects Altangi's belief that wisdom leads to happiness. A Persian slave describes a paradise known as "the valley of ignorance," whose inhabitants live in a state of bliss: "At length however, an unhappy youth, more aspiring than the rest undertook to climb the mountain's side, and examine the summits which were hitherto deemed inaccessible. The inhabitants from below, gazed with wonder at his intrepidity, some applauded his *courage, others censured his folly,* still however he proceeded towards the place where the earth and heavens seemed to unite, and at length arrived at the wished for height with extreme labour and assiduity" (II, 158; italics mine). Altangi glories in his own intrepidity, and the use of "intrepidity" and "courage" in the allegory clearly points toward his own travels. The syntactic arrangement, which pretends to praise bravery by the use of two honorific synonyms ("intrepidity" and "courage") and then undermines it with the pejorative word "folly," is an important device of irony in Goldsmith's writing. For the rest of the letter, any synonym for fortitude is automatically established as pejorative.

At this point in *The Citizen of the World* we can never be certain when truisms uttered by Altangi are intended to be ridiculous or to be equated with Goldsmith's point of view. Rather than being an artistic flaw, such subtlety in eighteenth-century satirical writing is all part of the awareness that order is always threatened by the complexity of experience. For example, in Letter XLIV, Altangi utters the stock neoclassical platitude that in order to find happiness one should concentrate on the present moment and not expect happiness elsewhere "but where we are": "The great source of calamity lies in regret or anticipation: he, therefore, is most wise who thinks of the present alone, regardless of the past or the future" (II, 189). Altangi adheres even now to the belief that the end of philosophy is happiness. But the real absurdity lies in the situation. The letter is addressed to Hingpo, "*a slave in Persia*," who is not in a position to find happiness in the present. Altangi's assertion that "misery is artificial" can hardly gain Hingpo's assent. By the same token, Letter XLVII, also addressed to Hingpo and entitled "Misery best relieved by dissipation," would appear on a first reading to be serious were it not for another editorial footnote: "This letter appears to be little more than a rhapsody of sentiments from Confucius. Vid. the Latin translation" (II, 200). This "rhapsody" footnote not only indicates a sarcastic attitude toward pseudo-oriental literature but reveals the rhetorical hollowness of Altangi's maxims. Now at last, Altangi admits that underlying his fortitude is pride: "I know but of two sects of philosophers in the world that have endeavoured to inculcate that fortitude is but an imaginary virtue; I mean the followers of Confucius, and those who profess the doctrines of Christ. All other sects teach pride under misfortunes; they alone teach humility" (II, 200–1).

This entire letter presents a complete reversal of all that Altangi has hitherto professed, and he stands condemned by his own rhetoric. If Altangi is indeed the representative of the pure light of reason and a relativist who utters platitudes on all subjects, then he can express points of view and be on all sides at once—but not without becoming an object of ridicule. If Altangi writes like a *philosophe* and a man of the Enlightenment, one needs to be reminded that English writers like Swift and Goldsmith in their best satirical writing are often anti-Enlightenment. Within the frame tale of *The Citizen of the World,* the role of Altangi as the foreign observer is con-

tinually undercut and made fun of by the point of view of
Hingpo, by the point of view of Fum Hoam, and by the
plot situations which reveal how ridiculously inappropriate Altangi's maxims are when confronted by experience.
There is a continuity of theme in the sustained satire on
Altangi's boasted "intrepidity" and on his excessive reliance on reason. By ironically undercutting this rationalism divorced from empiricism, Goldsmith ridicules what
he and some of his contemporaries (most notably Johnson) believed was an inadequate way of dealing with life.

Religion, Liberty, and Commerce: The Pursuit of Trifles

Man has long felt a profound dissatisfaction with the
inadequacy of natural language to describe existence. This
inadequacy was particularly noticeable to eighteenth-century thinkers and satirists because of Locke's discussion
of the abuse of words in the third book of the *Essay Concerning Human Understanding.*[13] The incongruity between things or ideas and the words used to describe
these things or ideas is but one variation of the contrast
between the actual and the ideal, which forms the basis
of comic satire. Goldsmith's keen awareness of this problem is demonstrated toward the end of *The Citizen of
the World,* in Letter CXXII, when Altangi sums up the
significance of his correspondence in the honorific idiom
of "colloquial ease":

> . . . to pursue trifles is the lot of humanity; and whether
> we bustle in a pantomime, or strut at a coronation;
> whether we shout at a bonefire, or harrangue in a senate-
> house; whatever object we follow, it will at last surely
> conduct us to futility and disappointment. The wise
> bustle and laugh as they walk in the pageant, but fools

[13] See Kenneth MacLean, *John Locke and English Literature of the
Eighteenth Century* (New Haven, 1936), pp. 103–18.

bustle and are important; and this probably is all the difference between them.

    This may be an apology for the levity of my former
correspondence; I talked of trifles, and I knew that they
were trifles; to make the things of this life ridiculous, it
was only sufficient to call them by their names.

                              (II, 470.)

Although Altangi purports to deal with this issue lightly, it
has great importance when seen in the context of Samuel
Johnson's famous review of Soame Jenyns' *A Free Inquiry
into the Nature and Origin of Evil:* "I do not mean to reproach this author for not knowing what is equally hidden
from learning and from ignorance. The shame is to impose words for ideas upon ourselves or others. To imagine
that we are going forward when we are only turning
round. To think that there is any difference between him
that gives no reason, and him that gives a reason, which
by his own confession, cannot be conceived." [14] In an
age that valued universal generalizations about life and
human nature, there was certain to be a considerable
amount of theorizing which would lack empirical verification; but if much in life could not be verified, the conservative point of view preferred an honest doubting to
a tissue of fabricated theories. While Johnson and many
of his contemporaries sought to discover those principles
unifying the particulars of experience, they were on the
other hand aware of the dangers of an excess cleavage
between language and experience. In an event-centered
world they despised verbal verification. For this reason,
Goldsmith directs his satire against the abuses of such
popular slogans and labels of the period as *intrepidity,
benevolence, liberty,* and *commerce,* all of which served
the purpose of propaganda. His contempt for such labels

---

[14] *Works of Johnson,* VI, 64. I have corrected the excessive punctua-
tion of the Oxford English Classics edition.

is revealed in the review of Murphy's *Orphan of China* which was referred to at the beginning of this chapter:

> And now we are mentioning faults, (faults which a single quotation from the play will happily expunge from the reader's memory), the author has, perhaps, too frequently mentioned the word *virtue*. This expression should, in the mouth of a philosopher, be husbanded, and only used on great occasions; to repeat it too often it loses its cabalistic power, and at last degenerates into contempt. This was actually the case at Athens, so that their *polythrylete arete* [much-spoken-of virtue], as it was called, became contemptible even among the most stupid of their neighbouring nations; and towards the latter end of their government they grew ashamed of it themselves.
>
> (I, 173. Transliteration of Greek is mine.)

It is worth noting that "*arete*" in its classical context more often than not refers to bravery; perhaps in this piece of dramatical criticism we have one of the germs from which developed Goldsmith's satire on Altangi's intrepidity.[15]

Goldsmith's skeptical attitude toward democracy is common knowledge, and in Letter IV (often found in essay anthologies) he satirizes the Englishman's extraordinary love of freedom. Motivated by pride, Englishmen, without realizing it, become easy victims for propaganda: "Liberty is ecchoed in all their assemblies, and thousands might be found ready to offer up their lives for the sound, though perhaps not one of all the number understands its meaning" (II, 27–28). This thesis is stated in such a deadpan fashion that we are not entirely certain whether to admire or to ridicule the passion of the lower classes for liberty. But by translating the thesis into a concrete anecdote, the ironic intention is unmistakably clear. Altangi

---

[15] See Werner Jaeger, *Paideia: The Ideals of Greek Culture,* trans. Gilbert Highet, 3 vols. (New York, 1945), I, 5.

stops by a prison to hear a conversation between a debtor inside the prison, a porter stopping to rest outside, and a soldier at the prison window, on the subject of a threatened invasion from France:

> "For my part, cries the prisoner, the greatest of my apprehensions is for our freedom; if the French should conquer, what would become of English liberty. My dear friends, liberty is the Englishman's prerogative; we must preserve that at the expense of our lives, of that the French shall never deprive us; it is not to be expected that men who are slaves themselves would preserve our freedom should they happen to conquer." "Ay, slaves, cries the porter, they are all slaves, fit only to carry burthens every one of them. Before I would stoop to slavery, may this be my poison (and he held the goblet in his hand) may this be my poison—but I would sooner list for a soldier."
>
> The soldier taking the goblet from his friend, with much awe fervently cried out, "It is not so much our liberties as our religion that would suffer by such a change: ay, our religion, my lads. May the devil sink me into flames, (such was the solemnity of his adjuration) if the French should come over, but our religion would be utterly undone." So saying, instead of a libation, he applied the goblet to his lips, and confirmed his sentiments with a ceremony of the most persevering devotion.
>
> (II, 28–29.)

That Goldsmith borrowed this anecdote from John Byrom's verse satire "Tom the Porter," first published November 25, 1746, does not diminish his artistic genius, when we realize that the anecdote would have been familiar to many of his readers. The real artistry is not in the originality of the essay but in how the anecdote with a certain political slant is adapted to a new historical context.

F. L. Lucas has summed up brilliantly the paradox

which Goldsmith dramatizes in Letter IV: "For example, there is the perennial sham of clap-trap about freedom (indeed 'Wilkes and Liberty' were shortly to turn London upside down). Goldsmith did not undervalue freedom; its praises were to form the climax of his *Traveller*. But he realized that some of those who shout loudest for freedom, are themselves the most enslaved by words; that political freedom is for many a mockery, when it goes with economic bondage (just as the modern dream of economic welfare in political bondage remains a selling of man's birthright for a mess of pottage)." [16] Lucas' allusion to "Wilkes and Liberty" raises a problem in literary history. Since *The Citizen of the World* was published in 1762 as a book and since John Wilkes's *North Briton* No. 45 did not appear until 1763, we need to know whether Goldsmith was merely attacking libertarian doctrines in general or whether he was parodying a specific abuse of the word *liberty*. An inspection of periodical literature in 1760 reveals that Goldsmith in Letter IV was ridiculing war slogans popularized by propagandists who desired the protraction of the war against the French. The war, begun in 1756, had by 1760 seemingly little purpose, particularly after the great naval victory in 1759, which should have quieted any British fears of a French invasion. By 1760 many Englishmen, including Goldsmith, were weary over the continuation of the war. This attitude is expressed in Letter XVII—"Of the war now carried on between France and England, with its frivolous motives": "The English and French seem to place themselves foremost among the champion states of Europe. Though parted by a narrow sea, yet are they entirely of opposite characters; and from their vicinity are taught to fear and admire each other. They are at present engaged in a very destructive war, have already spilled much blood, are ex-

[16] *The Search For Good Sense,* pp. 308–9.

cessively irritated; and all upon account of one side's desiring to wear greater quantities of *furs* than the other" (II, 72–73). To retain the popular support of the people, those in favor of continuing the war shouted in defense of "Religion, Liberty, and Commerce," or slight variations of this slogan. Ever since the early part of the eighteenth century the Whigs had attempted to smear the Tories by associating them with the restoration of the Stuarts, the restoration of Roman Catholicism, and the restoration of absolute monarchy with its subsequent threat to English liberties and the ownership of property. It was this same shopworn Whig propaganda that John Byrom had ridiculed in "Tom the Porter," so that to know the source of the anecdote in Goldsmith's essay is to enhance further its satire. Goldsmith's allusion should have reminded readers that the same stale Whig rhetoric was still being used to justify the continuation of the war.

A typical example of such propaganda is found in an anonymous pamphlet of 1757: "At a time when this Nation is necessarily engaged in a War, for the Preservation of her Commerce and Colonies against a dangerous and powerful enemy; and when, of consequence, it becomes the Duty of every *Briton* to steel his Breast, with a steady and determined Resolution, to hazard his Person and to sacrifice his Fortune, in Defence of his Religion, Liberty, Property, Posterity, Relations, Friends, and whatever else is dear and valuable in Society. . . ." [17] As late as 1761, letters in the *London Chronicle* arguing for continuing the war still used the same old clichés. One letter to the editor, however, pleads for peace and in its concluding paragraph attacks the slogan "Upon the whole, let me entreat my countrymen, to consider these things calmly; *if our Religion, our Laws, or Liberties* were concerned in this

---

[17] *Proposals for carrying on the war with vigour, raising the supplies within the year, and forming a national militia* (London, 1757), [p. 1].

contest, we ought to refuse no hazard or experience, to secure such inestimable blessings: but when these are entirely out of the question, and the end for which we entered into the war effectually answered, I confess, I can see no reasonable inducement to continue it; and I believe, dispassionate impartial persons will generally agree with me." [18] In *The Citizen of the World,* Letter IV is directed against smoke-screen propaganda promulgated by those who attempted to hide an ulterior motive of empire-building. The tragic irony is that those naïve thousands who accepted the slogans without understanding them would supply the cannon fodder for the war, which in part would be continued because of those slogans. Goldsmith's essay is not totally without meaning for twentieth-century citizens of the world.

"On the distresses of the poor, exemplified in the life of a private centinel" was published first in the *British Magazine* (June, 1760) and then later inserted into the first edition of *The Citizen of the World* as Letter CXVI (CXIX in modern editions). Both in theme and technique this essay resembles Letter IV. All of the problems of sense and sensibility in connection with Goldsmith are summed up in "Distresses of the Poor," and it is for this reason that Sherburn compares it to *The Vicar of Wakefield.* On the one hand Sherburn sees Goldsmith "lavishly" using distress as material; on the other, Sherburn recognizes that the "distresses of the Sentinel are so gross as to be absurd" and "far from moving tears," so that we "are not invited to weep" but "to admire intrepidity." Sherburn concludes that "submission, intrepidity," and

[18] *London Chronicle,* IX (Feb. 17–19, 1761), 171. See also other letters both pro ¬nd con with the same key phrases in March 3–5, IX, 220–21, and in March 5–7, IX, 227–28. For a valuable analysis of periodicals, see Robert D. Spector, *English Literary Periodicals and the Climate of Opinion During the Seven Years' War* (The Hague, 1966).

"fortitude" are the "lessons Goldsmith wishes us to learn from the distresses of the Virtuous." [19] Such an interpretation glosses over the function of the essay as satire. If the distresses of the sentinel are absurd, it is this very absurdity that provides the clue to the satirical meaning of Goldsmith's essay.

As in Letter IV, the essay begins with the exposition of the central thesis, but in the suspiciously grandiose style of what the "Editor" had warned in the preface would be Altangi's "Eastern sublimity":

> The misfortunes of the great, my friend, are held up to engage our attention, are enlarged upon in tones of declamation, and the world is called upon to gaze at the noble sufferers; they have at once the comfort of admiration and pity.
>
> Yet where is the magnanimity of bearing misfortunes when the whole world is looking on? Men in such circumstances can act bravely even from motives of vanity. *He only who, in the vale of obscurity, can brave adversity, who without friends to encourage, acquaintances to pity, or even without hope to alleviate his distresses, can behave with tranquillity and indifference, is truly great: whether peasant or courtier he deserves admiration, and should be held up for our imitation and respect.*
>
> The miseries of the poor are however entirely disregarded; tho' some undergo more real hardships in one day than the great in their whole lives. It is indeed inconceivable what difficulties the meanest English sailor or soldier endures without murmuring or regret. Every day is to him a day of misery, and yet he bears his hard fate without repining.
>
> (II, 458–59. Italics mine.)

The essential thesis appears to be that true courage does not stem from pride or vanity but from humility—he who displays courage in obscurity is truly great. The poor who

[19] *A Literary History of England*, p. 1061.

display great courage in obscurity deserve therefore to be more admired than they have been. But the thesis sentence in italics deserves another examination. Does "tranquillity and indifference" in the "vale of obscurity" and in the face of adversity really demand our admiration and respect? Nestled in the middle of four paragraphs of a seemingly direct exposition, this thesis sentence is easily skimmed over; and the reader may fail to ponder whether indifference be a true measure of intrepidity or merely a measure of dull insensibility. In short, the reader may fail to recognize the deliberate overstatement, always a favorite device of satire. But, if the fifty-three-word sentence is read aloud, one hears the unmistakable ring of the early *Rambler* style of Samuel Johnson! Goldsmith's deliberate parody through Altangi is intended to highlight the incongruities between the rhetoric and reality, between the use of the Johnsonian idiom and its bearing a meaning totally antithetical to what Johnson himself had professed. Furthermore, this overstatement has been prepared for, and undermined, by one of Altangi's earlier comments: "The fortitude of European sages is but a dream; for where lies the merit in being insensible to the strokes of fortune, or in dissembling our sensibility; if we are insensible, that arises only from an happy constitution; that is a blessing previously granted by heaven, and which no art can procure, no institutions improve" (II, 200).

Such reflection on the exaggeration of the thesis is not demanded this early in the essay, however, because Goldsmith plans to carry it to a *reductio ad absurdum* through the story of the disabled soldier. After the first four paragraphs Goldsmith's strategy could take two directions: (1) the presentation of a story which would win sympathy for the distresses of the poor and through pathos gain the reader's admiration for fortitude in the face of misery; and (2) the presentation of a story which by means of irony and comic devices would develop a humorous twist from the overt thesis. If, as I believe, Goldsmith intended satire, he could not develop his essay in both directions at once. Rather the hard edge of the second will slyly play on and ultimately exploit the surface-level appearances of the first. The transitional paragraph between the introductory exposition and the soldier's story is important in providing us with a clue to Goldsmith's intention:

> I have been led into these reflections from accidentally meeting some days ago a poor fellow begging at one of the outlets of this town, with a wooden leg. I was curious to learn what had reduced him to his present situation; and after giving him what I thought proper, desired to know the history of his life and misfortunes, and the manner in which he was reduced to his present distress. The disabled soldier, for such he was, with an intrepidity truly British, leaning on his crutch, put himself into an attitude to comply with my request, and gave me his history. . . .
>
> (II, 459–60.)

"Intrepidity truly British" is loaded with irony in the context of *The Citizen of the World* because of its earlier pejorative usage, a usage which Goldsmith had gone to great pains to establish. The soldier is telling his story as payment for a handout, and he has obviously rehearsed telling it often. His thespian talents are highlighted when he "*put* himself into an attitude to comply with my request." He acts the role of an inherent optimist with a chorus of thank heavens for having lost *only* a leg and being reduced to the status of a beggar. The soldier's attitude burlesques a particular eighteenth-century optimistic view of happiness which, recognizing the imperfection in the nature of created things, attempted to explain away this imperfection by making it ultimately a good. The earlier sentence parody of Johnson should have reminded one, then, of Johnson's seething comment in his review of Soame Jenyns' *A Free Inquiry into the Nature and Origin of Evil:* "The poor, indeed, are insensible of many little vexations, which sometimes imbitter the possessions, and pollute the enjoyments, of the rich. They are not pained by casual incivility, or mortified by the mutilation of a compliment; but this happiness is like that of a malefactor, who ceases to feel the cords that bind him, when the pincers are tearing his flesh." [20]

Of course, the soldier is continually explaining away his "distresses." For five years he works ten hours a day and receives only meat and drink, but he is fortunate in having "the liberty of the whole house, and the yard before the door" (II, 460). He finds Newgate "as agreeable a place as ever I was in" because he has enough to eat and drink and yet does not have to work. He is transported to the plantations and is favored by "providence" because of a fever which takes away his hunger, a fever most fortunate in that there is a shortage of provisions anyway. On returning to England after being bound for seven years, the soldier declaims his love of liberty: "O liberty, liberty, liberty! that is the property of every Englishman, and I will die in its defence" (II, 462). Coming after a life of forced labor, a prison term, and seven years of slavery overseas, such an encomium is ridiculous. The ironic contrast between what the soldier praises and the actual bondage of his life is the same device we observed earlier in Letter IV; only now Goldsmith has used the device in an essay completely original in content. The hollowness of the soldier's rhetoric is highlighted when, immediately afterward, he describes his involuntary induction into the army by the press-gang. This incongruity no doubt satirizes the hypocrisy of the Whig propaganda and the use of press-gangs. Even such

[20] *Works of Johnson,* VI, 55.

a Whig historian as George Trevelyan could remark on the hypocrisy of Pitt evoking "the spirit of freedom to save the Empire" (Pitt really meant to *build* the Empire) and on the hypocrisy of these words of a popular naval war song—"To glory we call you, as freemen, not slaves, / For who are so free as the sons of the waves"—when "the press-gang was then the one strikingly unfree element in the relation of government to the citizen." [21]

Goldsmith's syntactical technique is to have the soldier make cheerful assertions in the main clauses and then unconsciously undercut his own optimism by describing incredible misfortunes in succeeding parenthetical or subordinate clauses: " '. . . and received *but* one wound, through the breast, *which is troublesome to this day*. . . . When the peace came on, I was discharged; and *as I could not work, because my wound was sometimes painful,* I listed for a landman in the East India company's service' " (II, 462–63; italics mine.). The italicized phrases demonstrate this conventional device of irony: the soldier receives only a single wound, but the absurdity of this understatement lies in the contrast between what the soldier "with an intrepidity truly British" considers insignificant, and thus subordinates, and what readers would render most important. Later the soldier is again pressed into service, this time as a sailor, at the beginning of the Seven Years' War. He is ultimately captured and thrown into prison—he is perpetually in jail—and Goldsmith uses the situation to mimic another war slogan, "one Englishman is able to beat five French at any time." The soldier and a boatswain attempt to escape: "We had no arms; but one Englishman is able to beat five French at any time; so we went down to the door, where both the centries were posted, and rushing upon them, seized their arms in a moment, and knocked them down. From thence,

[21] *History of England* (London, 1926), p. 543.

nine of us ran together to the key, and seizing the first boat we met, got out of the harbour, and put to sea . . ." (II, 464). The soldier attempts to give the impression that he and the boatswain subdued a numerically superior force of French sentries, but the reader thinks otherwise after discovering in the next sentence that nine prisoners have escaped. It is important to see here how Goldsmith exploits an unreliable narrator through incongruities in his narration; the same technique is used in *The Vicar of Wakefield*. This discrepancy in the soldier's narrative is re-inforced when the soldier describes the defeat of his ship (twenty-three guns) by a French man-of-war (forty guns): "I verily believe we should have taken the Frenchman; but, unfortunately, we lost all our men just as we were going to get the victory" (II, 464). There can be little doubt that Goldsmith was parodying the Whig propagandists' lame alibis for British defeats.

The comic pattern of development in this essay, extreme intrepidity maintained in the face of extreme misfortune, reaches its climax in the final paragraph of the soldier's narrative, when in the casual manner of an almost forgotten afterthought the soldier remembers to relate the source of his battle wounds:

"I had almost forgot to tell you, that in this last engagement I was wounded in two places; I lost four fingers of the left hand, and my leg was shot off. Had I the good fortune to have lost my leg and use of my hand on board a king's ship, and not a privateer, I should have been entitled to cloathing and maintenance during the rest of my life, but that was not my chance; one man is born with a silver spoon in his mouth, and another with a wooden ladle. However, blessed be God, I enjoy good health, and will for ever love liberty and Old England."

(II, 464–65.)

His narrative completed, the soldier leaves, and the essay

is concluded with Altangi's point of view: "Thus saying, he limped off, leaving my friend and me in admiration at his intrepidity and content; nor could we avoid acknowledging, that an habitual acquaintance with misery is the truest school of fortitude and philosophy" (II, 465).

A major problem in interpreting this essay is to determine first, whether we are to accept Altangi's "admiration" of the soldier's intrepidity as serious or as ironic in the deadpan tradition, and second, whether Altangi's point of view is synonymous with Goldsmith's, thereby becoming a device designed to direct the reader's responses toward the essay in the way that Goldsmith intended. The editors of one short story anthology containing Goldsmith's essay equate the author's point of view with Altangi's: "In a traditional tale like Goldsmith's, the narrator provided a frame whose purpose it was to tell the reader exactly what the story meant and how he was to feel about it. In a modern story like Conrad Aiken's 'Strange Moonlight,' on the other hand, no explicit effort is made to hamstring the reader: neither the dialogue of the characters nor the narration of the author pretends to interpret the story fully." [22] Surely it is now apparent that eighteenth-century narrative techniques are more sophisticated than this. Altangi has already been the object of satire because of his own boasting of intrepidity. There is perhaps the rather lame possibility that Altangi has now learned his lesson and is himself being ironic in his "admiration" of the soldier's fortitude. Regardless of the narrator's attitude, however, the soldier's narrative contains its own signposts that indicate a satirical intention on the part of Goldsmith, and any attempt to view this essay as a comic moral lesson in praise of intrepidity is to fail to see its underlying strategy. If we are left dry-eyed

[22] Jack B. Ludwig and W. Richard Poirier, eds., *Stories: British and American* (Boston, 1953), p. iii.

at the distresses of the disabled soldier, it is because he has all of the artificiality of a recruiting poster come to life. Furthermore, "admiration," earlier exploited by Swift in a blame-by-praise sense not of liking but of mere amazement, is operating in a similar context here.[23] Patriotic slogans are ridiculed by being parroted by a vagabond who has been the victim of them. The entire complex of British jingoism in 1760 is here being satirized, and the ironic method of undercutting verbal platitudes with concrete situations (a contrast between the ideal and the real) is double edged. False ideals expressed in terms of propaganda are attacked as well as the immorality of English legalism, untempered by mercy, adhering to forms, and lacking compassion. We remain detached from the disabled soldier because, as Goldsmith knew, we cannot easily feel sorry for those who do not feel sorry for themselves. That "misery" is the truest school of fortitude and philosophy is, in the context of the essay, as absurd a deduction as the original thesis that the truly great man is one who can remain tranquil and indifferent to his miseries even in obscurity. The disabled soldier, for that matter, like the actors of heroic tragedy whom he imitates, has *his* audience and can hardly be said to suffer in a "vale of obscurity." The underlying moral issue in both Letter IV and this essay is that on which we quoted Johnson earlier: "The shame is to impose words for ideas upon ourselves or others."

The Man in Black and the Pathology of Universal Benevolence

Before examining Letter XXVI, "The character of the man in black; with some instances of his inconsistent con-

[23] See John M. Bullitt, *Jonathan Swift and the Anatomy of Satire* (Cambridge, Mass., 1953), p. 54.

duct," we might, at the risk of oversimplification, review briefly eighteenth-century attitudes toward benevolence. As an ethical ideal benevolence was certainly the object of praise; as an overused slogan it was the object of satire by such writers as Fielding and Goldsmith, who delighted in showing how those who professed to be charitable to an extreme often revealed their hypocrisy by their actions. There were also those theologians and philosophers, optimistic in outlook, who sought to demonstrate that benevolence was an inherent universal law, that man was naturally good, and that benevolence was therefore naturally easy. From the conservative point of view, the error of these optimists was their belief that an ethical ideal was an actual law of nature. Skeptics such as Mandeville and Augustinian Christians such as Johnson attacked such facile optimism by maintaining that man was not naturally good or benevolent, that the act of charity was frequently motivated by vanity or self-interest, and that man was indeed a very selfish creature. For Johnson, any theory of life extolling the natural goodness of man would in turn threaten the orthodox Christian view of man as a sinful being badly in need of grace and redemption: for the Augustinian, virtue is not natural, and therefore easy, but rather a constant struggle. This attitude explains Johnson's discussion of Mrs. Montagu's conspicuous benevolence:

A literary lady of large fortune was mentioned, as one who did good to many, but by no means 'by stealth,' and instead of 'blushing to find it fame,' acted evidently from vanity. JOHNSON. 'I have seen no beings who do as much good from benevolence, as she does, from whatever motive. If there are such under the earth, or in the clouds, I wish they would come up, or come down. What Soame Jenyns says upon this subject is not to be minded; he is a wit. No, Sir; to act from pure benevolence is not possible for finite beings. Human benevolence is mingled with vanity, interest, or some other motive.[24]

Johnson attacks an overly scrupulous attitude toward benevolence put forth by those optimists who, once they had made benevolence an inherent law in the universe, then defined it so narrowly that few individuals, if any, could truly be said to have practiced it. The theory that self-love and benevolence are incompatible was probably associated by most eighteenth-century gentlemen with Shaftesbury's disciple, Francis Hutcheson: "As to the *Love* of *Benevolence*, the very Name excludes *Self-Interest*. We never call that Man *benevolent*, who is in fact useful to others, but at the same time only intends *his own Interest*, without any ultimate desire of the *Good of others*. If there be any *Benevolence* at all, it must be *disinterested*; for the most useful Action imaginable, loses all appearance of *Benevolence*, as soon as we discern that it only flowed from Self-Love, or Interest." [25]

The second sense of benevolence as defined in the *Oxford English Dictionary* is that of a "Favourable feeling or disposition, as an emotion manifested towards another; affection; goodwill (towards a particular person or on a particular occasion)." The important factor in this definition is the emphasis on feeling. Given a character who is virtuous and benevolent, and given a prolonged and repeated emphasis on the benevolent feelings of that character designed to win readers' sympathy toward the character, a novel or an essay will then contain an essential ingredient for the development of sentimentalism. Sentimental literature, then, in part grows out of an underlying philosophical optimism that believed in benevolence both as a law of nature and as a state of emotion in

---

[24] Boswell, *Life*, III, 48.

[25] *An Inquiry into the Original of our Ideas of Beauty and Virtue*, 3d ed. (London, 1739), p. 135.

individuals.[26] If the empirical comic moralists satirized the excessive emphasis on reason divorced from the emotions (Goldsmith's satire of Altangi's rationalism), so these writers would also attack the excessive emphasis on emotions divorced from reason. Benevolence unchecked by prudence (a regard for self-interest) was a violation of the golden mean; prudence too was considered a supreme virtue: "It [prudence] necessarily supposes the utmost perfection of all the intellectual and of all the moral virtues. It is the best head joined to the best heart. It is the most perfect wisdom combined with the most perfect virtue."[27]

Goldsmith's own attitude on the subject of benevolence was hinted at in an essay entitled "On Justice and Generosity," which was published in the Bee (October 20, 1759). Although over half of the essay is a translation from an essay by Justus Van Effen, the very fact that Goldsmith translated it and later reprinted it in a collection of his essays in 1765 indicates how strongly the essential theme appealed to him: "The qualities of candour, fortitude, charity, and generosity, for instance, are not in their own nature, virtues; and, if ever they deserve the title, it is owing only to justice, which impels and directs them. Without such a moderator, candour might become indiscretion, fortitude obstinacy, charity imprudence, and generosity mistaken profusion" (I, 406).

A more original treatment of this theme is found in "The Proceedings of Providence vindicated. An Eastern Tale,"

[26] See Ronald S. Crane, "Suggestions towards a Genealogy of the Man of Feeling," ELH, I (1934), 205–30. It has been brought to my attention, however, that Crane's essay ought to be reconsidered on two points: (1) the definition of Latitudinarianism and (2) the full sermon contexts of some of the passages selected to illustrate an emphasis on intense feeling and which apparently describe the Christian *after* the individual is in a state of grace.

[27] Adam Smith, The Theory of Moral Sentiments (London, 1857), p. 348.

published in the 1765 collection of essays. Asem practices a life of benevolence until he loses his entire fortune. When his friends fail to respond with equal benevolence, Asem becomes a man-hater and withdraws from civilization. About to drown himself, Asem is stopped by a genie, who then shows him a land of "rational inhabitants" without vice. It is, however, a society without polite arts, wisdom, or friendship. Asem discovers an inhabitant starving to death along the road because, since all inhabitants possess only enough provisions for a single meal, it would be an injustice for them to give food to the starving man. The country bewilders Asem, for, as the genie points out, "Nothing less than universal benevolence is free from vice, and that you see is practised here" (III, 65). Asem then goes back to the world of men, having learned the lesson that in a world of universal benevolence in which there is no vice, neither is there any virtue. He will now control his benevolence by prudence.[28]

Robert Heilman has shown how in *The Good-Natured Man* (1768) Goldsmith's central character Honeywood was created as a sentimental hero not to be admired but rather to be ridiculed. Heilman recognizes the similarity between "On Justice and Generosity" and Goldsmith's satire on Honeywood: "In *GNM* Goldsmith dramatizes the generalities of *The Bee*: Young Honeywood is prodigality, disguised as generosity and justified with magniloquence. So close is the parallel that it is difficult to imagine Goldsmith's writing the play without having in mind the earlier essay. It is so tonic and unsentimental that Goldsmith could hardly now turn sentimental or fall short of his intention to use the materials of sentimental plays for the sake of ridiculing them. What he attacked so often, he could hardly yield to, even unconsciously."[29] Heilman's

---

[28] This benevolence-ruled-by-prudence thesis has been perceptively discussed by Sherburn in *A Literary History of England*, p. 1058.

[29] "The Sentimentalism of Goldsmith's *Good-Natured Man*," p. 243.

analysis is a pioneering but seldom-quoted corrective of traditional Goldsmith criticism which views this play as sentimental in spite of an antisentimental intention. Goldsmith's ridicule of a blindly benevolent central character will remind many readers of Johnson's essay *Rambler* No. 99:

> To love all men is our duty, so far as it includes a general habit of benevolence, and readiness of occasional kindness; but to love all equally is impossible; at least impossible without the extinction of those passions which now produce all our pains and all our pleasures; without the disuse, if not the abolition, of some of our faculties, and the suppression of all our hopes and fears in apathy and indifference.
>
> The necessities of our condition require a thousand offices of tenderness, which mere regard for the species will never dictate. Every man has frequent grievances which only the solicitude of friendship will discover and remedy, and which would remain for ever unheeded in the mighty heap of human calamity, were it only surveyed by the eye of general benevolence equally attentive to every misery.[30]

All of this background material is necessary if we are to understand Goldsmith's ironic treatment of the Man in Black in *The Citizen of the World*. Letter XXVI—"The character of the man in black; with some instances of his inconsistent conduct"—represents one of the cleverest and most misunderstood essays of the entire eighteenth century. The story is narrated by Altangi so that the Man in Black is described in the third-person point of view. Whereas Goldsmith has elsewhere satirized the mounting of universal benevolence, in this essay there appears to be a completely different approach: the Man in Black de-

---

[30] *Works of Johnson*, II, 469–70. Published on February 26, 1751, Johnson's essay may have suggested to Goldsmith the theme for "Asem the Man Hater."

tests overt boasting about benevolence and extols the virtues of prudence, while in his actions he practices an extravagant benevolence that he attempts to conceal from others. He is described as a "humourist in a nation of humourists" and as the only man known to Altangi who seems "ashamed of his natural benevolence" (II, 109). This expository portrayal of the Man in Black is then dramatized by a narration of an excursion into the country. John Forster's interpretation is the traditional (sentimental) interpretation of this country ramble: "The country ramble of the Man in Black, wherein, to accompaniment of the most angry invective, he performs acts of the most exquisite charity; where with harsh loud voice he denounces the poor, while with wistful compassionate face he relieves them; where, by way of detecting imposture, he domineeringly buys a shilling's worth of matches, receives the astonished beggar's whole bundle and blessing, and, intimating that he has taken in the seller and shall make money of his bargain, bestows them next moment on a tramper with an objurgation; is surely never to be read unmoved." [31] If we were to accept this interpretation, the country excursion would present a comic contrast between the Man in Black's stern professions of the virtue of prudence and his generous charity to the three poor people. If we were to read the story this way, we might even shed a tear or be deeply touched at the Man in Black's generosity in alleviating the poverty of the woman in rags. Such an interpretation would reduce the story to pathos, the moral intention would appear to be that of praising benevolence, and the conclusion would be sentimental in that the reader would indulge in a luxury of feeling in admiration for the muddled but well-intended actions of the Man in Black. Such an interpretation then leads to a superficial analogy between the Man in Black

[31] *The Life and Times of Oliver Goldsmith*, I, 261.

and the Vicar of Wakefield, both of whom we are to admire for their benevolence.

What has happened, however, to the satirical significance, if there is any, of Goldsmith's essay? If the essay has a moral, the moral as traditionally interpreted is too easily gained, and Goldsmith is playing on our sensibility. If, on the other hand, there is a conflict between sense and sensibility, the real moral is not so readily obvious. After declaiming against charity to the poor, the Man in Black meets the first beggar:

> . . . an old man who still had about him the remnants of tattered finery, implored our compassion. He assured us that he was no common beggar, but forced into the shameful profession, to support a dying wife and five hungry children. *Being prepossessed against such false-hoods, his story had not the least influence upon me;* but it was quite otherwise with the man in black; I could see it visibly operate upon his countenance, and effectually interrupt his harrangue. I could easily perceive that his heart burned to relieve the five starving children, but he seemed ashamed to discover his weakness to me. While he thus hesitated between compassion and pride, I pretended to look another way, and he seized this opportunity of giving the poor petitioner a piece of silver bidding him at the same time, in order that I should hear, go work for his bread, and not teize passengers with such impertinent falsehoods for the future.
>
> (II, 110; italics mine.)

We may infer that this beggar is a fraud on the basis of Altangi's point of view, which I have italicized. The presentation of a piece of silver to the beggar by the Man in Black is extraordinarily generous, to say the least. It is only on the surface that the comic contrast exists between the Man in Black's charity to the beggar and his frantic attempts to hide his act from Altangi. The underlying satire relies on the reader's awareness of the blindness of this charity—charity that by its very blindness is false. Earlier in *The Citizen of the World*, in Letter XXIII, "The English Subscription in Favour of the French Prisoners Commended," Altangi had provided the reader with an example of true benevolence—emotion controlled by reason: "In other countries the giver is generally influenced by the immediate impulse of pity; his generosity is exerted as much to relieve his own uneasy sensations, as to comfort the object in distress: in England benefactions are of a more general nature; some men of fortune and universal benevolence propose the proper objects; the wants and the merits of the petitioners are canvassed by the people; neither passion nor pity find a place in the cool discussion; and charity is then only exerted when it has received the approbation of reason" (II, 97–98). Since Altangi's concept of benevolence is here not an object of ridicule, his point of view undercuts the Man in Black's charity, which we can now recognize as a therapeutic means of relieving "his own uneasy sensations." After giving the piece of silver, the Man in Black maintains his prudent mask, expounding "on his own amazing prudence and œconomy, . . . his profound skill in discovering imposters." His rhetoric is immediately undercut by the appearance of a sailor with a wooden leg, who petitions for charity:

> I was for going on without taking any notice, but my friend looking wishfully upon the poor petitioner, bid me stop, and he would shew me with how much ease he could at any time detect an impostor. He now therefore assumed a look of importance, and in an angry tone began to examine the sailor, demanding in what engagement he was thus disabled and rendered unfit for service. The sailor replied in a tone as angrily as he, that he had been an officer on board a private ship of war, and that he had lost his leg abroad in defence of those who did nothing at home. At this reply, all my friend's importance vanished in a moment; he had not a single question more

to ask; he now only studied what method he should take
to relieve him unobserved. He had however no easy part
to act, as he was obliged to preserve the appearance of
ill nature before me, and yet relieve himself by relieving
the sailor. Casting therefore a furious look upon some
bundles of chips which the fellow carried in a string at
his back, my friend demanded how he sold his matches;
but not waiting for a reply, desired, in a surly tone, to
have a shilling's worth. The sailor seemed at first surprised at his demand, but soon recollecting himself, and
presenting his whole bundle, Here, master, says he, take
all my cargo, and a blessing into the bargain.

(II, 111.)

The Man in Black's assertions about his skill in discovering impostors are preposterous, particularly after he has
just been duped by one. The sailor, at least, possesses a
genuine wooden leg and peddles matches in return for
charity. When the attempt to show that the sailor is an
impostor backfires, the Man in Black tries to conceal his
compulsive charity by purchasing the bundle of chips for
a shilling. No wonder the sailor is surprised and hands over
his entire merchandise! The bundle of chips is at best
worth only a few pence, but once the Man in Black performs this second act of charity, he is forced to convince
both himself and Altangi that he was not performing an
act of benevolence and that the chips are worth more
than a shilling. He now boasts of his frugality:

. . . he informed me of several different uses to which
those chips might be applied, he expatiated largely upon
the savings that would result from lighting candles with
a match instead of thrusting them into the fire. He
averred, that he would as soon have parted with a tooth
as his money to those vagabonds, unless for some valuable consideration. I cannot tell how long this panegyric
upon frugality and matches might have continued, had
not his attention been called off by another object more

[133]

distressful than either of the former. A woman in rags, with one child in her arms, and another on her back, was attempting to sing ballads, but with such a mournful voice that it was difficult to determine whether she was singing or crying. A wretch, who, in the deepest distress still aimed at good humour, was an object my friend was by no means capable of withstanding, his vivacity, and his discourse were instantly interrupted, upon this occasion his very dissimulation had forsaken him. Even, in my presence, he immediately applied his hands to his pockets, in order to relieve her, but guess his confusion, when he found he had already given away all the money he carried about him to former objects. The misery painted in the woman's visage, was not half so strongly expressed as the agony in his. He continued to search for some time, but to no purpose, 'till, at length, recollecting himself, with a face of ineffable good nature, as he had no money, he put into her hands his shilling's worth of matches.

(II, 111–12.)

The Man in Black gives a piece of silver to an obvious impostor, pays a shilling for a bundle of chips worth only a few pence, and then gives the bundle of chips to the woman with two children, deluding himself into the belief that she is getting the equivalent of a shilling; for he assumes a "face of ineffable good nature." In the process of relieving "his own uneasy sensations," the Man in Black fails to relieve "the object in distress." This essay is not a sentimental treatment of true benevolence which leaves us moved, but is rather a masterpiece of subtle satire directed against blind benevolence unchecked by prudence.[32]

[32] Robert Voitle refers to this essay when he writes perceptively, "According to Goldsmith, the sentimentalist is wrong not because he exaggerates the importance of benevolent emotions but because he perverts them." See *Samuel Johnson the Moralist* (Cambridge, Mass., 1961), p. 131. See also Thomas R. Preston, "Smollett and the Benevolent Misanthrope," *PMLA*, LXXIX (1964), 51–57.

This attack on the Hutchesonian doctrine of universal benevolence is continued in Letter XXVII, "The History of the Man in Black," which presents the case history of a patient suffering from the pathological effects of compulsive benevolence. The real villain is not the Man in Black, who is merely the victim of his environment, but rather his clergyman father:

"As his fortune was but small, he lived up to the very extent of it; he had no intentions of leaving his children money, for that was dross; he was resolved they should have learning; for learning he used to observe, was better than silver or gold. For this purpose he undertook to instruct us himself; and took as much pains to form our morals, as to improve our understanding. We were told that universal benevolence was what first cemented society; we were taught to consider all the wants of mankind as our own; to regard the *human face divine* with affection and esteem; he wound us up to be mere machines of pity, and rendered us incapable of withstanding the slightest impulse made either by real or fictitious distress; in a word, we were perfectly instructed in the art of *giving away* thousands, before we were taught the more necessary qualifications of *getting* a farthing."

(II, 114.)

The bitter tone which the Man in Black uses to describe his father's optimism and gross imprudence is one with which the reader tends to sympathize. If any analogies are to be made, one should compare the Vicar of Wakefield to the Man in Black's father rather than to the Man in Black himself. Indeed, the Man in Black's description of his education leads directly to the foolish discussions between the Vicar and his son Moses:

"I resembled, upon my first entrance into the busy and insidious world, one of those gladiators who were exposed without armour in the amphitheatre at Rome. My father,

[135]

however, who had only seen the world on one side, seemed to triumph in my superior discernment; though my whole stock of wisdom consisted in being able to talk like himself upon subjects that once were useful, because they were then topics of the busy world; but that now were utterly useless, because connected with the busy world no longer."

(II, 114.)

To see *The Vicar of Wakefield* as a panegyric rather than as a satire is to obscure the likenesses between the novel and the description in Letter XXVII. Extremes beget extremes, and the blind benevolence of the Man in Black in youth leads to the mask of extraordinary prudence in maturity; yet he remains a helpless practitioner of false benevolence because habit has been too strong.

Finally, to sentimentalize the Man in Black essays is to ignore the occasional tough-minded attitude toward indiscriminate charity found in the periodicals and magazines of the day. Two illustrations will demonstrate this point. In the *Annual Register* for 1758 the following account appears under a recapitulation of interesting news items from March: "A notorious imposter was detected at Edinburgh: when taken up, he had four pair of thick coarse stockings, a pillow under his waistcoat, and, by an affected motion in his head and hands, has had the address, for some time past, to pass upon the inhabitants as both dropsical and paralytical, and a very great object of charity. When freed of his dressings, he comes out to be a strong well-made fellow; and was immediately sent to the Castle, as very fit to serve as a soldier." [33] A week and a half after the appearance of "The Character of the Man in Black," the *Public Ledger* (April 12, 1760) carried the following news item under "London":

[33] *Annual Register*, 9th ed., I (1758), 86.

The comparatively few maimed beggars that have for some weeks past appeared in our streets, is no doubt owing to the commendable activity of some of our magistrates, who have lately taken upon them to see that the laws were duly enforced.

It is to be wished that some part of the same zeal was applied to the removal and proper correction of a woman, that is become an intolerable nuisance. This mendicant usually places herself in the most frequented streets of Westminster, not only in the day, but by candle-light, with a child at her breast, and three or four around her, where she soon collects a staring crowd, to the no small obstruction of the passengers. She has followed this trade for some time; and by her numerous train of infants, which are borrowed at a certain stipend per day, she moves the compassion of the weak and credulous. It is affirmed this woman has got in six hours upwards of three pounds. She has lately frequented about Great Queen-street, St. Martin's-lane, Northumberland House, and took her station on Thursday night at the end of Beufort Buildings in the Strand.[34]

This news item adds a delightful touch and another potential reversal to the Man in Black's pathological benevolence. The possibility that the woman to whom he gives the chips is also a fraud would be the final straw. In a world in which appearances are so deceiving, properly applied charity is difficult enough without committing oneself to *universal* benevolence.

[34] *Public Ledger*, I (April 12, 1760), 314.

Chapter Four

THE CRAFT OF HUMOR

*Goldsmith's Theory of Humor and the Shabby
Beau—A Caricature of Aristocratic Taste*

Humor in eighteenth-century literature has by no
means been described exhaustively. Critics have either
dealt with the term on a linguistic level or have dealt with
humor in psychologistic terms as it gives us an inside view
of character. If, however, we examine those characters in
the literary works themselves who are supposed to illustrate humor in practice, we may discover an incongruity
between literary theory and actual practice. Sir Roger de
Coverley illustrates this incongruity. Edward N. Hooker,
in his discussion of humor, stated that Addison and Steele
were "interested in humor that is endearing as well as singular," and that the *Spectator* "gives us aplenty the amiable idiosyncrasies which lift characters out of stereotypes
and which reflect the abundance of life that shines out to a
sensitive and sympathetic observer." [1] Although John Butt
recognized the difficulty of Addison and Steele portraying
a Tory squire sympathetically and recognized that the
country squire who had been a traditional object of satire

[1] "Humour in the Age of Pope," *Huntington Library Quarterly*, XI
(1948), 378. For a valuable study of the theory of humor and the
transition from corrosive satire to amiable humor in the eighteenth
and nineteenth centuries, see Stuart M. Tave, *The Amiable Humorist*
(Chicago, 1960).

on the Restoration stage "was still an object of contempt in the City, and in fashionable London society," he concluded that by "showing the humanity of the feudal relationship between squire and retainer, Addison tried to bring the town into closer sympathy with the country, to substitute affection for ridicule and to convert contempt into respect."[2] Both Hooker and Butt, then, see Roger de Coverley as a lovable eccentric character. They do not reconcile the contradiction between Addison and Steele's political affiliations and their creation of an apparently lovable Tory squire, nor do they support their opinions with a detailed analysis of the *Spectator* essays in which Sir Roger appears.

C. S. Lewis, on the other hand, in his classic essay on Addison, argued convincingly that Sir Roger de Coverley is a masterpiece of subtle satire. Instead of vilifying (the technique of the Tory satirists), Addison and Steele, observed Lewis, turn Sir Roger into "a dear old man": "The thought that he could ever be dangerous has been erased from our minds; but so also the thought that anything he said could ever be taken seriously. . . . What we might have been urged to attack as a fortress we are tricked into admiring as a ruin."[3] If Lewis' thesis that Addison and Steele are both patronizing and sly in their deliberately low-keyed portrayal of Sir Roger is correct, then Hooker has left out an important ingredient in his otherwise valuable sketch of eighteenth-century humor. Nor is Lewis alone in his interpretation. Donald J. Greene, in his discussion of the Tory myth, sees the need for a separate study of "Fielding's Squire Western, Addison's sly portraits of Sir Roger de Coverley and the Tory Fox-Hunter, and Macaulay's brutal and illiterate squire of 1685" and refers

---

[2] *The Augustan Age* (London, 1950), p. 39.
[3] "Addison," in *Eighteenth-Century English Literature: Modern Essays in Criticism*, ed. James L. Clifford (New York, 1959), p. 146.

to "Tory" as "the least fashionable of political labels, which Addison, most skillfully subtle of propagandists, had indelibly associated with stupid country squires."[4] And, in his magnificent edition of the *Spectator*, Donald F. Bond unequivocally sees Sir Roger as an object of satire.[5] Even if there is a trend in the eighteenth century away from corrosive satire to increasingly amiable humor (at least in theory), one must still recognize the satirical function in the very works that supposedly represent amiable humor. It is the crux of the critical problem involved in the interpretation of Sir Roger de Coverley. Because the *Spectator* had promised to avoid "party" from its very beginning, a direct frontal assault would be out. In a discussion of works of humor in the *Spectator*, No. 35, Addison had complained about their distorted fantasy and lack of realism. When viewed as a satirical character creation who is designed to undermine subversively the Tory ideology in an overtly nonpartisan context, Sir Roger de Coverley serves a satirical function of humor and is also portrayed realistically, i.e., believably. In the light of Addison's concept of a realistic humor, the subtlety of the satirical portrayal of Sir Roger becomes even more understandable. Rather than directly satirizing the sophisticated urban Tory aristocrats and leaders, Addison and Steele chose to use as a low character a country squire (the embodiment of humor) to reflect and satirize Tory attitudes. Even in its later usage in the eighteenth century, as Greene has indicated, humor may be used to serve a similar satirical end. All of this discussion suggests that at the root of some of his most original character creations resides Goldsmith's own self-consciously formulated theory of humor.

To understand Goldsmith's treatment of character, we

[4] *The Politics of Samuel Johnson* (New Haven, 1960), pp. 231, 236. See also my " 'The Good Old Cause' in Pope, Addison, and Steele," *Review of English Studies*, XVII (1966), 62–68.
[5] (Oxford, 1965), I, xxxvi.

must understand his distinction between "wit" and "humor," and his defense of the latter:

HOWEVER, by the power of one single monosyllable, our critics have almost got the victory over humour amongst us. Does the poet paint the absurdities of the vulgar; then he is *low:* does he exaggerate the features of folly, to render it more thoroughly ridiculous, he is then very *low*. In short, they have proscribed the comic or satyrical muse from every walk but high life, which, though abounding in fools as well as the humblest station, is by no means so fruitful in absurdity. Among well-bred fools we may despise much, but have little to laugh at; nature seems to present us with an universal blank of silk, ribbands, smiles and whispers; absurdity is the poet's game, and good breeding is the nice concealment of absurdities. The truth is, the critic generally mistakes humour for wit, which is a very different excellence. Wit raises human nature above its level; humour acts a contrary part, and equally depresses it. To expect exalted humour, is a contradiction in terms. . . .

(I, 320–21.)

It is not sufficient to say that this theory explains Goldsmith's use of "low" comic characters in his fiction and in his stage productions, for such an explanation ignores the moral nature of his satire. A good case in point is Beau Tibbs.

Beau Tibbs is a three-dimensional character attesting to Goldsmith's fully developed craftsmanship. He is not a mere mouthpiece or an abstraction—he is an individual:

Ah, Tibbs thou art an happy fellow, cried my companion with looks of infinite pity, I hope your fortune is as much improved as your understanding in such company? *Improved,* replied the other; *You shall know,— but let it go no further,—a great secret—five hundred a year to begin with.—My Lord's word of honour for it— His lordship took me down in his own chariot yesterday, and we had a tete-a-tete dinner in the country; where we talked of nothing else.* I fancy you forget sir, cried I, you told us but this moment of your dining yesterday in town! *Did I say so, replied he, cooly, to be sure if I said so; it was so—Dined in town; egad now I do remember, I did dine in town; but I dined in the country too; for you must know my boys I eat two dinners. By the bye, I am grown as nice as the Devil in my eating. I'll tell you a pleasant affair about that, we were a select party of us to dine at Lady Grogram's, an affected piece, but let it go no farther; a secret. . . .*

(II, 227.)

The flighty shifting of topics to avoid being pinned down, the staccato sentence fragments so characteristic of actual conversation, and the repetition of a favorite phrase to identify character, "Let it go no further—a secret," demonstrate that Goldsmith was by now a consummate artist able to write dialogue that could both vivify and reveal character. It is in fact the vivid concreteness of Beau Tibbs that may make him appear to be lovable. Lovable though he may be, however, Beau Tibbs embodies Goldsmith's theory of humor and serves a satirical function which a mere surface view of Beau Tibbs will fail to comprehend. Goldsmith believed that his age had witnessed a considerable decline in contemporary aristocratic manners and taste. The basic problem was how to ridicule this taste. The creation of an aristocratic fop was not the answer for Goldsmith because this device was worn out and because high society presented a "universal blank of silk, ribbands, smiles and whispers." But to take a character originating in a lower level of society and to use this character as a mirror reflecting in an exaggerated manner the affectations of the aristocrats would be a brilliant solution, one of its antecedents being John Gay's use in *The Beggar's Opera* of highwaymen and fences to parody the Whig administration of Walpole, and another being Hogarth's engravings. Beau Tibbs is more than a mere satire, however, against the aristocratic *nouveaux riches* themselves; he represents the potential corruption in taste and fashion of the entire middle class.

Throughout *The Citizen of the World* there is a sustained attack against those members of the aristocratic class who possessed neither merit nor virtue. In Letter XXXII, "Of the degeneracy of some of the English nobility . . . ," Altangi and the Man in Black see a nobleman pass by in a chariot drawn by six horses, attended by a retinue of coaches and followers. Altangi, greatly impressed, cannot understand his friend's disgust, for in China such a retinue indicates the merit of a mandarin. The Man in Black explains that the nobleman is a fool who, though descended from a "race of statesmen and heroes," is known remarkably only for "his kitchen and stable." With the ironic naïveté of the foreign observer, Altangi protests that such a man deserves not scorn but pity; for, lacking personal merit, the nobleman by reason of his position must be the more exposed to contempt, despised by his equals, and neglected by his inferiors. The Man in Black enlightens his friend: this aristocrat lacks taste, wit, and conversation and yet his company is eagerly sought after:

> Quality and title have such allurements, that hundreds are ready to give up all their own importance to cringe, to flatter, to look little, and to pall every pleasure in constraint merely to be among the great, though without the least hopes of improving their understanding or sharing their generosity: they might be happy among their equals, but those are despised for company, where they are despised in turn. You saw what a crowd of humble cousins, card-ruined beaux, and captains on half pay, were willing to make up this great man's retinue down to his country seat.
>
> (II, 139.)

In this attack on a degenerate aristocracy Goldsmith takes full advantage of the pejorative connotation of "great" established by the attack on Walpole's administration in earlier eighteenth-century satire. Like many another satirist of this period Goldsmith was familiar with conspicuous consumption as a means of seeking status. In Letter LII, "The impossibility of distinguishing men in England, by their dress . . . ," Altangi has become "a convert to English simplicity"; for earlier in his sojourn in Britain he was introduced to a company of extraordinarily "best dressed men" whom he assumed were nobility until informed that they were "a dancing master, two fiddlers, and a third rate actor." Altangi protests indignantly and suggests that the English copy a Chinese custom by making these paltry fellows wear the "instruments of their profession strung round their necks." The Man in Black retorts sarcastically:

Hold, my friend, replied my companion, were your reformation to take place, as dancing masters and fidlers now mimic gentlemen in appearance, we should then find our fine gentlemen conforming to theirs. A beau might be introduced to a lady of fashion with a fiddle case hanging at his neck by a red ribbon; and, instead of a cane, might carry a fiddle stick. Tho' to be as dull as a first rate dancing master might be used with proverbial justice; yet, dull as he is, many a fine gentleman sets him up as the proper standard of politeness, copies not only the pert vivacity of his air, but the flat insipidity of his conversation. In short, if you make a law against dancing masters imitating the fine gentleman, you should with as much reason enact, That no fine gentleman shall imitate the dancing master.

(II, 219.)

The aristocracy of the Augustan age, well bred and well educated, patronizing the scholar and the man of letters, setting the criteria of manners and of the arts for society, was the ideal against which Goldsmith set the taste of the aristocracy of his day and found it wanting: "Since the days of a certain prime minister of inglorious memory, the learned have been kept pretty much at a distance. A jockey, or a laced player, supplies the place of the scholar, poet, or the man of virtue. Those conversations, once the result of wisdom, wit, and innocence, are now turned to humbler topics, little more being expected from a companion than a laced coat, a pliant bow, and an immoderate friendship for—a well served table" (I, 311).

Howard J. Bell, Jr., has shown how Goldsmith consistently attacked the rich commercial class as a menace to the social stability of Britain: "It was not the power (such as it was) of the old noble families of which he wrote so bitterly, but rather the increasing influence of the newly rich commercial class. The members of this class, as he conceived of them, were unscrupulous, scheming, and power-mad: they pillaged from slaves the wealth of uncivilized lands in order to enslave Englishmen. So strong was his feeling against them that he lost no opportunity to get in a blow in his histories, his essays, his poems, even in his novel." [6] Once we accept Bell's thesis, amply supported by Goldsmith's works, and once we understand the full implications of Goldsmith's theory of humor, there can be no doubt as to the satirical function that Beau Tibbs serves. Tibbs's dress is the very caricature of aristocratic garb: "His hat was pinch'd up with peculiar smartness; his looks were pale, thin, and sharp; round his neck he wore a broad black ribbon, and in his bosom a buckle studded with glass; his coat was trimmed with tarnish'd twist; he wore by his side a sword with a black hilt, and his stockings of silk, though newly wash'd, were grown yel-

[6] "*The Deserted Village* and Goldsmith's Social Doctrines," *PMLA*, LIX (1944), 759.

low by long service" (II, 226). The "pale, thin, and sharp" looks, the "broad black ribbon" round Tibbs's neck, the coat trimmed with twist, and the focus on the silk stockings—all have a remarkable visual parallel in Joshua Reynolds' caricature of Lord Ailesbury (1751).[7] There is no reason to believe that Goldsmith knew of Reynolds' caricature at the time he was writing the "Chinese letters." Rather, the parallel demonstrates how stereotyped the English aristocratic mode was and how two great artists in different media arrived at an almost identical caricature of this stereotype. The order of Goldsmith's description, culminating with a focus on the silk stockings, is precisely the manner in which the eye follows Reynolds' caricature (Figure I) from head to foot, pausing to scan the highly stylized position of the front leg of Lord Ailesbury. Both Goldsmith's and Reynolds' caricatures may stem from Hogarth's portrayal of the French dancing master in Plate Two of A Rake's Progress (Figure II): the dancing master's posture is too stylized, and, as C. J. Rawson has written, "the gentleman should learn to dance well, yet not like a dancing-master." [8] The difference between Reynolds' caricature and Goldsmith's description of Beau Tibbs is that Reynolds could have actually presented his as a gift to Lord Ailesbury had he wished, an amiable comic tribute to the real thing. Goldsmith's portrayal, like that of Hogarth's French dancing master, satirizes through a low character the false taste of a segment of the aristocracy and primarily the prosperous middle class's attempt to imitate that taste.[9]

Beau Tibbs caricatures in the flesh aristocratic affecta-

[7] See Ellis K. Waterhouse, Reynolds (London, 1941), plate 15.
[8] "Gentlemen and Dancing-Masters," Eighteenth-Century Studies, I (1967), 156.
[9] As Ronald Paulson observes, "Hogarth's second 'Progress' is of the wealthy bourgeois who tries to ape the aristocratic rake. . . ." Hogarth's Graphic Works, ed. Paulson, 2 vols. (New Haven, 1965), I, 161.

Figure I. Joshua Reynolds, *Caricature* (Lords Ailesbury and Milltown, Mr. Henry, and Mr. Ward),
1751. Courtesy of the National Gallery of Ireland.

tions which elsewhere in *The Citizen of the World* are attacked by Altangi himself or by his companion. Thus, when
in Letter LIV, "The character of an important trifler,"
Beau Tibbs makes the ridiculous criticism that at Lady

Figure II. William Hogarth, A *Rake's Progress*. Reproduced by permission of the Huntington Library, San Marino, California.

Grogram's *"there happened to be no Assa-foetida in the sauce to a turkey,"* he caricatures the lord's taste in cookery that the Man in Black mocked in Letter XXXII. When Altangi visits Beau Tibbs's apartment, the gimcracks mock the more expensive gimcracks of the aristocrats: "We waited some time for Mrs. Tibbs's arrival, during which interval I had a full opportunity of surveying the chamber, and all its furniture; which consisted of four chairs with old wrought bottoms, that he assured me were his wife's embroidery; a square table that had been once japanned, a cradle in one corner, a lumbering cabinet in the other; a broken shepherdess, and a mandarine without an head, were stuck over the chimney; and round the walls several paltry, unframed pictures, which he observed, were all of his own drawing . . ." (II, 231). The "mandarine without an head" reflects the English fad for pseudo-Chinese culture, which Altangi attacks in Letter XIV, "The reception of the Chinese from a lady of distinction": "She took me through several rooms all furnished, as she told me, in the Chinese manner; sprawling draggons, squatting pagods, and clumsy mandarines, were stuck upon every shelf: in turning round one must have used caution not to demolish a part of the precarious furniture" (II, 65). When the lady informs Altangi that her favorite mandarine had its head snapped off by a careless servant, we are justified in wondering if it is the same broken mandarine perched on Beau Tibbs's mantelpiece. The pride taken by Beau Tibbs in his supposed own drawings reflects the current fad among the nobility for painting, a fad ridiculed in Letter XXXIV, "Of the present ridiculous passion of the nobility for painting."

Painting is now become the sole object of fashionable care; the title of connoisseur in that art is at present the safest passport into every fashionable society; a well timed shrug, an admiring attitude, and one or two exotic tones of exclamation are sufficient qualifications for men of low circumstances to curry favour; even some of the young nobility are themselves early instructed in handling the pencil, while their happy parents, big with expectation, foresee the walls of every apartment covered with the manufactures of their posterity.

(II, 148–49.)

The same fad is mocked in Letter XLVIII, "The absurdity of persons in high station pursuing employments beneath them. . . ." Altangi discovers a young prince learning to paint in a workshop: "Need I tell, that it struck me with very disagreeable sensations *to see a youth who, by his station in life, had it in his power to be useful to thousands, thus letting his mind run to waste upon canvas, at the same time fancying himself improving in taste, and filling his rank with proper decorum"* (II, 202).

Certainly one of the most entertaining essays in *The Citizen of the World* is Letter LXXI, "The shabby beau, the man in black, the Chinese philosopher, &. at Vauxhall." The caricature of aristocratic taste is found in the Tibbses' refusal to be pleased by anything: thus the aristocrat by wealth, too uncultured to be committed to any criterion of taste, can bluff by pretending to reject all criteria. F. L. Lucas asserts that this essay attacks one of Goldsmith's lifelong abominations, "the aesthetic snob." [10] Beau Tibbs and his wife are lovable only in that they obliquely ridicule their social peers. We scorn more an aristocratic fool who has more opportunity for self-knowledge than the ignorant fool who tries to emulate him.

Goldsmith adds a further level of irony to this essay by having Beau Tibbs and his wife set the standards of propriety for the widow, who, having come primarily to see the waterworks display, is forced by her own inhibitions and ignorance of social propriety to miss the display because Mrs. Tibbs is singing: "The widow's face, I own, gave me high entertainment; in it I could plainly read the struggle she felt between good breeding and curiosity; she had talked of the water-works the whole evening before, and seemed to have come merely in order to see them, but then she could not bounce out in the very middle of a

---

[10] *The Search for Good Sense*, p. 310.

song, for that would be forfeiting all pretensions to high life, or high-lived company ever after . . ." (II, 297). It is indeed a rare occasion when Beau Tibbs is considered "high life"! The situation ridicules the chain reaction (a chain of being of etiquette) in the imitation of "proper decorum" from the top level of society to the bottom. The most delightful touch of all is the description of Beau Tibbs and his wife making preparations for the wedding in the concluding letter of *The Citizen of the World*: "The little beau was constituted Master of the Ceremonies, and his wife Mrs. Tibbs conducted the entertainment with *proper* decorum. The man in black and the pawnbroker's widow, were very sprightly and tender upon this occasion. The widow was dressed up under the direction of Mrs. Tibbs, and as for her lover, his face was set off by the assistance of a pig-tail wig, which was lent by the little beau, to fit him for making love with *proper* formality" (II, 474; italics mine). "Proper" in the context of the letters we have been quoting is a pejorative word: it is the perfect adjective to describe the obsession of Beau Tibbs and of those whom he caricatures. It is the perfect adjective to describe a standard of fashion and taste based on a morally hollow social ideal. "Proper" sums up perfectly the paradox in Letter LII that the little beaux, the "triflers," define what is proper by the fashions and manners of the "great," and the "great" define what is "proper" by looking to their dancing masters. This relativity of social and cultural standards was a very real problem for Goldsmith's age, and by creating Beau Tibbs he sought to reform through ridicule and laughter the false taste and senseless manners of a segment of British aristocracy and of a middle class uncritically copying that aristocracy. Twentieth-century readers above all should be able to appreciate Goldsmith's achievement, for if we accept the premises of Thorstein Veblen's *Theory of the Leisure Class* and Vance Packard's *The Status Seekers*, his century's problem is now ours.

"Little" Beau Nash: The Monarch of Genteel Fashion

Unless we see how Beau Tibbs embodies Goldsmith's theory of humor, we shall fail to see that *The Life of Richard Nash*, despite its prefatory comments, is primarily satire. In the past this biography has been praised for putting into practice Samuel Johnson's theory of biography:

> Thus Goldsmith in advance of most of his contemporaries accepted in theory—and illustrated in practice . . . a conception of biography that was soon to be further perfected in *The Lives of the Poets* and Boswell's *Life of Johnson,* and was even to become the basis of present-day methods. The ideal of truth rather than panegyric, the will to pierce through the outer vestments of public acts to the real man within, the importance of the trivial and of the shadows as well as the lights of character to the moralist and the artist seeking convincing, rounded portraiture—such, in general, were the principles of these three biographies. And the dominating influence upon Goldsmith as well as upon Boswell was that of Johnson.[11]

Such an interpretation of *The Life of Richard Nash* is based on Goldsmith's avowed intention in the "Preface": "Instead therefore of a romantic history filled with warm pictures and fanciful adventures, the reader of the following account must rest satisfied with a genuine and candid recital compiled from the papers he left behind, and others equally authentic; a recital neither written with a spirit of satire nor panegyric, and with scarce any other

[11] Joseph E. Brown, "Goldsmith and Johnson on Biography," *Modern Language Notes,* XLII (1927), 171.

art, than that of arranging the materials in their natural order" (III, 288). Goldsmith's motive for emphasizing authenticity may have been, as Donald A. Stauffer suggests, to prevent the reader from associating the biography with "the life-and-amours school for scandal to which his subject might so readily have lent itself." [12] Stauffer himself is forced to admit that the biography contains more irony than the "Preface" would lead us to expect: "If he is not satiric, as he assures us, he is at least detached and superior. Something of the irony of the modern biographer may be detected, given more seriousness in Goldsmith by his careful scrutiny of the rise and fall of a figure with whose interests and ambitions the biographer cannot fully sympathize." [13]

Unfortunately, Stauffer does not go far enough. If on the surface Goldsmith seems to treat Richard Nash as an interesting biographical study, he provides sufficient clues to the underlying satire. Goldsmith's belief that the writer ought to be the monitor of his age should make us suspicious of his prefatory statement that *The Life of Richard Nash* "is well enough calculated to supply a *vacant* hour with innocent amusement, however it may fail to open the heart, or improve the understanding" (italics mine). *Spectator* Nos. 93 and 228, Johnson's *Idler* No. 67, and his *Dictionary* definitions of *vacant* as "empty of thought; not busy" and of *vacuity* as "inanity; want of reality," should all suggest the irony of the professed motive in writing *The Life*. The city of Bath during the latter half of the eighteenth century was, after all, a favorite setting for writers portraying the corruption of English manners and taste. To Goldsmith, Richard Nash was a paradoxical symbol of corrupt aristocratic taste, paradoxical because

[12] *The Art of Biography in Eighteenth-Century England* (Princeton, 1941), p. 382.
[13] *Ibid.*, p. 383.

although Nash actually *does* refine the manners of Bath
society it is absurd that *he* should be the *"Arbiter Elegan-
tiarum* of his time.*"* Smollett's *The Expedition of Humphry Clinker* (1771) will help us to understand Goldsmith's biography if we equate Goldsmith's underlying
attitude with that of Matthew Bramble:

> . . . men of low birth, and no breeding, have found
> themselves suddenly translated into a state of affluence,
> unknown to former ages; and no wonder that their brains
> should be intoxicated with pride, vanity, and presump-
> tion. Knowing no other criterion of greatness, but the
> ostentation of wealth, they discharge their affluence with-
> out taste or conduct, through every channel of the most
> absurd extravagance; and all of them hurry to Bath,
> because here, without any further qualification, they can
> mingle with the princes and nobles of the land.[14]

Goldsmith's use of irony in *The Life* is based in large part
on his maintaining the pose of the detached impartial
biographer, just as Smollett had ridiculed Bath society
through the voice of Jerry Melford, who, though seemingly more detached and impartial than his uncle, was no
less satirical:

> Here we have ministers of state, judges, generals, bishops,
> projectors, philosophers, wits, poets, players, *chemists,*
> *fiddlers,* and *buffoons.* If he makes any considerable stay
> in the place, he is sure of meeting with some particular
> friend, whom he did not expect to see; and to me there is
> nothing more agreeable, than such casual rencounters—
> Another entertainment, peculiar to Bath, arises from the
> general mixture of all degrees assembled in our public
> rooms, without distinction of rank or fortune. This is
> what my uncle reprobates, as a monstrous jumble of
> heterogeneous principles; a vile mob of noise and imperti-

[14] *The Expedition of Humphry Clinker,* ed. Knapp, pp. 36–37.

nence, without decency or subordination. But this chaos is to me a source of infinite amusement.[15]

Diminution is the primary device of irony and satire that Goldsmith uses in *The Life*.[16] Compared to Swift's corrosive use of debasing imagery, i.e., excretory and animal imagery, Goldsmith's method of diminution is extraordinarily mild, relying on the adjectives "little" and "some" to depress Nash and Bath society beneath the moral standard of the reader. This technique is begun in the "Preface": ". . . he [Nash] will be found to be a weak man, governing weaker subjects, and may be considered as resembling a monarch of *Cappadocia*, whom *Cicero* somewhere calls, *the little king of a little people*" (III, 289). "Little" is then related to "great" in the first paragraph of *The Life*: "The great and the little, as they have the same senses, and the same affections, generally present the same picture to the hand of the draughtsman; and whether the heroe or the clown be the subject of the memoir, it is only man that appears with all his native minuteness about him, for nothing very great was ever yet formed from the little materials of humanity" (III, 290). By reducing "the great" to the level of "the little," Goldsmith sets up an interchangeability of terms that carries the brunt of the satire. Traditionally in English society the lower classes look to the aristocrats, "the great," for social and cultural standards; but now the roles are reversed, and Richard Nash fulfills the role formerly played by the aristocrat. Goldsmith pretends to mock the reader who would still read biographies of the great in a search for heroic ideals to be emulated: "Yet if there

[15] *Ibid.*, pp. 48–49.
[16] See John M. Bullitt's definition of diminution as "any kind of speech which tends, either by the force of low or vulgar imagery, or by other suggestion, to depress an object below its usually accepted status." *Jonathan Swift and the Anatomy of Satire*, p. 45.

be any who think the subject of too little importance to command attention, and had rather gaze at the actions of the great, than be directed in guiding their own, I have one undeniable claim to their attention. Mr. *Nash* was himself a King. In this particular, perhaps no Biographer has been so happy as I. They who are for a delineation of men and manners may find some satisfaction that way, and those who delight in adventures of Kings and Queens, may perhaps find their hopes satisfied in another" (III, 291–92). In reality, of course, it is not the reader but the split between manners and aristocratic virtue in eighteenth-century society which is satirized here.

"Little" is repeated throughout the first part of the biography as a device conditioning, and thus controlling, the reader's point of view:

> It is a matter of very little importance who were the parents, or what was the education of a man who owed so little of his advancement to either. He seldom boasted of family or learning, and his father's name and circumstances were so little known, that Doctor *Cheyne* used frequently to say that *Nash* had no father.
>
> (III, 292.)
>
> His father had strained his little income to give his son such an education. . . .
>
> (III, 292.)
>
> In the neighbourhood of every university there are girls who with *some* beauty, *some coquettry*, and *little* fortune, lie upon the watch for every raw amorous youth, more inclined to make love than to study.
>
> (III, 293. Italics mine.)
>
> Though very poor he was very fine; he spread the little gold he had, in the most ostentatious manner, and though

the gilding was but thin, he laid it on as far as it would
go.

(III, 294.)

Throughout *The Life of Richard Nash* verbal irony
demonstrates the great incongruity between appearance
and reality: "Genteel" takes on sarcastic implications because it is equated with the outward appearance of clothes
and not with innate social grace.

> In this manner Mr. *Nash* spent some years about town,
> till at last his *genteel appearance*, his constant civility,
> and still more, his assiduity, gained him the acquaintance
> of several persons qualified to lead the fashion both by
> birth and fortune. To gain the friendship of the young
> nobility little more is requisite than much submission and
> very fine cloaths; dress has a mechanical influence upon
> the mind, and we naturally are awed into respect and
> esteem at the elegance of those, whom even our reason
> would teach us to contemn. He seemed early sensible of
> human weakness in this respect, he brought a person
> *genteely* dressed to every assembly, he always made one
> of those who are called very good company, and assur-
> ance gave him an air of elegance and ease.
>
> (III, 294. Italics mine.)

There is subtle irony in the position of "assiduity" in the
first sentence, last in the order of Nash's virtues but in
reality the most effective of his techniques for working
his way into "high" society. To reinforce this point, Goldsmith intrudes with an outright didactic comment on the
corrupt influence which appearances have on "the young
nobility," and then in the next sentence he disassociates
himself from social approval of Nash by the phrases "who
are *called* very good company" and "assurance gave him
an *air* of elegance and ease." At this stage the sensitive
reader perceives that Richard Nash is merely a Beau

Tibbs who has made good! Even if the impetus to write
this biography came from a commission by John Newbery, Goldsmith certainly must have realized quickly that
Richard Nash would serve admirably the identical satirical
function that Beau Tibbs had performed in *The Citizen
of the World*.[17] Fairly conclusive proof for this interpretation is found in Goldsmith's use of the same pejorative
phrases that he had previously used in the description of
Beau Tibbs and his wife:

> This ceremony which has been at length totally dis-
> continued, was last exhibited in honour of King *William,*
> and Mr. *Nash* was chosen to conduct the whole with
> *proper decorum.* He was then but a very young man, but
> we see at how early an age he was thought *proper* to
> guide the amusements of his country, and be the *Arbiter
> Elegantiarum* of his time; we see how early he gave
> proofs of that spirit of regularity, for which he after-
> wards became famous, and shewed an attention to those
> *little* circumstances, of which tho' the observance be
> *trifling,* the neglect has often interrupted men of the
> greatest abilities in the progress of their fortunes.
> (III, 294–95. Italics mine.)

"Proper decorum" was used sarcastically in Letter XLVIII
and somewhat less sarcastically in the concluding letter of
The Citizen of the World. The pejorative words "little"
and "trifling" satirize the incongruity between manners
and merit. That neglect of "little circumstances" should
handicap "men of the greatest abilities" while a beau like
Nash succeeds because of "trifling" observance of such
details demonstrates the monstrous perversion of cultural

[17] Goldsmith received from Newbery fourteen guineas for the life of
Nash, according to a receipt dated March 5, 1762. *The Life* was first
published in October, 1762, but a second edition with important additional material was published in December, 1762. Edmund Gosse con-
jectured that Newbury may not have been satisfied with the first edition.
See *Gossip in a Library* (London, 1891), p. 231.

values in English society. An intrusive moral comment by Goldsmith only two paragraphs later hammers home his point: "How many little Things do we see, without merit, or without friends, push themselves forward into public notice, and by self-advertizing, attract the attention of the day. The wise despise them, but the public are not all wise. Thus they succeed, rise upon the wing of folly, or of fashion, and by their success give a new sanction to effrontery" (III, 295). Eventually Nash becomes the monarch of the kingdom of manners, and by the juxtaposition of "great" and "little" Goldsmith portrays the breakdown of all traditional standards of value and discrimination: "Some of the nobility regarded him as an inoffensive, useful companion, the size of whose understanding was, in general, *level with their own;* but their *little* imitators admired him as a person of fine sense, and *great* good breeding" (III, 302; italics mine). The stunning impact of this passage stems from the understatement that those nobles who do not see Nash as a model to be emulated see him at least as an equal and not as an inferior. The pattern now becomes clear. Richard Nash has been "littlefied" in the early part of his biography so that when he becomes the monarch of Bath and "some nobility" consider his understanding on a "level" with their own, the so-called "great" become reduced to littleness and the "little" monarch in the eyes of his even littler imitators is seen as great. We are back to the social paradox of Letter LII in *The Citizen of the World,* in which beaux imitate gentlemen and gentlemen imitate their dancing masters. Richard Nash becomes a living embodiment of Goldsmith's theory of humor designed to penetrate and expose the hollowness of high society's "universal blank of silk, ribbons, smiles and whispers."

The most obvious signposts indicating satire in *The*

Life of Richard Nash are Goldsmith's direct moral reflections. Even some of these are ironic, however, and must be read with care. Thus, after sarcastically condemning Nash's authoritarianism in the realm of manners, Goldsmith pretends to defend him:

> Let the morose and grave censure an attention to forms and ceremonies, and rail at those, whose only business it is to regulate them; but tho' ceremony is very different from politeness, no country was ever yet polite, that was not first ceremonious. The natural gradation of breeding begins in savage disgust, proceeds to indifference, improves into attention, by degrees refines into ceremonious observance, and the trouble of being ceremonious at length produces politeness, elegance and ease. There is therefor some merit in mending society, even in one of the inferior steps of this gradation; and no man was more happy in this respect than Mr. *Nash.* In every nation there are enough who have no other business or care but that of buying pleasure; and he taught them, who bid at such an auction, the art of procuring what they sought without diminishing the pleasure of others.
>
> (III, 307.)

The repetition of "ceremonious" renders the word pejorative: the connotation is that of mere form or ritual without content or spirit. This sketch of social improvement is more akin to the civilizing of a society of Hottentots than to a supposedly already refined English society. Ultimately, the satire is directed at those whose only business is "*buying* pleasure," an indirect castigation of the wealthy leisure class devoid of any sense of moral or social responsibility. Goldsmith's ironic moral intrusion gains its effect because, as David Worcester has remarked, "Irony is never so sweet as when a character seems to defend his cause with consistency but in reality gives it completely away." [18] Much of the deadpan irony in *The Life of Richard Nash* is not very obvious until it is compared with points of view contained in certain letters in *The Citizen of the World:* "Concert breakfasts at the assembly-house, sometimes make also a part of the morning's amusement here, the expences of which are defrayed by a subscription among the men. Persons of rank and fortune who can perform are admitted into the orchestra, and find a pleasure in joining with the performers" (III, 309). While this passage is borrowed from another source, Goldsmith's attitude toward cultural dilettantism by those who should be contributing more profoundly to society was one of disgust and is reflected in Letter XLVIII, "The absurdity of persons in high station pursuing employments beneath them. . . ." [19] The description of Richard Nash traveling to *Tunbridge* "in a post chariot and six greys, with outriders, footmen, *French* horns, and every other appendage of expensive parade" (III, 311), is a caricature of the extraordinary equipage of the aristocrat satirized in Letter XXXII, "On the degeneracy of some of the English nobility. . . ."

Another object of satire in *The Life of Richard Nash* continued from *The Citizen of the World* is false benevolence. Richard Nash is described as having "generosity for the wretched in the highest degree, at a time when his creditors complained of his justice" (III, 295–96). One anecdote tells of a friend who collects a debt from Nash by having another friend borrow the sum in an appeal to the beau's generosity. Arthur Sherbo has suggested that Goldsmith invented the anecdote by developing it out of two sentences in the essay "On Justice and

---

[18] *The Art of Satire* (Cambridge, Mass., 1940), p. 87.
[19] Arthur Friedman estimates that one-tenth of *The Life* is taken from John Wood's *Essay Towards a Description of Bath* (1749). See his *Works of Goldsmith,* III, 281.

Generosity." [20] If Sherbo is right, this illustrates again
Goldsmith's ability to translate themes into concrete anec-
dotes and also warns us not to take Goldsmith too seriously when he claims in the "Preface" to be merely arranging his material "with little art."

There are times when Goldsmith drops the pose of the
detached biographer and uses sheer invective: "The duch-
ess of *Marlborough* seems not to be a much better writer
than Mr. *Nash*; but she was worth many hundred thousand pounds, and that might console her. It may give
splenetic philosophy, however, some scope for meditation, when it considers, what a parcel of stupid trifles
the world is ready to admire" (III, 333). He mocks the
imitators who hang around the great. As lords would have
their circle of admirers, so Richard Nash has his: "I have
before me a bundle of letters, all addressed from a pack
of flattering reptiles, to his *Honour* [Nash]; and even
some printed dedications, in the same servile strain" (III,
346). The tone of such passages as these is more that of
the righteous indignation of Swift than what we would
normally call Goldsmith's amiability. When a critic writes
that Goldsmith "liked Nash," "had a fellow-feeling for
the Beau," or that "towards such a man Goldsmith could
not possibly be harshly critical," his impressionistic criticism is simply not supported by a careful reading of *The
Life*.[21]

The final third of the biography presents another problem of interpretation. One critic observes that this section
"is overweight and anticlimactic" owing to the inclusion
of many of Nash's papers.[22] These documents not only add

[20] "A Manufactured Anecdote in Goldsmith's *Life of Richard Nash*,"
Modern Language Notes, LXX (1955), 20–22.
[21] Temple Scott, *Oliver Goldsmith Bibliographically and Biographically
Considered* (New York, 1928), p. 93.
[22] Wardle, *Oliver Goldsmith*, p. 136.

an air of authenticity but actually keep the reader more
detached from Nash's misfortunes than he might otherwise be. Stauffer, in spite of this, sees pathos in the conclusion: "Then, loading his palette with darker tones,
Goldsmith draws the octogenarian in which Goldsmith's
achievements in pathos and moralizing seem more certain
and moving than in comparable scenes in *The Vicar of
Wakefield* or—may it be hazarded?—in *The Deserted
Village*." [23] Pathos is of course a relative matter depending on the reaction of each reader to the text, but Goldsmith himself attempts to direct the reader into attitudes
other than pathos: "An old man thus striving after pleasure
is indeed an object of pity; but a man at once old and
poor, running on in this pursuit, might excite astonishment" (III, 361). There is a corrosive strain here which
in fact prevents sympathy: "a sight like this might well
serve as a satire on humanity; might shew that man is
the only preposterous creature alive, who pursues the
shadow of pleasure without temptation" (III, 361). That
Goldsmith tried to avoid the effect of pathos is demonstrated by the manner in which he quickly passes over
Nash's death. This is followed by a mock elegiac description of Nash's funeral:

> The crowd was so great, that not only the streets were
> filled, but, as one of the journals in a *Rant* expresses it,
> "even the tops of the houses were covered with spec-
> tators, each thought the occasion affected themselves
> most; as when a real King dies, they asked each other,
> *where shall we find such another;* sorrow sate upon every
> face, and even children lisped that their Sovereign was
> no more. The awfulness of the solemnity made the deep-
> est impression on the minds of the distressed inhabi-
> tants. The peasant discontinued his toil, the ox rested

---

[23] *The Art of Biography,* p. 385.

from the plough, all nature seemed to sympathize with
their loss, and the muffled bells rung a peal of Bob
Major."

(III, 366.)

This rhapsodic passage is followed by the moral reflection that "our deepest solemnities have something truly
ridiculous in them." Goldsmith does not hesitate to parody
epitaph-writing as well by means of an egregious pun on
the word "grave": "I remember one of those character
writers, and a very grave one too, after observing, alas!
that *Richard Nash,* Esq; was no more, went on to assure
us, that he was *sagacious, debonair, and commode;* and
concluded with gravely declaring, *that impotent posterity
would in vain fumble to produce his fellow*" (III, 367).
Goldsmith mocks in the biography what he had mocked
previously in Letter XII, "The funeral solemnities of the
English. Their passion for flattering epitaphs." The pathos
which many readers find in *The Life of Richard Nash* is
perhaps inherent in the situation of a doddering old fool
dying—certainly not in Goldsmith's treatment of it. And
while in the conclusion Goldsmith appears to soften good-
naturedly the corrosiveness of his satire by asserting that
Nash's "faults raise rather our mirth than our detestation"
(III, 378), still, the satire remains and the biography can
by no stretch of the imagination be called impartial.

The response of at least one contemporary review may
offer another bit of evidence that Goldsmith intended
satire in *The Life.* The majority of reviews quoted in
Friedman's introduction to *The Life* are unfavorable, but
one in the *Critical Review* for October, 1762, is, in Friedman's words, "kinder to the author than to the book":
"There is something in the manner in which the Memoirs
are written, that convinces us the author's talents are
equal to a greater subject. He has contrived to render his
narration amusing . . . to give his hero a degree of im-

portance, without painting a feature in his character to engage our esteem; and to make folly, dissipation, and profusion, appear not only venial, but in some measure amiable." The reviewer is shrewdly perceptive. His clinching remarks are that he pities the writer of *The Life*, "thus tortured to give substance to inanity," and that he thinks it "no injustice to the writer to consider him as a satyrist, who holds up the mirror of folly to the present generation." [24]

In view of this interpretation, *The Life of Richard Nash* will have to be given more emphasis in any assessment of Goldsmith's satire. The biography for the most part continues the same techniques of irony and diminution that Goldsmith used in *The Citizen of the World*.[25] Structurally, *The Life* is uneven and does tend to bog down toward the conclusion. By modern standards of biography or of ironic fiction Goldsmith makes too many intrusive moral observations in order to control the reader's point of view. There is a slight parallel here between Fielding's *Jonathan Wild* and *The Life of Richard Nash*, in that both are important in the development of the author's artistry, but both may tend to be weakened by being overly sustained. Yet it is no exaggeration to suggest that if Goldsmith had not sharpened his satirical techniques in *The Citizen of the World* and *The Life of Richard Nash*, *The Vicar of Wakefield* would not have been the superb comic masterpiece that it is.

[24] *Critical Review*, XIV (October, 1762), 270–71.

[25] For a similar and earlier use of diminution, see Letter LXXIV, "The Description of a Little Great Man." Valuable as his article on sources is, I cannot agree with Oliver Ferguson's conclusions about the "tact and humanity" of Goldsmith's treatment of Nash. Ferguson's conclusion is the traditional one that Goldsmith is having it both ways; I agree with the reviewer in the *Critical Review*. See "The Materials of History: Goldsmith's *Life of Nash*," PMLA, LXXX (1965), 372–86.

Chapter Five

FORTUNE AND THE HEAVENLY BANK:
THE VICAR OF WAKEFIELD AS
SUSTAINED SATIRE

A survey of interpretations of *The Vicar of Wakefield* from 1766 to the present will reveal that we have inherited an approach to *The Vicar* that judges the novel in terms of morality rather than in terms of narrative art. This moral approach appeared first in the *Monthly Review*, XXXIV (May, 1766), in a review of *The Vicar* which is of considerable importance. The reviewer frankly admits his inability to understand the novel and then retreats to the safe expedient of praising *The Vicar* for its morality:

Through the whole course of our travels in the wild regions of romance, we never met with any thing more difficult to characterize, than the Vicar of Wakefield; a performance which contains beauties sufficient to entitle it to almost the highest applause, and defects enough to put the discerning reader out of all patience with an author capable of so strangely under-writing himself.— With marks of genius equal, in some respects, to those which distinguish our most celebrated novel-writers, there are in this work, such palpable indications of the want of a thorough acquaintance with mankind, as might go near to prove the Author totally unqualified for success in this species of composition, were it not that he finds such resources in his own extraordinary natural talents, as may, in the judgment of many readers, in a great measure, compensate for his limited knowledge of men, manners, and characters, as they really appear in the living world.—In brief, with all its faults, there is much rational entertainment to be met with in this very singular tale: but it deserves our warmer approbation, for its moral tendency; particularly for the exemplary manner in which it recommends and enforces the great obligations of universal BENEVOLENCE: the most amiable quality that can possibly distinguish and adorn the WORTHY MAN and the GOOD CHRISTIAN! [1]

The phrases "strangely under-writing himself," "rational entertainment," and "this very singular tale" indicate that the critic was suspicious of satire. And in the light of our own analysis of *The Citizen of the World*, the reviewer's praise of the novel for its recommendation of "universal BENEVOLENCE" should indeed make us skeptical.[2] This uncritical attitude is characteristic of what was to follow in nineteenth-century criticism. Later critics differed only in being more emphatic about the moral value of *The Vicar* and thereby further undermined its artistic achievement.[3]

The danger of such an approach to *The Vicar* is demonstrated in the candid observation by Walter Allen: "Its popularity, indeed, has been quite disproportionate to its achievement as a novel, and much of it has undoubtedly been due to its 'niceness', which allowed adults to put it in the hands of young people when *Tom Jones* was considered improper."[4] This dichotomy between popularity and achievement cannot be ignored by any conscientious critic, nor is the label of morality sufficient for most con-

[1] *Monthly Review*, XXXIV (May, 1766), 407.
[2] See pp. 124–37 in this book for a discussion of Goldsmith's satire on universal benevolence in *The Citizen of the World*.
[3] The adjectival, syrupy, impressionistic tradition of nineteenth-century criticism of *The Vicar* has been documented in my 1961 University of Pennsylvania dissertation, "The Creative Genius of Oliver Goldsmith."
[4] *The English Novel* (London, 1954), p. 77.

temporary readers.[5] When compared to other major novels of the eighteenth century, *The Vicar of Wakefield* has been neglected by modern critics. Perhaps this critical neglect is due in part to traditional criticism which has placed *The Vicar* on a level of appreciation totally unacceptable to modern-day critics, who themselves have not given Goldsmith his artistic due because they have accepted the implicit corollary that the novel is an artistic failure.

Fortunately, in the last forty years a few critics have suggested that *The Vicar* is more of an artistic achievement than has been recognized in the past. In 1933 W. F. Gallaway, Jr., on the basis of a study of antisentimentalism in Goldsmith's works, suggested that Dr. Primrose, heretofore regarded as a hero, might have been originally conceived as an object of satire and that *The Vicar* might be "a satire on idealism comparable to *The Good Natured Man*—a satire broken in the end by an indulgence of the novelist to his own heart and to the hearts of a sentimental reading public."[6] Because Gallaway's pioneering study was concerned with the thematic study of sentimentalism in all of Goldsmith's works, his observations on the novel raise important questions without answering them. In 1934 Ernest Baker also argued vigorously for an interpretation of *The Vicar* as satire—satire broken in the end because Goldsmith lost artistic control of his materials:

. . . Goldsmith started in one direction, lost his way before he had gone far, and presently found himself going, without being able to stop, in a direction entirely

---

[5] The position that anyone who would truly appreciate *The Vicar* "should not try to criticize it, but should read and enjoy it as people have been doing ever since it was published" is surely an untenable one (Wardle, *Oliver Goldsmith*, p. 171). My own experience has been that students find *The Vicar* to be a very bad novel when interpreted along traditional lines.

[6] "The Sentimentalism of Goldsmith," *PMLA*, XLVIII (1933), 1181.

opposite. The idyll was to have been a comic idyll, a bitter-sweet pastoral, the bitterness concealed in the irony. Fielding had shown the possibility of a comic epic in prose, but whether the comic and the idyllic will go together is another question, assuredly not settled by Goldsmith. It was to be a fable at the expense of sentimental optimism, complacent trust in the supremacy of good, confidence that honesty will have its reward without a cautious sense of the wickedness of the world and the guile and unscrupulousness of others. The Vicar, so full of sound maxims, out of conceit in his own sagacity, out of the overweening optimism that he is always reproving, out of blindness to the perils which he loves to point out to his wife and children, is chiefly responsible for bringing calamity upon his own head and theirs.[7]

Working against a critical tradition over a hundred and fifty years old, Baker revealed his personal frustration when he complained, "There is a sort of conspiracy among critics to ignore the irony which was assuredly Goldsmith's intention, though he found it difficult to sustain." [8] Baker's observations have never been refuted, but neither do they appear to have gained general acceptance. It is illuminating, moreover, to see how Baker, in reacting against the homiletic tradition, unintentionally continued to undermine Goldsmith's artistry by assuming that the irony and satire in *The Vicar* were not sustained to the very end. On the positive side, Baker's interpretation in conjunction with Gallaway's study established a strong argument for viewing at least the first half of *The Vicar* as satirical. In 1950 D. W. Jefferson concentrated on Goldsmith's use of diminution, which reduces the emotional effect of Dr. Primrose's misfortunes on the reader. While Jefferson's analysis hinted at satire, he did not really come

[7] *The History of the English Novel,* 10 vols. (London, 1934), V, 81.
[8] *Ibid.,* V, 82n.

to any affirmative conclusions and in fact undermined his own astute examination of Goldsmith's subtle artistry by apologetically writing that "no claim to greatness is made for Goldsmith's novel." [9] Nonetheless, Jefferson's essay is important because of its close examination of the text in terms of art and not of morality. In 1951 this genuine critical approach was employed by Frederick W. Hilles, who in the introduction to his American Everyman edition of *The Vicar* demonstrated Goldsmith's artistry by showing how carefully the narrative structure was put together[10] and who thereby conclusively destroyed the traditional opinion that Goldsmith wrote *The Vicar* hastily—an opinion whereby critics could excuse what appeared to be many inconsistencies in the text. In 1958 Curtis Dahl found "a strong thematic unity" in *The Vicar* presented in patterns of "disguise, truth and appearance, blindness and sight." [11] Dahl does attempt to analyze *The Vicar,* but his conclusions are too mythic and generalized, while his analysis is not minute enough to explain individual cruxes. Dahl concludes: "Clearly no one interpretation can do justice to all facets of so rich a book as the *Vicar of Wakefield.* But if out of an analysis of the novel's complex but strong thematic structure any one principal meaning emerges, it is that unhappiness springs from an imperfect perception of truth while happiness is born of a capacity to see the real truth that lies behind appearance and disguise. Complete comprehension of absolute truth is never possible, but he who honestly and sincerely seeks to find the moral reality that is concealed behind worldly

[9] "Observations on *The Vicar of Wakefield,*" *Cambridge Journal,* III (1949–50), 626.

[10] *The Vicar of Wakefield,* introduction by F. W. Hilles, Everyman's Library, New American Edition (New York, 1951).

[11] "Patterns of Disguise in *The Vicar of Wakefield,*" *ELH,* XXV (1958), 96.

appearance will be *happy in his own heart,* however miserable he may appear in the eyes of others." [12] By now, it should be evident that a happiness consisting in any form of egoism, such as Dahl seems to be suggesting, would be alien to Goldsmith's previous satire in *The Citizen of the World.* It was not until 1964 that Ricardo Quintana could suggest in print that *The Vicar* is satire sustained to the very conclusion "by an irony which places in doubt the mood generated by a too-fortunate turn of events." [13] In 1965 W. O. S. Sutherland, Jr., viewed the novel as "kindly satire," although Goldsmith "makes ambiguous the degree to which the Vicar is satirized," and although he "shifts his satiric object during the course of the book" from a satire on Christian optimism to a satire on Primrose's "lack of knowledge of men." [14] Sutherland's curious thesis that a "sentimental author would not agree with Goldsmith, for it is characteristic of sentimentalism that it does not allow an ambivalent attitude toward its ideals," ignores the whole sad history of criticism of *The Vicar* that refused to see any ambivalence in it at all and that *did* read it as a sentimental novel. When Sutherland writes that Primrose "may cause difficulty to his friends and fam-

---

[12] *Ibid.,* XXV, 120.

[13] "The Deserted Village: Its Logical and Rhetorical Elements," *College English,* XXVI (1964), 214. See also Quintana's important discussion of *The Vicar* in Chapter Six of his *Oliver Goldsmith: A Georgian Study* (New York, 1967), pp. 99–115. Michael Adelstein's 1961 essay in *College English,* which sees the first part of the novel as a satire on Primrose's idealism and lack of prudence and the second part as an almost tragic celebration of Primrose's fortitude, returns one to the old cliché that Goldsmith changed his mind in the middle of the novel. Adelstein ignores Goldsmith's earlier satire on "fortitude" in *The Citizen of the World.* Macdonald Emslie's 1963 paperback guide to *The Vicar* seems to lack any sense of *The Vicar* as a unity, and it regrettably omits Hilles' American Everyman Edition discussion of the novel.

[14] *The Art of the Satirist* (Austin, Texas, 1965), pp. 83–91.

ily but he is not a threat to his society," he ignores Goldsmith's own earlier statements on the Anglican church and its complacent clergymen.[15]

Any analysis of *The Vicar of Wakefield* must operate on the premise that by 1762 Goldsmith was a mature creative artist not apt to be guilty of the artistic flaws that critics usually associate with the novel. Nor should such an analysis be hampered by traditional interpretations of *The Vicar*, which, as we have seen, are the result of a petrified impressionism that by its continuation as a dogma of literary history into the first half of the twentieth century has distorted our understanding of Goldsmith. *The Vicar* will be analyzed in this chapter, first, by studying the narrator's point of view and his relationship to other characters; second, by treating the structure of the novel as parody; and third, by treating the second half of the novel as aesthetically and logically prepared for in the first half so that satire is retained until the very end.

The Integrity of Dr. Primrose

The Vicar of Wakefield is perhaps the first English novel in which a clergyman becomes the narrator of an entire story. While it seems painfully obvious to remind ourselves that this first-person point of view does not necessarily represent Goldsmith's, critics of *The Vicar* have stumbled on this point from the very beginning. This confusion is found early in a review of the novel in the *Critical Review* (1776): "If it be objected, that there is not a sufficient variety of character, or a larger display of what is called Knowledge of the world, it is to be remembered that the whole is supposed to be written by the Vicar himself. . . ."[16] The anonymous critic seems to rec-

---

[15] *Ibid.*, p. 90.
[16] *Critical Review*, XXI (June, 1766), 439–41.

ognize that the naïve tone of the novel is due to a naïve
narrator, but later in this same review he fails to dissociate the narrative of Dr. Primrose from the point of
view of Goldsmith: "But pray, Dr. Goldsmith, was it necessary to bring the concluding calamities so thick upon
your old venerable friend; or in your impatience to get
to the end of your task, was you not rather disposed to
hurry the catastrophe?" The inconsistency shown by this
reviewer has persisted to the present day, yet the subtitle
of *The Vicar* clearly states, "A TALE Supposed to be written by HIMSELF." We might wonder why Goldsmith
uses "supposed" instead of "A Tale Written by Himself." [17] In his review of Thyer's *Genuine Remains of
Samuel Butler,* Goldsmith had quoted from Butler, "There
is a kind of physiognomy in the titles of books, no less
than in the faces of men, by which a skillful observer will
as well know what to expect from the one as the other"
(I, 212). In view of the importance which Goldsmith
placed on titles, this subtitle provides a clue for the reader
to detect that the first-person point of view of Dr. Primrose is not the controlling point of view of the novel and
certainly not the point of view of Goldsmith.

The central problem involved in this first-person point
of view narrative is whether Dr. Primrose is to be viewed
as a hero to be admired (Sir Walter Scott's attitude) or as
a narrator from whom the reader remains detached. If the
reader is to remain detached from the Vicar, then the text
should provide specific examples that will explain this
detachment and indicate another, more objective point of
view. One such example is given in Chapter Sixteen in
the ludicrous portrait of the Primrose family. Dr. Primrose
is depicted presenting his books on the Whistonian con-

---

[17] This subtitle was dropped from most of the editions of *The Vicar*
in the nineteenth century, an interesting example of how interpretation
tends to color textual editing.

troversy to his wife, who is dressed as Venus. In the first edition of *The Vicar* Goldsmith wrote "Bangorean controversy" (IV, 83). This allusion raises the problem of why Goldsmith would create as a hero in this novel a clergyman who spent so much time writing on a clerical controversy that had begun in 1717 and was indeed a dead issue by 1762. Furthermore, Goldsmith disliked intensely those clergymen who concerned themselves in such disputes to the neglect of more important duties:

> The vulgar of England are without exception, the most barbarous and the most unknowing of any in Europe. A great part of their ignorance may be chiefly ascribed to their teachers, who, with the most pretty gentlemen-like serenity, deliver their cool discourses, and address the reason of men, who have never reasoned in all their lives. They are told of cause and effect, of beings self existent, and the universal scale of beings. They are informed of the excellence of the Bangorian controversy, and the absurdity of an intermediate state. The spruce preacher reads his lucubration without lifting his nose from the text, and never ventures to earn the shame of an enthusiast.
>
> (I, 480.)

> Yet upon the whole our clergy might employ themselves more to the benefit of society, by declining all controversy, than by exhibiting even the profoundest skill in polemic disputes; their contests with each other often turn on speculative trifles, and their disputes with the deists are almost at an end, since they can have no more than victory. . . .
>
> (III, 154–55.)

Goldsmith's statements would indicate that he did not intend Dr. Primrose to be viewed as heroic. The Bangorian allusion brings out the Vicar's pedantic love of controversy, and his great interest in this graveyard of clerical tracts reveals his tendency to look to the past rather than to the present. The change in the second edition from "Bangorean controversy" to "Whistonian controversy" might seem to be an attempt by Goldsmith to weaken the satirical implications of the allusion: Hilles, for instance, believes that "Goldsmith's alteration narrows the Vicar's writings to those concerned with monogamy." [18] But we should not ignore the odious connotation which the name of Whiston had for any orthodox Anglican clergyman by the middle of the eighteenth century. An object of ridicule and so absurd that he was pitied rather than feared, Whiston was a religious quack who had been expelled from his professorship of mathematics at Cambridge on charges of Arianism. [19] By narrowing the issue to the Whistonian tenet that it was unlawful for a priest of the Church of England, after the death of his first wife, to take a second, Goldsmith fixes the ruling passion of Dr. Primrose on the most trifling religious issue possible. By linking the Vicar with the name of Whiston (even if only on such a trifle), Goldsmith marks the religious orthodoxy of his narrator as suspect to the discerning eighteenth-century reader.

We have already mentioned the tendency to label certain incongruities in the text as artistic lapses. There is one such incongruity which can be explained once we recognize that the Vicar's point of view is not the controlling point of view in the novel. In Chapter Three, Dr.

[18] Hilles does not link it, however, to Goldsmith's allusion to the Bangorean controversy in the *Bee*. See *The Vicar of Wakefield and Other Writings*, pp. 577–78.

[19] See Leslie Stephen's discussion of Whiston in his *History of English Thought in the Eighteenth Century*, 2 vols. (London, 1902), I, 212–14. In "Mr. Collins's Discourse of Freethinking," Swift had ridiculed Whiston by having the narrator refer to him as denying the divinity of Christ. In his edition of Swift, Temple Scott reprinted a pamphlet satirizing Whiston, which was attributed to Pope and Gay in the *Miscellanies* (1747). *The Prose Works of Jonathan Swift*, 12 vols. (London, 1910), IV, 275–85.

Primrose professes to leave voluntarily a thirty-five-pound benefice for a "small Cure of fifteen pounds a year": "During this interval, my thoughts were employed on some future means of supporting them; and at last a small Cure of fifteen pounds a year was offered me in a distant neighbourhood, where I could still enjoy my principles without molestation. With this proposal I joyfully closed, having determined to encrease my salary by managing a little farm" (IV, 25). Critics have pointed out the inadequate motivation here and have attributed this apparent flaw to poor artistry. In 1883 Edward Ford suggested that Goldsmith left out material which for some reason he never finished:

> Why did the Vicar leave Wakefield, where he had a good income, "An elegant house situated in a fine country, and a good neighbourhood"? Why did he "at last accept a small cure in a distant part of the country, worth only 15 a year"? What was the story which he afterwards told at the fair, to his "old acquaintance—a brother clergyman—of the result of 'the Whistonean controversy,' 'my last pamphlet,' the archdeacon's reply, and the hard measure that was dealt me"?
>
> There must have been some unfinished account of all this, which Goldsmith had intended to insert, but (as Mrs. Thrale says) "could not get it done for distraction. . . ." [20]

In his introduction to *The Vicar* Doughty describes Ford's hypothesis and then evaluates it: "Without more evidence, it is impossible to decide whether these weaknesses are merely due to carelessness or are the result of a hasty sale before the work was finally revised and polished." [21] Clearly, Doughty judges this textual incongruity as an ar-

[20] "Names and Characters in *The Vicar of Wakefield*," *National Review*, I (1883), 387–88.

[21] *The Vicar of Wakefield*, ed. Oswald Doughty (London, 1928), p. xxvi.

tistic weakness on the part of Goldsmith. Even Friedman, who has intentionally refrained from interpretive editorial commentary, states that "these references . . . have no meaning in the present state of the novel" (IV, 8). But Friedman then admits that Goldsmith "in his extensive stylistic revisions for the second edition" did leave these references "unchanged." Here it seems to me is an editorial crux, the solution of which requires interpretation. Either critics have missed Goldsmith's point entirely or they are prejudging his intention here by assuming that he did not know what he was doing, even in the second edition. Such a position is patently ridiculous.

Most readers expect adequate motivation in the novel as a genre, but surely sound criticism will exhaust all possible reasons for such seeming discrepancies in terms of narrative structure before assuming that they are weaknesses or before hypothesizing a missing chapter. By refusing to see Dr. Primrose as an object of satire, we have failed to realize that the "hard measure" dealt to him may have been his *forced* resignation from the thirty-five-pound benefice at Wakefield. This is the most logical interpretation of the phrase in its context: "my friend and I discoursed on the various turns of fortune we had met: the Whistonean controversy, my last pamphlet, the archdeacon's reply, and the hard measure that was dealt me" (IV, 72). "Hard measure" could conceivably refer to the loss of Dr. Primrose's fortune, but the phrase occurs at the end of a sentence in which theological matters only are discussed. Syntactically "hard measure" would be more apt to refer to disciplinary action by the archdeacon (note that Miss Arabella Wilmot's father is "a dignitary in the church" [IV, 23]), and in fact this interpretation is reinforced when later in the same paragraph Dr. Primrose describes himself as that "unfortunate Divine, who has so long, and it would ill become me to say, successfully, fought against the deuterogamy of the age" (IV, 73). To make the narrator of a novel an object of satire is a difficult task, and one method of presenting another point of view is to present incongruities in the narrator's story that the alert reader is expected to perceive. It is unfortunate that while such deliberate incongruities are accepted as part of the highly refined irony of Swift and Fielding and are taken for granted in modern literature, we have predicated the absurd theory of an intended additional chapter for *The Vicar* to explain incongruities perfectly understandable and functional as they are. If we realize that the Vicar is *forced* to go to a poorer cure by virtue of his dismissal *and* his financial losses, then the apparent lack of motivation is a mark not of hasty writing but rather of subtle artistry. This discrepancy adds to the comedy in the novel: Dr. Primrose is not being perfectly candid with his readers; he is not telling a vicious lie, but he is omitting certain facts that reflect unfavorably on his self-image of his character. This incongruity reflects somewhat on the narrative integrity of Dr. Primrose and warns the reader to be on guard against similar slips.

Such a slip is found in Chapter Twenty-one when Dr. Primrose gives his blessing to his son George, who is about to leave for town in order to secure an ensign's commission: "After he had taken leave of the rest of the company, I gave him all I had, my blessing. 'And now, my boy,' cried I, 'thou art going to fight for thy country, remember how thy brave grandfather fought for his sacred king, when loyalty among Britons was a virtue. Go, my boy, and immitate him in all but his misfortunes, if it was a misfortune to die with Lord Falkland. Go, my boy, and if you fall, tho' distant, exposed and unwept by those that love you, the most precious tears are those with which heaven bedews the unburied head of a soldier' " (IV, 124).

Critics have commented on the Vicar's lack of discretion in mentioning George's possible death before his former fiancée, Arabella Wilmot, but have not attempted to explain in terms of artistic function the significance of the Falkland allusion. James Prior was astute enough, however, to perceive an unusual discrepancy: "A few inadvertencies and legal errors, though of no moment, required little trouble to amend. Thus George Primrose is told on departing to join his regiment, to emulate his grandfather, who fell in the same field with Lord Falkland: this if taken literally would make the Vicar more than a century old." [22] Prior's assumption that this discrepancy would *not* be obvious to Goldsmith is absurd. Obviously, Prior's conception of Dr. Primrose as a hero would not allow him to perceive that the Vicar is a quixotic character who lives in the past and exaggerates his ancestry accordingly. We are again faced with two alternatives: either Goldsmith is guilty of an inadvertent error, or he is providing the reader with a clever clue toward an intention of satire.

The duplicating structure of *The Vicar of Wakefield* is such that the situation containing the Falkland allusion mimics an earlier situation in Chapter Three, in which George is sent off to London in order to earn a living:

My son, after taking leave of his mother and the rest, who mingled their tears with their kisses, came to ask a blessing from me. This I gave him from my heart, and which, added to five guineas, was all the patrimony I had now to bestow. "You are going, my boy," cried I, "to London on foot, in the manner Hooker, your great ancestor, travelled there before you. Take from me the same horse that was given him by the good bishop Jewel, this staff, and take this book too, it will be your comfort on the way: these two lines in it are worth a million, *I have*

---

[22] Prior, *Life of Goldsmith*, II, 114.

been young, and now am old; yet never saw I the righteous man forsaken, or his seed begging their bread. Let this be your consolation as you travel on.

(IV, 26.)

The biblical verse both foreshadows the happy ending of the novel and reflects the smug optimism of Dr. Primrose that because he is possessed of the grace of God he will eventually triumph over misfortune. The Hooker–Bishop Jewel allusion is also ironic, for the analogy drawn by Dr. Primrose is unfavorable to his own character, if the relevant passage is read in Izaak Walton's *The Life of Richard Hooker*:

As soon as he [Hooker] was perfectly recovered from this Sickness, he took a journey from *Oxford* to *Exeter*, to satisfie and see his good Mother, being accompanied with a Countreyman and Companion of his own Colledge, and both on foot; which was then either more in fashion, or want of money, or their humility made it so: But on foot they went, and took *Salisbury* in their way, purposely to see the good Bishop, who made Mr. *Hooker* and his Companion dine with him at his own Table; which Mr. *Hooker* boasted of with much joy and gratitude when he saw his Mother and Friends: And at the Bishops parting with him, the Bishop gave him good Counsel, and his Benediction, but forgot to give him money; which when the Bishop had considered, he sent a Servant in all haste to call *Richard* back to him, and at *Richard's* return, the Bishop said to him, *Richard, I sent for you back to lend you my Horse; be sure you be honest, and bring my Horse back to me at your return this way to Oxford. And I do now give you Ten Groats to bear your charges to Exeter; and here is Ten Groats more, which I charge you to deliver to your Mother, and tell her, I send her a Bishops Benediction with it, and beg the continuance of her prayers for me. And if you bring my Horse back to me, I will give you Ten Groats more to carry you on foot to the Colledge, and so God bless you, good Richard.*[23]

Bishop Jewel's stingy concern for his walking staff is certainly treated comically, and Goldsmith uses this allusion as an ironic indication of Dr. Primrose's own stinginess in giving George only five guineas to go to London, while he is able to set aside four hundred pounds as a potential dowry in order to marry his daughters into wealth and society.[24] Dr. Primrose's blessings are singularly ineffective in defending George against the cruel misfortunes of the world, and the five-guinea patrimony shows that the Vicar's professed benevolence elsewhere is badly misdirected if charity begins at home. This interpretation is reinforced by a letter that Goldsmith wrote to Daniel Hodson, his brother-in-law, imploring him to receive his nephew when he returned from London and to "endeavour to serve the young man effectually not by foolish fond caresses but by either advancing him in his business or setling him in life."[25]

When examined in terms of narrative structure, the allusions to the Whistonian controversy, Lord Falkland, and Bishop Jewel can be understood best as serving the artistic function of satire. They also provide us with a marvelous insight into Dr. Primrose's position in the eighteenth-century English social chain of being as it has been described by J. H. Plumb:

[23] *Walton's Lives,* ed. S. B. Carter (London, 1951), p. 131.
[24] Both the oak-staff allusion in *The Vicar* and a similar episode cited in Goldsmith's letters are clearly adapted from the Bishop Jewel episode. See Katharine Balderston's comment in *The Collected Letters of Oliver Goldsmith,* pp. xxiii–xxix.
[25] *The Collected Letters of Goldsmith,* pp. 101–2. Thackeray accused Goldsmith's father of impoverishing his family in order to provide one of his daughters with a dowry. *The Works of Thackeray,* 20 vols. (New York, 1910–11), XI, 328. See also Temple Scott's *Oliver Goldsmith Bibliographically and Biographically Considered,* p. 8.

The lesser gentry were in a dilemma. It was difficult for them to suppress either their envy or their desire to emulate their betters. Their envy was further quickened because the possession of vast estates carried greater significance than the ownership of land. For with this ownership went a host of social and political privileges which drew to their possessors the anxious and devoted attention of all aspiring men. As the social and political power of the magnates grew, that of the lesser gentry diminished. Those who had once been courted were now ignored. Naturally, they began to look back to a world of the past in which they believed they had possessed undisputed control of their countryside. So men whose fathers had voted for Shaftesbury or welcomed William III as a deliverer turned Tory.[26]

The dilemma of the "lesser gentry" in the latter half of the eighteenth century is symbolized by Dr. Primrose's dependency on the country squire, Mr. Thornhill, for temporal support. But he is also a clergyman with spiritual obligations to his poor parishioners. No doubt this dilemma explains somewhat Dr. Primrose's inability to make decisive choices. D. W. Jefferson comments on the ease with which eighteenth-century novelists "negotiate transitions between different levels of moral attitude":

> Much of the charm of Goldsmith's novel lies in the perfect relationship between opposing values: between Christian rectitude and social conformity, between the humorous and the moral, between the official and the unofficial self of the vicar. The vicar's polite and friendly relations with his new patron, Mr. Thornhill, whom he knows to be wicked, is an interesting case of eighteenth-century manners. It may be argued that his Christian integrity is not compromised, because his duty to Caesar is governed by conventions which enjoy a generous measure of autonomy under the higher law of duty to God. The plea is a sound

[26] *England in the Eighteenth Century* (Baltimore, 1950), p. 19.

one, yet we may smile to see Christian zeal so nicely regulated.[27]

In *The Vicar of Wakefield* the "ease" with which different levels or moral attitudes are brought together must be attributed not to Goldsmith but to Dr. Primrose, the narrator, and the "perfect relationship between opposing values" is not so perfect for the reader who sees Dr. Primrose as an object of satire. Much of the irony in *The Vicar* does in fact stem from the incongruities between opposing values, incongruities that Dr. Primrose himself tries to avoid seeing.

The first-person point of view in *The Vicar* can become a trap for the reader, just as Gulliver's first-person point of view has in the past ensnared critics, who equated Gulliver's attitudes totally with Swift's. If the reader identifies himself with Dr. Primrose's attitudes, he will fail to understand the artistic function of the allusions and textual incongruities we have already discussed. Such a reader will then accuse Goldsmith of poor craftsmanship, as does Boris Ford: ". . . the radical weakness of the novel lies in Goldsmith's ambiguous attitude towards the Vicar himself. The novel, to some extent because it is related by the Vicar in the first person, is never able to present the Vicar with the gentle irony that he deserves." [28] Because Ernest Baker recognized that the Vicar was an object of satire, he was able to perceive that the first-person point of view is an asset: "Note, however, that the Vicar, writing the story himself, is able to tell us what he thinks, and hopes, and intends. This makes the lesson of his self-deception the more unmistakable." [29] Goldsmith's originality here has been stressed by Ronald Paulson, who writes that *The Vicar* "is the first of the early novels to use an ironic nar-

[27] "Observations on *The Vicar of Wakefield*," III, 626–27.
[28] *From Dryden to Johnson*, ed. Ford, p. 378.
[29] *The History of the English Novel*, V, 85.

rator who is a central character of the action as well—both an ironist and the object of dramatic irony." [30]

Incongruities in the narrative and allusions that seem harmless to the narrator but meaningful to the reader are but two of the many devices whereby an author can inject another, more dominant objective point of view into first-person narration. The narrator himself may undermine his point of view through actions that belie his words, or he may use words with dual meanings that seem insignificant to himself but significant to the reader. The actions and dialogue of other characters also present multiple points of view that frequently undermine that of the narrator. Indeed, most of the obviously contrived manipulation of characters in *The Vicar of Wakefield* can be understood and artistically justified only as satirical technique used to disparage Dr. Primrose.

We might ask, for example, how critically sound it is to set the Vicar apart from the rest of his family as a moral judge or to fail to see how the snobbery and petty practicality of Mrs. Primrose merely reflect the same traits in her husband. At the beginning of his narrative the Vicar selects his wife because she is "notable," an adjective that Hilles points out could mean capable in business.[31] "She prided herself also upon being an excellent contriver in house-keeping; tho' I could never find that we grew richer with all her contrivances. However, we loved each other tenderly, and our fondness encreased as we grew old" (IV, 18). This passage demonstrates the clever shift in point of view from the singular "I" to the third person plural when Dr. Primrose wishes to dissociate himself from moral responsibility.[32] The Vicar shows his own concern

---

[30] *Satire and the Novel in Eighteenth-Century England* (New Haven, 1967), p. 271.

[31] *The Vicar of Wakefield and Other Writings*, p. xvii.

[32] The Vicar takes safety in numbers in Chapter Nine when he refuses to let his daughters accompany Mr. Thornhill's lady friends home:

for temporal matters; then by the use of "however" he makes it appear that he loves his wife in spite of her failure to make the family any richer. For a clergyman Dr. Primrose seems to take an unusual snobbish pride in his social status: "We had an *elegant* house, situated in a *fine* country, and a *good* neighbourhood. The year was spent in moral or rural amusements; in visiting our *rich* neighbours, and relieving such as were poor" (IV, 18; italics mine). Although the italicized adjectives need not indicate snobbery when spoken by an eighteenth-century gentleman, the Vicar's language when viewed in retrospect reveals a serious moral shortcoming. The yoking effect of "moral" and "amusements" (zeugma) illustrates an attitude of which Primrose is blissfully unconscious—the attitude that manners are more important than morals. We observe also that the Vicar visits not merely neighbors but "rich neighbours." The full impact of Goldsmith's verbal irony here comes *after* a first reading of the novel as a whole. Ronald Paulson has only recently reminded us that any comprehensive rhetoric of fiction cannot ignore "the possibility of a second reading as well as the general complexity of a reader's response as his mind ranges back and forth in memory and anticipation." [33] I would suggest that some such retrospective process is absolutely essential to a complete interpretation of *The Vicar*.

Primrose's money-consciousness is revealed by his attitude toward his children:

> When I stood in the midst of the little circle, which promised to be the supports of my declining age, I could not avoid repeating the famous story of Count Abensberg, who, in Henry II's progress through Germany, while other

---

"I was obliged to give a peremptory refusal; for which *we* had nothing but sullen looks and short answers the whole day ensuing" (IV, 56; italics mine).

[33] Review article, *Journal of English and Germanic Philology*, LXV (1966), 604.

courtiers came with their treasures, brought his thirty-two children, and presented them to his sovereign as the most valuable offering he had to bestow. In this manner, though I had but six, I considered them as a very valuable present made to my country, and consequently looked upon it as my debtor.

(IV, 19–20.)

At first this anecdote appears to be mirthful jesting, but as the reader progresses through the novel, he eventually realizes that its artistic function is to set up a pattern of verbal irony. "Treasures" and "supports" appear at first to be nothing more than endearing names for the Vicar's children, but with the development of the plot the literal meaning of these words becomes so conspicuous as to remind the reader that the father looks upon his children as annuities for old age.

Because such materialism seems comically incompatible with his spiritual vocation, Dr. Primrose attempts to relegate responsibility to his wife: "The temporal concerns of our family were chiefly committed to my wife's management, as to the spiritual I took them entirely under my own direction" (IV, 21). Such a relegation is comically inconsistent with the epitaph which the Vicar wrote for his wife and which hangs over the fireplace; it extols "her prudence, œconomy, and obedience till death" (IV, 22). Dr. Primrose can hardly be absolved from responsibility for his wife's fortune-seeking and social climbing, particularly when we realize that by turning money matters over to her he attempts to free his conscience of the immoralities which later occur in *his* pursuit of fortune.

There are other examples of the Vicar dissociating himself from his wife and revealing his hypocrisy in doing so. Thus he is critical of her false pride:

. . . as Mr. Burchell was going to a different part of the country, he took leave; and we pursued our journey. My wife observing as we went, that she liked him extremely, and protesting, that if he had birth and fortune to entitle him to match into such a family as our's, she knew no man she would sooner fix upon. I could not but smile to hear her talk in this lofty strain: but I was never much displeased with those harmless delusions that tend to make us more happy.

(IV, 31.)

The irony in this passage is, of course, that Mrs. Primrose's delusion foreshadows the ending of the novel; and earlier in the chapter Mr. Burchell's true identity as Sir Thornhill has been provided in his rhetorical slip from "he" to "I" (IV, 30). Furthermore, knowing Burchell's true identity, the reader finds the Vicar's snobbery to be as flagrant as his wife's:

> When he [Burchell] had finished his own, he would join in her's, and enter into a close conversation: but I had too good an opinion of Sophia's understanding, *and was too well convinced of her ambition, to be under any uneasiness from a man of broken fortune.*
>
> (IV, 40. Italics mine.)

> . . . nor could I conceive how so sensible a girl as my youngest, could thus prefer a man of broken fortune to one whose expectations were much greater.
>
> (IV, 52.)

Again, the full impact of the Vicar's attitude comes retrospectively. In Chapter Thirteen the Vicar's attitude is shown to be more than mere snobbery. While his wife insults Mr. Burchell until he leaves in anger, Dr. Primrose remains silent and "neutral." He upbraids his wife, but only briefly, and his real underlying plans for Sophia are brought out in his advice to her: " '. . . I hope you have been taught to judge properly of such men, and that it would be even madness to expect happiness from one who has been so very bad an *œconomist* of his own. Your mother and I have now better *prospects* for you. The next winter, which you will probably spend in town, will give you opportunities of making a more *prudent* choice'" (IV, 71; italics mine). Dr. Primrose's equation of happiness with material prosperity is hardly what we would expect from a clergyman. The words "oeconomist," "prospects," and "prudent"—all terms more appropriate for commercial discourse—reveal that for the Vicar marriage is more a business investment than a sacred spiritual bond.

It is ludicrous how Dr. Primrose's benevolence has been praised in the past. His benevolence lies in his rhetoric, and his actions often belie what he professes. His hypocrisy reflects his dual vocation as both a clergyman and an entrepreneur. Under the subterfuge of Christian humility he exercises a *petty* practicality—a practicality which shows that his spontaneous generosity is not so spontaneous as has often been supposed. When his wife offers to feed the Squire's servants, it is the Vicar who acidly comments, "for which, by the bye, our family was pinched for three weeks after" (IV, 41–42). When Moses brings back the copper spectacles from the fair, it is Mrs. Primrose who would have thrown them in the fire but for her husband's thrift, "for though they be copper, we will keep them by us, as copper spectacles, you know, are better than nothing" (IV, 68). At the beginning of the novel Dr. Primrose performs an apparent act of benevolence by signing over "the profits" of his living to the orphans and widows of clergymen of his diocese, "for having a sufficient fortune of my own, I was careless of temporalities, and felt a secret pleasure in doing my duty without reward" (IV, 21–22). But the act involves no real sacrifice; there is considerable smugness in the Vicar's telling the reader of the motives, particularly when they indicate vanity rather than a genuine concern for the widows and orphans themselves. To be sure, the Vicar's loan of his purse to Mr.

Burchell is the impulsive, generous act of a benevolent and credulous man. But this is undercut by Primrose's comment the next day on Burchell's independence in argument: "But what surprised me most was, that though he was a money-borrower, he defended his opinions with as much obstinacy as if he had been my patron" (IV, 28).[34] Aside from informing the reader of Burchell's true identity, the reference to him as a "money-borrower" acting like a patron reveals that the benevolent act is really a loan, not a gift, and that through benevolence the Vicar gains a sense of power.[35] The heading of Chapter Thirty-one is the most incriminating passage of all: "Former benevolence now repaid with unexpected interest" (IV, 170). Referring to Primrose's lending of his purse to Burchell, this chapter heading at the end of the novel shows the Vicar's final attitude toward benevolence (as toward his daughters' marriages) to be that of a good business investment. And it is the Vicar's final attitude, because he is retelling his narrative.

The only moral choice in *The Vicar* that might seem to refute this interpretation of Dr. Primrose's materialism is his decision during his debate with Mr. Wilmot not to conceal the loss of his fortune until after Miss Wilmot has signed over her settlement to George. We can hardly call this a significant moral choice for a clergyman, and the Vicar's refusal "to disavow my principles" (IV, 24) is not a willed choice but the result of his ruling passion, or what

[34] The reader discovers later in Chapter Six that Mr. Burchell won the argument, when Mrs. Primrose informs her husband that Burchell is coming "that run you down fairly in the argument" (IV, 38).

[35] Abraham Tucker writes: "There is likewise a spurious benevolence which flows from vanity; it makes men helpful and obliging to show their power and importance, or gain the incense of applause, or bring others into dependence upon them." See his *The Light of Nature Pursued*, 2 vols. (London, 1852), I, 251. Goldsmith sets out, I would suggest, to show the Vicar's benevolence to be spurious, and this in turn undercuts the Vicar's smugness as the narrative is developed.

an eighteenth-century reader would understand as a humor.[36]

When Squire Thornhill first visits the Primroses, Mrs. Primrose, anticipating a marriage between him and one of her daughters, calls it "a most fortunate hit" (IV, 37). Dr. Primrose is at first skeptical, suggesting that they keep to companions of their own rank and moralizing: "There is no character more contemptible than a man that is a fortune-hunter, and I can see no reason why fortune-hunting women should not be contemptible too" (IV, 38). The Vicar is of course condemning explicitly not only his wife's later actions but implicitly and unconsciously his own as well. Throughout *The Vicar* there is a verbal pattern of ironic wordplay on *fortune* and *misfortune* based on the constant interchange of meanings between fate, good or bad luck, and financial wealth or poverty. The underlying quest of Dr. Primrose is revealed by his equation of fortune (good luck) with economic prosperity and misfortune (bad luck) with poverty. In terms of this satire the major theme of the novel is found in George's assertion that "travelling after fortune, is not the way to secure her" (IV, 106). Only after Dr. Primrose believes that he will die in prison, only after he renounces temporal ties, does fortune's wheel both in the sense of good luck and financial prosperity ironically turn upward.

We cannot, then, logically absolve Dr. Primrose from responsibility for his wife's decisions (as he would have us do); for by his deliberate acquiescence he does in effect approve immoral choices. Such a situation as this occurs in Chapter Fifteen when Dr. Primrose allows Mr.

[36] For a valuable discussion of humor as a character trait and a narrative technique, see Alan D. McKillop, *The Early Masters of English Fiction* (Lawrence, Kan., 1956), p. 104. As I have already shown, Goldsmith's theory of humor serves a satirical function, and Dr. Primrose's ruling passion may be seen to reveal the lethargy and complacency (in its pejorative sense) of many eighteenth-century clergymen.

Burchell's sealed note to be opened and read: "It instantly occurred that he was the base informer, and we deliberated whether the note should not be broke open. I was against it; but Sophia, who said she was sure that of all men he would be the last to be guilty of so much baseness, insisted upon its being read. In this she was seconded by the rest of the family, and, at their joint solicitation, I read as follows . . ." (IV, 77). That the Vicar himself reads the note aloud is especially compromising—he has already informed the reader that the spiritual concerns of the Primrose family are "entirely under my own direction" (IV, 21). The most serious of all of the Vicar's acquiescences is that with his wife's scheme to use farmer Williams as a pawn in order to induce Squire Thornhill to propose marriage to Olivia. Once the scheme has been put into effect Dr. Primrose uses his role as a clergyman to warn Olivia that if Thornhill does not propose to her, she will have to marry Mr. Williams, since "the character which I have hitherto supported in life demands this from me, and my tenderness, as a parent, shall never influence my integrity as a man" (IV, 87). The obvious dishonesty of the scheme being supported by Dr. Primrose's "integrity as a man" is surely a corrosive piece of satire against hypocrisy. In the light of his previous actions the exuberance of the Vicar and his coarse joking about the marriage market while under the influence of gooseberry wine (*in vino veritas*) hardly do credit to his role as a clergyman or qualify him to be a valid judge of the morality of his wife's actions.

The use of multiple points of view to undercut the narrator's point of view explains much of the relationship between the Vicar and his family. The heading of Chapter One, "The description of the family of Wakefield; in which a kindred likeness prevails as well of minds as of persons" (IV, 18), suggests that the Primrose family functions as a mirror reflecting those more unfavorable traits of Dr. Primrose's character which he does not directly tell us about or which he distorts in his narrative. In no other character is the mirror function so clearly drawn as in Moses. In the past Moses has been singled out as the most flagrant example of Goldsmith's inconsistency in the delineation of character: "There are also inconsistencies of characterization. Moses at one time talks with the wit and wisdom of an experienced town gallant, at another, reveals himself as simple and gullible as a village idiot. The contradictions in his character are not the least of Goldsmith's inconsistencies in his novel." [37] Such inconsistency need not be seen as an artistic weakness if it can be shown to be functional. Unless we see that Dr. Primrose is an object of satire, we shall fail to see that when Moses is simple and gullible he reflects a similar trait in his father, and when Moses is witty and wise he undercuts his father by an unfavorable contrast. Traditionally, obvious manipulation of character in the novel is considered bad technique; in satire, however, such manipulation is perfectly acceptable. When judged by the standards of satire, as *The Vicar* should be, Moses (even his name is ironic) is a delightful fictional creation. His mirror function is established in Chapter Four: Dr. Primrose mentions setting aside a certain amount of time for meals, which was also taken up "in philosophical arguments between my son and me" (IV, 33). The nature of these "philosophical arguments" is brought out in the debate between Squire Thornhill and Moses in Chapter Seven. Thornhill's ridiculing of Moses' pedantry causes the rest of the company to laugh, but Dr. Primrose, whose pedantry is reflected by Moses, gets no pleasure from his son's comeuppance. It is the Vicar who designed Moses "for business," but when Moses and his father are swindled at the fair, both are shown to be

[37] *The Vicar of Wakefield*, ed. Doughty, p. xlv.

yokels. On the other hand, when Dr. Primrose loses control of himself and forgets his moral reflections, Moses is the one who repeats these reflections, in the form of a reprimand. Such a situation occurs immediately after the Vicar discovers that Olivia has run away from home; he is plunged into despair, and Moses reminds him of his cue:

"Father," cried my son, "is this your fortitude?"—"Fortitude, child! Yes, he shall see I have fortitude! Bring me my pistols. I'll pursue the traitor. While he is on earth I'll pursue him. Old as I am, he shall find I can sting him yet. The villain! The perfidious villain!"—I had by this time reached down my pistols, when my poor wife, whose passions were not so strong as mine, caught me in her arms. "My dearest, dearest husband," cried she, "the bible is the only weapon that is fit for your old hands now. Open that, my love, and read our anguish into patience, for she has vilely deceived us."—"Indeed, Sir," resumed my son, after a pause, "your rage is too violent and unbecoming. You should be my mother's comforter, and you encrease her pain. It ill suited you and your reverend character thus to curse your greatest enemy: you should not have curst him, villain as he is."

(IV, 91–92.)

There is genuine comedy in this undercutting of the Vicar's actions by Moses' echoing (if not parodying) his moral platitudes, and, if we recognize the satirical intention, the manipulation of character appears fully justified.

Dr. Primrose's criticism of Olivia as "a girl, who by education was taught to value an appearance in herself, and consequently to set a value upon it in another" (IV, 43), is in reality a criticism of himself as well. That he values appearances yet is easily fooled by them is demonstrated when he first sees Jenkinson, the swindler, at the fair: "I never in my life saw a figure that prepossessed me more favourably. His locks of silver grey venerably shaded his temples, and his green old age seemed to be the result of health and benevolence" (IV, 72). It soon becomes apparent to the reader that Olivia's reliance on appearances reflects a similar trait in her father. The Vicar's assertion in Chapter Two that the spiritual management of the family was "entirely under his own direction" makes him more responsible for Olivia's indiscretions. When he and his wife discuss Squire Thornhill's erroneous religious views, Mrs. Primrose points with pride to Olivia's skill at polemics:

> "Why, my dear, what controversy can she have read?" cried I. "It does not occur to me that I ever put such books into her hands: you certainly over-rate her merit." "Indeed, pappa," replied Olivia, "she does not: I have read a great deal of controversy. I have read the disputes between Thwackum and Square; the controversy between Robinson Crusoe and Friday the savage, and I am now employed in reading the controversy in Religious courtship."—"Very well," cried I, "that's a good girl, I find you are perfectly qualified for making converts, and so go help your mother to make the gooseberry-pye."
>
> (IV, 45.)

The Vicar's casual treatment of Olivia's religious instruction most assuredly denigrates his "spiritual management" of his family. Robinson Crusoe's own comment on the quality of his religious indoctrination of Friday, "I had, God knows, more Sincerity than Knowledge," perhaps pinpoints Dr. Primrose's real inability to instruct. Dr. Primrose implies that Olivia's deception by appearances is due to her reading of romances, but the blame rests equally on his own romantic nature.[38] In fact, while professing to dislike romances, the Vicar himself tells us a romance of which he is the hero.

[38] The Vicar tries to avoid his share of the responsibility for his daughter's actions by saying that Mrs. Primrose was reading romances during Olivia's pregnancy (IV, 20).

George and Sophia are actually the two most admirable characters in the Primrose family, so much so that they seem wiser than their father. The predominant aspect of his father that George subtly mirrors is the Vicar as actor. This function is brought out early in the novel, when the Vicar sends his son to London: "As he was possest of integrity and honour, I was under no apprehensions from throwing him naked into the *amphitheatre of life*; for I knew *he would act a good part* whether vanquished or victorious" (IV, 26–27; italics mine). Later, when in his search for Olivia Dr. Primrose falls in with a strolling company's cart, we learn that he "once had some theatrical powers" (IV, 95) and that his favorite dramatists are Dryden and Otway. In Chapter Nineteen the manager of the strolling company describes a promising new player:

> In this manner we spent the forenoon, till the bell summoned us in to dinner, where we found the manager of the strolling company that I mentioned before, who was come to dispose of tickets for the Fair Penitent, which was to be acted that evening, the part of Horatio by a young gentleman *who had never appeared on any stage*. He seemed to be very warm in the praises of the new performer, and averred, that he never saw any who bid so fair for excellence. *Acting, he observed, was not learned in a day;* "But this gentleman," continued he, *"seems born to tread the stage."*
>
> (IV, 105. Italics mine.)

The new performer turns out to be George, and after George narrates his adventures, the assertion that "acting was not to be learnt in a day" (IV, 122) is repeated. We learn also that the company has had difficulty fitting George for a role because "almost every character was in keeping." While it is true that this motif stresses the large number of roles George has been forced to play since leaving home, Dr. Primrose's original assurance before his son went to London that he would play a good role hints that the father himself is essentially an actor.

Dr. Primrose is continually conscious of his *role* as a clergyman: "The character which I have hitherto supported in life demands this from me . . ." (IV, 87). While under great emotional stress, he forgets his lines, and it is the rest of his family that provides him with the proper cues; yet he does not always make the proper responses to these cues. The Vicar bursts into tears upon hearing of Olivia's death; the two youngest children Dick and Bill try to comfort him: " 'And is not my sister an angel, now, pappa,' cried the eldest, 'And why then are you sorry for her? I wish I were an angel out of this frightful place, if my pappa were with me.' 'Yes,' added my youngest darling, 'Heaven, where my sister is, is a finer place than this, and there are none but good people there, and the people here are very bad' " (IV, 154). Dr. Primrose's subsequent dismissal of his own moral platitudes echoed by his children as "harmless prattle" is magnificent comedy.[39] To say that this concept of Dr. Primrose as actor shows conscious insincerity on his part does not seem entirely fair; throughout the narrative he appears to mean well and to have good intentions. Nonetheless, he is acting a role— a preconceived ideal of a clergyman that never becomes an integral part of his personality—and what D. W. Jefferson calls the "official and the unofficial self of the vicar" are never fully reconciled.[40] The attitude which Goldsmith takes toward Dr. Primrose may not be so far removed from William Hazlitt's attitude expressed in his famous essay "On the Clerical Character":

[39] Dr. Primrose's own comment satirizes the potential sentimentality of this scene, which is, I suspect, a burlesque of the literary and stage conventions of using children for pathetic effects. See Arthur Sherbo, *English Sentimental Drama* (East Lansing, Mich., 1957), pp. 53–59.

[40] For Jefferson's comments see pp. 182–83 of this book.

The Priest is not a negative character; he is something positive and disagreeable. . . . He is proud with an affectation of humility; bigotted, from a pretended zeal for truth; greedy, with an ostentation of entire contempt for the things of this world; professing self-denial, and always thinking of self-gratification; censorious, and blind to his own faults; intolerant, unrelenting, impatient of opposition, insolent to those below, and cringing to those above him, with nothing but Christian meekness and brotherly love in his mouth. He thinks more of external appearances than of his internal convictions. . . . He plays a part through life. He is an actor upon a stage. The public are a spy upon him, and he wears a mask the better to deceive them.[41]

One objection to this view of Dr. Primrose as an object of satire might be based on his political harangue in Chapter Nineteen. Here the Vicar's attitudes are identical with those which Goldsmith defends elsewhere. Internal industry is opposed to external commerce; the middle class must be maintained in order to keep the balance between the rich and the poor; the monarchy must be kept strong in order to defend the middle class against a potential plutocracy; and wealth should not be excessively accumulated in the hands of a few.[42] If the Vicar is being satirized, why did Goldsmith make him a spokesman for these attitudes? To answer this question we need to examine closely the style or form of the speech:

Now, the state may be so circumstanced, or its laws may be so disposed, or its men of opulence so minded, as all to conspire in carrying on this business of undermining monarchy. For, in the first place, if the circumstances of our state be such, as to favour the accumulation of wealth, and make the opulent still more rich, this will encrease

---

[41] *The Complete Works of William Hazlitt,* ed. E. P. Howe, 21 vols. (London, 1930–34), VII, 247–48.
[42] See Goldsmith's "The Revolution in Low Life" (III, 195–98).

their ambition. An accumulation of wealth, however, must necessarily be the consequence, when as at present more riches flow in from external commerce, than arise from internal industry: for external commerce can only be managed to advantage by the rich, and they have also at the same time all the emoluments arising from internal industry: so that the rich, with us, have two sources of wealth, whereas the poor have but one.

(IV, 100.)

In its excessive repetition of polysyllabic words borrowed from the jargon of political tracts, the Vicar's oratory is incredibly heavy handed; and the unintentional rhyme of "managed to advantage" calls the reader's attention to the Vicar's lack of sensitivity to his language. Dr. Primrose's pomposity enables the reader to understand why in the church at Wakefield "the 'Squire would sometimes fall asleep in the most pathetic [exciting] parts of my sermon, or his lady return my wife's civilities at church with a mutilated curtesy" (IV, 19). The Vicar's defense of Goldsmith's beliefs is analogous to Samuel Johnson's technique in *Idlers* No. 60 and 61, in which Dick Minim, a coffee-house critic, repeats all of the neoclassical critical attitudes that Johnson elsewhere defended. And most important of all, within the context of the chapter, Dr. Primrose's harangue is the straight build-up for the comic letdown that follows when immediately afterward we discover that the owner of the mansion is merely the butler. The Vicar's comment on the butler's ability to talk politics is the most appropriate commentary on his own harangue: "It seems my entertainer was all this while only the butler, who, in his master's absence, had a mind to cut a figure, and be for a while the gentleman himself; and, to say the truth, he talked politics as well as most country gentlemen do" (IV, 103).

The Vicar of Wakefield *as Burlesque*

The narrative structure of *The Vicar of Wakefield* is what has been criticized most often. We have already read the critic who objected to Goldsmith's bringing the "concluding calamities so thick upon" Dr. Primrose and then hurrying to the conclusion; we have already commented on this same critic's failure to recognize that this is the Vicar's story—not Goldsmith's (see pp. 172–73). The consensus of traditional critical opinion toward the plot of *The Vicar* is contained in Macaulay's well known objection, which because it has appeared in so many editions of *The Encyclopaedia Britannica* has had an important conditioning effect on readers' attitudes toward the novel: "The fable is indeed one of the worst that ever was constructed. It wants not merely that probability which ought to be found in a tale of common English life, but that consistency which ought to be found even in the wildest fiction about witches, giants and fairies. But the earliest chapters have all the sweetness of pastoral poetry together with all the vivacity of comedy.[43]

Macaulay's criticism is hardly just because he evaluates the structure in terms of the naturalistic criteria of the novel. If, on the other hand, Dr. Primrose is an object of satire, the very story which he tells must be considered part of the satirical technique. Northrop Frye has shown how fiction from the point of view of form is bound together by four chief strands—the novel, the confession, the anatomy, and the romance. Much of the critical confusion in analyzing fiction, according to Frye, stems from critics judging one form of fiction by the standards of another or failing to see that a prose work may contain a combination of these forms.[44] I would suggest that, instead of being

[43] *Encyclopedia Britannica*, 11th ed., p. 216.
[44] *Anatomy of Criticism* (Princeton, 1957), pp. 312–13. Frye uses the term *anatomy* to refer to prose satire.

an artistic weakness, the structure of *The Vicar* is an artistic masterpiece, provided we recognize in it strains of novel, romance, and anatomy.

Most emphatically, the improbability of plot cannot be attributed to Goldsmith's shoddy craftsmanship. Hilles has shown how all of the foreshadowing devices which anticipate the ending advertise "the Aristotelian concept of Recognition and Reversal"—a pattern of such devices proving that *The Vicar* was "put together with considerable care." [45] These foreshadowing devices could serve another function as well: anticipating the happy ending, the reader will not become so involved with the Vicar's misfortunes and will remain as detached from the narrative structure as from the narrator himself. A few critics have suggested, but without exploring the implications, that *The Vicar of Wakefield* is not only a satire on complacent optimism but also a burlesque of the shallow, optimistic, inferior romances and possibly of the "weeping" comedy of Goldsmith's day. If this interpretation is right, then the improbability of plot, instead of being a weakness, is in reality a deliberate stratagem on the part of Goldsmith.

Such an interpretation is not so startling or original as it may at first seem. As early as 1932, Lovett and Hughes had remarked, "Goldsmith has joined with Sterne in laughing at the conventions of the novel." [46] In 1933 Gallaway hinted several times at the possibility of parody. The first hint concerns Sir William Thornhill, "who comes to the rescue in an unintentional parody of the happy ending that the novel-reading public expected"; the second hint concerns the Primroses, whom Goldsmith did not intend "as models for action" because he was "writing to

[45] *The Vicar of Wakefield*, Everyman New American Edition, xi.
[46] Robert M. Lovett and Helen L. Hughes, *The History of the Novel in England* (New York, 1932), p. 154.

counteract the effects of sentimental novels, as later he was to attack the drama of sensibility in essay and play"; and the third hint concerns Jenkinson's role, in that "seeing the trickster tricked in *The Vicar of Wakefield* is an even worse parody of probability than the good fortune showered on the Primrose family by an indulgent providence masquerading as Sir William Thornhill." [47] In 1950 Jefferson also recognized parody in *The Vicar*: first, in connection with the episode in which Dick first brings the news of Olivia's abduction, "the vicar's moral reflections and the reported speeches in Dick's narration . . . echo literary convention with a triteness which is half way towards parody"; and second, in connection with the artificial role played by Mr. Burchell, "the denouement and happy ending follow tradition to the verge of parody." [48]

Long before *The Vicar* was published, Goldsmith had expressed his contempt for the superficial romances of his day. In July, 1757, Goldsmith published two reviews of novels in the *Monthly Review*:

> The story contains the Adventures of a couple of true *Lovyers*, in indigent circumstances; the Lady, obliged to go to service; the Gentleman, in quest of fortune, to the East-Indies. After some vicissitudes, they at length meet again; wallow in riches; and the Lady lives to this day under her husband's *wing*, as we are told, in Gloucestershire. Where we shall leave them in the full enjoyment of all the felicity that a bounteous *Author* can bestow.
> (I, 82.)

> As Miss Bellmour is now happily married, to the very agreeable Mr. Frankly, we would not interrupt her present felicity, by any strictures upon her Authorship. But

[47] "The Sentimentalism of Goldsmith," pp. 1168, 1178, 1180.
[48] "Observations on *The Vicar of Wakefield*," III, 622, 626.

we must beg leave to offer her one hint, at parting, which she may profit from, if she does not too much mistake her talents; viz. that one good Pudding is worth fifty modern Romances.

(I, 82.)

Both reviews sum up the triteness of much of mid-eighteenth-century fiction, and it is clear that "felicity" when applied to romances was a pejorative, sarcastic word for Goldsmith. Goldsmith also expressed his dislike of excessive improbability of plot—the same criticism that Macaulay made against *The Vicar of Wakefield*: "By the title-page some Readers may be induced to search into this performance for hidden satire, or political allegory; but it contains nothing more than an harmless tale, loaded with uninteresting episodes, and professedly wrote in the manner and stile of the old Romances; equally improbable indeed with the wildest of them, but falling far short of their glowing imagery, and strong colouring, which often captivate the fancy, of *young* Readers especially, and please in spite of sense and reason" (I, 57).[49] Even more important, this review shows Goldsmith's awareness of the possibilities for "hidden satire" in works of fiction.

That critics have praised *The Vicar* for some of the very qualities that Goldsmith himself abhorred is one of the ironies of literary history. Gallaway's conjecture that Goldsmith fell in love with his own character creation implies that he lost control of his artistry; at the same time, such a conjecture leaves *The Vicar* in the realm of homily. If *The Vicar* is a burlesque of trite fiction and perhaps of sentimental stage comedy, then a consistent burlesque would retain the happy ending. The numerous foreshadowing devices of the recognition and reversal

[49] This criticism again shows the significance Goldsmith would place on title pages as clues to satire.

pattern at the conclusion of *The Vicar* are themselves a parody of the conclusion, and the conclusion is a parody of the happy, prosperous endings found in most eighteenth-century novels. In this connection, Alan McKillop's conjecture about the ending of *Joseph Andrews* may be equally valid for the ending of *The Vicar of Wakefield*: "Technically the discovery that Joseph is Wilson's son, and so not of mean birth, is the 'recognition' that produces the final 'reversal,' but a hundred deservedly forgotten storytellers could have used this device for resolving the plot. It may even be taken as a burlesque of the stock recognition ending of romance, an instance in which Fielding extends the burlesque method from form to content. On the same level are the numerous coincidences and accidental meetings in the book." [50] Because generations of readers have preconceived of *The Vicar* as homily rather than satire, the plot exaggeration has been considered a flaw. When the novel is considered as satire, the plot exaggeration becomes the obvious signpost of the burlesque of literary form.

Burlesque of the romance is suggested in Chapter One when Dr. Primrose describes how his children received their names:

> Our eldest son was named George, after his uncle, who left us ten thousand pounds. Our second child, a girl, I intended to call after her aunt Grissel; but my wife, who during her pregnancy had been reading romances, insisted upon her being called Olivia. In less than another year we had another daughter, and now I was determined that Grissel should be her name; but a rich relation taking a fancy to stand godmother, the girl was, by her directions, called Sophia; so that we had two romantic names in the family; but I solemnly protest I had no hand in it.
> (IV, 20.)

---

[50] *The Early Masters of English Fiction*, p. 109.

The naming of both George and Sophia after, or at the request of, rich relatives leads us to suspect that the Vicar has ulterior motives in his preference for the name "Grissel." Is Aunt Grissel the widow of the uncle who left the Primroses ten thousand pounds? Furthermore, the Grissel motif with its sudden reversal leading to a happy ending is itself a romantic theme.

In Chapter Eight there is a clever burlesque of the pastoral setting of romance. The scenic description appears at first to contain what Macaulay calls "the sweetness of pastoral poetry":

> Our family dined in the field, and we sate, or rather reclined, round a temperate repast, our cloth spread upon the hay, while Mr. Burchell gave chearfulness to the feast. To heighten our satisfaction two blackbirds answered each other from opposite hedges, the familiar redbreast came and pecked the crumbs from our hands, and every sound seemed but the echo of tranquillity. "I never sit thus," says Sophia, "but I think of the two lovers, so sweetly described by Mr. Gay, who were struck dead in each other's arms. There is something so pathetic in the description, that I have read it an hundred times with new rapture."
>
> (IV, 45–46.)

Mr. Burchell objects to the epithetical poetry of Gay and Ovid and recites his own ballad of Edwin and Angelina, which foreshadows the happy ending of the novel. The total effect of this idyllic setting followed by a pastoral ballad must indeed seem to verge upon the sentimental, but immediately after the reading of the ballad the situation is comically undermined by the shooting of one of the two blackbirds symbolic of Gay's lovers and of Edwin and Angelina.

> While this ballad was reading, Sophia seemed to mix an air of tenderness with her approbation. But our tran-

quillity was soon disturbed by the report of a gun just
by us, and immediately after a man was seen bursting
through the hedge, to take up the game he had killed.
This sportsman was the 'Squire's chaplain, who had shot
one of the blackbirds that so agreeably entertained us.
So loud a report, and so near, startled my daughters; and
I could perceive that Sophia in the fright had thrown
herself into Mr. Burchell's arms for protection.

(IV, 52.)

Sophia's rapture over lovers "struck dead in each other's
arms" turns into startled fear when put to the practical
test of reality. Goldsmith does not, as some have implied,
merely place a sentimental situation side by side with a
comical situation so as to have it both ways. Rather, it is
no exaggeration to assert that every seemingly sentimental
situation in *The Vicar* is ironically undermined by one
device or another.

The most important signpost in *The Vicar* indicating
the burlesque of literary form is "An Elegy on the Death
of a Mad Dog" in Chapter Seventeen. Sung just before
the Vicar's calamities begin in earnest, the ballad represents not only a burlesque of contemporary elegies but,
even more importantly, a satire on the vogue of sentimentality—emotion for emotion's sake: " 'The great fault of
these elegiasts is, that they are in despair for griefs that
give the sensible part of mankind very little pain. A lady
loses her muff, her fan, or her lapdog, and so the silly poet
runs home to versify the disaster' " (IV, 90). Not only
does "An Elegy" foreshadow the reversal of the end of
the novel but, most significantly, the reader is warned
about the intensified structural burlesque that is about
to ensue in *The Vicar* itself. When Bill asks his father
whether he prefers to hear *"the Dying Swan, or the Elegy
on the death of a mad dog,"* Dr. Primrose replies, " 'The
elegy, child, by all means' " (IV, 88). "The Dying Swan"

refers to a sentimental serious ending whereas "An Elegy" refers to a recognition and reversal ending that will be a burlesque—as "An Elegy" is a burlesque—of sentimentality. Immediately afterwards, the narrative structure becomes extremely exaggerated with fluctuations between states of happiness and misery.

It is absurd to assume that Goldsmith himself was unaware that the piling up of misfortunes and sudden fluctuations of emotional states would seem contrived and improbable. Smollett had already commented on such artificial reversal patterns in *The Adventures of Gil Blas* in the preface to *Roderick Random*: "The disgraces of Gil Blas are, for the most part, such as rather excite mirth than compassion: he himself laughs at them; and his transitions from distress to happiness, or at least ease, are so sudden, that neither the reader has time to pity him, nor himself to be acquainted with affliction. This conduct, in my opinion, not only deviates from probability, but prevents that generous indignation which ought to animate the reader against the sordid and vicious disposition of the world." [51] The reference to *The Vicar* as a "tale" in the subtitle might well be interpreted as a warning to the reader to expect not a realistic novel but rather a fable-satire, to be judged by the criteria of satire. The hurried treatment of episodes in the latter half of *The Vicar* can be interpreted as a deliberate device to burlesque situations usually treated sentimentally and to keep the reader detached from the misfortunes of the Primrose family.[52] And if we are prepared to view *The Vicar of Wakefield* as burlesque, we need no longer be-

[51] *Roderick Random*, Shakespeare Head Press Edition, 2 vols. (Oxford, 1926), I, ix.

[52] Arthur Sherbo observes that sentimentality in drama relies on prolonged treatment of certain situations and that, conversely, hurried treatment of potentially sentimental situations can avoid it. *English Sentimental Drama*, p. 71.

lieve that Goldsmith changed his mind and imposed a sentimental conclusion on a narrative structure originally intended for satire. We shall also recognize the remarkable verbal irony in the latter part of the novel as a legitimate ingredient in its structure.

The "Dying Swan" or Satire?

Before examining the latter half of *The Vicar* in order to determine whether or not satire is maintained to the very end, we need to sum up the levels of meaning contained in the structure. To recapitulate, on the surface level *The Vicar* seems to be a sentimental romance—a homily illustrating the Job motif, told by a lovable, very human clergyman who suffers many misfortunes without loss of his optimistic faith. The frame of reference is essentially humorous, but there are elements of the tragic when the reader suffers vicariously through the narrator's misfortunes. Although the structure on this level is full of inconsistencies that can be attributed to Goldsmith's poor artistry, *The Vicar*, judged not by its faults but by its virtues, is to be rated one of the great moral novels of English literature. On the second level of meaning, another point of view is presented through the first-person narration by means of ironical allusions, inconsistencies in the Vicar's own story, incongruities between the Vicar's rhetoric and his actions, verbal irony, and the undermining effect of other characters' points of view. In terms of this objective point of view, Dr. Primrose is an object of satire who is both a clergyman and a fortune-hunter, as well as a professor of optimistic platitudes. His complacency is nauseous, and there is a smugness about the Vicar, who is writing his own romance with himself as the hero, who has seen his platitudes vindicated by experience, and who is in effect telling us that he was right all along.[53] The exaggeration of structure, particularly toward the conclusion, represents Dr. Primrose's being carried away by his own story: he uses all the stock situations normally used in sentimental romance and stage comedy, but Goldsmith's hurried treatment of these situations keeps the reader detached from the Vicar's misfortunes while it burlesques trite fiction and perhaps "weeping" comedy. On this second level narrative structure is seen to be thoroughly functional both in revealing the narrator's character and in burlesquing literary form, while the surface level itself is best understood as a trap for the naive reader who responds only to literature that appears to reflect his own sentimental attitudes.

The decisive proof of this second level of meaning must rely on evidence that the satire of *The Vicar of Wakefield* is not "broken in the end." The problem must be solved by measuring the reader's responses to the misfortunes of Dr. Primrose. By the end of the novel is the reader sympathetic toward Dr. Primrose? Does the reader admire him? If the Vicar was at first an object of satire (as suggested by Baker, Gallaway, and Hilles), does he vindicate himself by his "heroic" conduct in prison? Or is he still an object of satire to be viewed with comic detachment?

Critics who reject the interpretation of *The Vicar* as satire will immediately point to Mr. Burchell's criterion for judging men: "As the reputation of books is raised not by their freedom from defect, but the greatness of their beauties; so should that of men be prized not for their exemption from fault, but the size of those virtues

---

[53] Boris Ford writes, "This note of smugness is pervasive, and it is unqualified by any suggestion of implicit criticism." See his *From Dryden to Johnson*, p. 378. Ford's assumption that Goldsmith himself would not have been aware of the Vicar's smugness in untenable, and my entire interpretation of *The Vicar* is intended to show Goldsmith's "implicit criticism" through the rhetoric of his fiction.

they are possessed of" (IV, 79). The crux of the problem is not, however, that Dr. Primrose has virtues, but rather that they are much smaller than his rhetoric would lead us to believe. The Vicar's hypocrisy is inextricably interwoven with his sentimental (optimistic) attitude toward life—a hypocrisy of which, as W. F. Gallaway has shown, Goldsmith was fully aware.

Whereas in the first half of *The Vicar* the satire of Dr. Primrose is obvious, in the second half the satire becomes more subtle and goes underground as Primrose's narration becomes more subjective. It is a pattern which Goldsmith had already exploited in *The Citizen of the World* in his satirical essay on the Man in Black's pathological benevolence. This underground satire takes the form of verbal irony both in the text and in the chapter headings—patterns of verbal irony that reflect the ambivalent attitudes of Dr. Primrose in looking upon his children as annuities and upon benevolence as a good business investment. These verbal clusters have been prepared for, however, in the earlier part of *The Vicar*.

The use of farce and verbal irony to undercut a potentially sentimental situation is found in the reconciliation of Dr. Primrose and Olivia, which most nineteenth-century readers undoubtedly interpreted in the same pathetic manner as they would interpret the Peggotty-Emily reconciliation episode in *David Copperfield*:

> I instantly knew the voice of my poor ruined child Olivia. I flew to her rescue, while the woman was *dragging her along by the hair*, and I caught the dear forlorn wretch in my arms.—"Welcome, *any way welcome*, my dearest lost one, *my treasure*, to your poor old father's bosom. Tho' the vicious forsake thee, there is yet one in the world that will never forsake thee; tho' thou hadst ten thousand crimes to answer for, he will forget them all."— "O my own dear"—for minutes she could no more—"my

own dearest good papa! Could angels be kinder! How do I deserve so much! The villain, I hate him and myself, to be a reproach to such goodness. You can't forgive me. I know you cannot."—"Yes, my child, from my heart I do forgive thee! Only repent, and we both shall yet be happy. We shall see many pleasant days yet, my Olivia!"—"Ah! never, sir, never. The rest of my wretched life must be infamy abroad and shame at home. But, alas! papa, you look much paler than you used to do. Could such a thing as I am give you so much uneasiness? Sure you have too much wisdom to take the miseries of my guilt upon yourself."—"Our wisdom, *young woman,*" replied I.—*"Ah, why so cold a name, papa?"* cried she. *"This is the first time you ever called me by so cold a name."*—"I ask pardon, my darling," returned I; "but I was going to observe, that wisdom makes but a slow defence against trouble, though at last a sure one."

(IV, 126. Italics mine.)

Immediately after Olivia insinuates that she is no longer a virgin, thus preventing herself from marrying into society—and wealth—Dr. Primrose calls his daughter "young woman." By having Olivia repeat the phrase "so cold a name," Goldsmith reminds the alert reader that verbal irony is present in the endearing name "treasure." If the reader harks back to the Count Abensberg anecdote in Chapter One (see p. 185), the dual meaning of "treasure" in its literal significance as wealth and its dead metaphorical function as a term of endearment should evoke only a comic response.

The next chapter contains another potentially sentimental situation in which the same wordplay on "treasure," in conjunction with exaggerated fluctuations from happiness to misery and back to happiness, presents a comic frame of reference to the discerning reader. An excellent example of what Hilles calls "obviously stylized sentiment" is found in the Vicar's optimistic expectations when he returns home after leaving Olivia back at the inn:

And now my heart caught new sensations of pleasure the nearer I approached that peaceful mansion. As a bird that had been frighted from its nest, my affections outwent my haste, and hovered round my little fire-side, with all the rapture of expectation. I called up the many fond things I had to say, and anticipated the welcome I was to receive. I already felt my wife's tender embrace, and smiled at the joy of my little ones.

(IV, 129–30.)

This passage, a deadpan parody of stilted style ("rapture" by neoclassical standards was a pejorative word), is nothing more than the optimistic build-up for the comic letdown when the Vicar discovers his cottage is afire: "It was now near mid-night that I came to knock at my door: all was still and silent: my heart dilated with unutterable happiness, when, to my amazement, I saw the house bursting out in a blaze of fire, and every apperture red with conflagration! I gave a loud convulsive outcry, and fell upon the pavement insensible" (IV, 130). It is incredible that these passages be taken seriously. Conclusive proof of comic intention is found several sentences later, after Dr. Primrose rescues his children from the fire:

"Now," cried I, holding up my children, "now let the flames burn on, and all my possessions perish. Here they are, *I have saved my treasure. Here, my dearest, here are our treasures, and we shall yet be happy.*" We kissed our little darlings a thousand times, they clasped us round the neck, and seemed to share our transports, while their mother laughed and wept by turns.

(IV, 130–31. Italics mine.)

The repetition of "treasure" calls attention to the verbal irony just as the repetition of "so cold a name" did in he previous chapter. This passage does not imply that Dr. Primrose failed to love his children, but it does reveal again his equation of earthly happiness with material prosperity and his reliance on his children to provide eventually for his future happiness by marrying into money. The entire episode can best be interpreted as satire.[54]

The exodus of Dr. Primrose from his estate to the prison can also be viewed as mock heroic. In his stand on principles against the wicked Squire Thornhill (if Thornhill gives in, Olivia gets her husband and the booty), Dr. Primrose is analogous to the dwarf in the fable found in Chapter Thirteen:

> The Dwarf was now without an arm, a leg, and an eye, while the Giant was without a single wound. Upon which he cried out to his little companion, My little heroe, this is glorious sport; let us get one victory more, and then we shall have honour for ever. No, cries the Dwarf, who was by this time grown wiser, no, I declare off; I'll fight no more: for I find in every battle that you get all the honour and rewards, but all the blows fall upon me.
>
> (IV, 69.)

This fable serves to foreshadow the Vicar's attempt to preserve the honor of his family by refusing to sanction the approaching marriage of the Squire to Arabella Wilmot, and in consequence going to jail. The Vicar is mor-

---

[54] Certainly D. W. Jefferson responds to this episode as comical: "The passage is full of words which ought to suggest emotional intensity— 'amazement', 'alarmed', 'wild with apprehension', 'anguish', 'terror', 'agony', 'misery'—but they are quite without emotiveness: they are used as counters as the vocabulary proper to the occasion. Conventionality dominates the detail as well as the language. . . . The fire, starting at the moment of the vicar's arrival in an obvious story-book contrivance." See "Observations on *The Vicar of Wakefield,*" III, 624.

ally right in principle, of course, but the pride exhibited in his ludicrously mock heroic account of his heroism renders him absurd: " 'My friends,' said I, 'this is severe weather on which you have come to take me to a prison; and it is particularly unfortunate at this time, as one of my arms has lately been burnt in a terrible manner, and it has thrown me into a slight fever, and I want cloaths to cover me, and I am now too weak and old to walk far in such deep snow: but if it must be so—' " (IV, 139). The exaggeration of the Vicar's plight is remarkably similar to Goldsmith's comic treatment of the plight of the sentinel in *The Citizen of the World* (II, 458–65). If we did not interpret this passage as a satire of a stock device of trite sentimentality, we could become deeply involved with Dr. Primrose's misfortunes. In the next chapter, the Vicar's rejection of the unlawful attempts of his parishioners to free him would then seem to mark him as heroic to the point of martyrdom. Again his pride is revealed, however, in his last words to his parishioners: "But let it at least be my comfort when I pen my fold for immortality, that not one here shall be wanting" (IV, 141). Another point of view attacking Dr. Primrose's complacency may be observed in the conservative attitude found in Boswell's *Life of Johnson*: "Johnson, talking of the fear of death, said, 'Some people are not afraid, because they look upon salvation as the effect of an absolute decree, and think they feel in themselves the marks of sanctification. Others, and those the most rational in my opinion, look upon salvation as conditional; and as they can never be sure that they have complied with the conditions, they are afraid.' " [55]

Even the Vicar's entrance into prison is not without its comic elements. He has steeled himself to be a hero and a martyr in spite of misfortune. He conceives of himself

[55] Boswell, *Life*, IV, 278.

as a virtuous man, and, according to the heading of Chapter Twenty-three, "None but the guilty can be long and completely miserable" (IV, 132). Upon entering the jail, Dr. Primrose discovers not at all what he had expected: "I expected upon my entrance to find nothing but lamentations, and various sounds of misery; but it was very different. The prisoners seemed all employed in one common design, that of forgetting thought in merriment or clamour" (IV, 141). After contributing his perquisite, Dr. Primrose becomes thoroughly nonplused when the prison is soon "filled with riot, laughter, and prophaneness": " 'How,' cried I to myself, 'shall men so very wicked be chearful, and shall I be melancholy! I feel only the same confinement with them, and I think I have more reason to be happy.' With such reflections I laboured to become chearful; but such chearfulness was never yet produced by effort, which is itself painful" (IV, 141). Disconcerted as he is by the merriment of his fellow prisoners, Dr. Primrose decides to reform them in spite of the disapproval of his family; and "in less than six days some were penitent, and all attentive" (IV, 148). He institutes the manufacturing of wooden pegs by the prisoners to be sold to "tobacconists and shoemakers," and a utopian reform is accomplished "in less than a fortnight"—and in not more than three paragraphs: "I did not stop here, but instituted fines for the punishment of immorality, and rewards for peculiar industry. Thus in less than a fortnight I had formed them into something social and humane, and had the pleasure of regarding myself as a legislator, who had brought men from their native ferocity into friendship and obedience" (IV, 149). Dr. Primrose launches into a lengthy digression on the necessity for the reform of English penal laws. The basic concepts in his harangue, and such key words as "natural law," "compact," "savages," and "untutored nature," have led some critics to believe that Goldsmith was favorably influenced by Rousseau's ideas to the extent of having the Vicar extol them.[56] There is no reason to doubt that Goldsmith actually did believe in the need for prison reform, but this entire chapter is a burlesque of optimistic idealism that underrates the difficulty of putting theory into practice because it fails to take into consideration the fallibility of human nature. The rapidity with which Dr. Primrose *claims* to have reformed his fellow prisoners is too improbable—he is telling tales, and the reader may legitimately suspect that the narrator is a man who deludes himself and whose rhetoric can delude us as well.

The sentimental interpretation of the Vicar as a hero is based on his moral choice to refuse to sacrifice principle for expediency, even when the security of his family and his own life are at stake. Another point of view is presented twice in Chapter Twenty-eight by Mr. Jenkinson. After Olivia departs from the prison, Jenkinson suggests to Dr. Primrose that the rest of his family should not be sacrificed to the peace of one child alone, and she the only one who had offended him (IV, 152). After Olivia is supposedly dead, Jenkinson again suggests to Primrose that it is now incumbent on him to sacrifice any pride or resentment of his own to the welfare of those who depend on him for support (IV, 154). The implication is, of course, that the Vicar's heroic choice is dictated as much by pride and resentment as by moral principle. Dr. Primrose replies that there is no pride left in him: "On the contrary, as my oppressor has been once my

---

[56] See Sells, *Les Sources Françaises*, pp. 125–32. Ernest Baker quite correctly, however, shows Rousseau's influence to be negative. *The History of the English Novel*, V, 84. In *An Enquiry* Goldsmith calls Rousseau "a professed man-hater, or more properly speaking, a philosopher enraged with one half of mankind, because they unavoidably make the other half unhappy. Such sentiments are generally the result of much good-nature, and little experience" (I, 301).

parishioner, I hope one day to present him up an un-
polluted soul at the eternal tribunal" (IV, 154). The
Vicar's lack of humility is revealed by his attitude that he
is already one of the chosen. He tenaciously sticks to his
principles, for in his rose-colored optimism the virtuous
man must ultimately triumph over vice on this earth. He
is unable to realize that the Primrose path (the sentimental view of life) more often than not leads to spiritual
if not physical destruction. His belief is weakened when
he is told of Olivia's death. And when he is told of Sophia's
abduction, his belief in goodness always triumphant is so
shaken that Mrs. Primrose exclaims: "Alas! my husband
. . . you seem to want comfort even more than I" (IV,
156). In the comic-burlesque frame of reference the misfortunes are so unbelievable that they are ludicrous—
in fact we desire to see the Vicar's inflated optimism
punctured.

Verbal irony is still an important device when Moses
informs his mother that George, who is supposedly in the
service, "is perfectly gay, chearful, and happy": " 'But
are you sure,' still repeated she, 'that the letter is from
himself, and that he is really so happy?'—'Yes, Madam,'
replied he, 'it is certainly his, and he will one day be
the credit and the support of our family " (IV, 156;
italics mine). The usage of terms of commerce reminds
the reader again that the satire is still sustained: first
Olivia, then Sophia, and finally George—all are involved
in misfortunes until it appears that Dr. Primrose is totally bankrupt. The appearance of George, "all bloody,
wounded and fettered with the heaviest irons" (this description is comically overdone) causes the Vicar to
plunge into the deepest despair. In a scene duplicating
the one in Chapter Seventeen when Moses has to remind
his father of his role as a clergyman, George twice has to
ask his father to display his fortitude, while displaying

remarkable courage of his own: " 'Where, Sir, is your fortitude,' returned my son with an intrepid voice. 'I must suffer, my life is forfeited, and let them take it' (IV, 158). " '. . . as I am the first transgressor upon the statute, I see no hope of pardon. But you have often charmed me with your lessons of fortitude, let me now, Sir, find them in your example' " (IV, 159). This episode not only reminds the reader of the incongruities between the Vicar's rhetoric and his actions, but it also undermines the father's fortitude by contrasting it with his son's.[57]

Dr. Primrose complies with his son's request by renouncing all earthly ties: "From this moment I break from my heart all the ties that held it down to earth, and will prepare to fit us both for eternity. Yes, my son, I will point out the way, and my soul shall guide yours in the ascent, for we will take our flight together" (IV, 159). The Vicar's soaring rhetoric is too much for his sinking physical state, so that his last sermon to the prisoners has to be delivered from the unheroic position of reclining against the wall. If the sermon itself contains no overt signs of irony in either style or content, yet it seems singularly inappropriate to the situation and appears to reach a *reductio ad absurdum* when Dr. Primrose proclaims, "Yes, my friends, we must be miserable" (IV, 162). In the comic frame of reference the sermon can best be interpreted as the straight build-up for the comic letdown; after the reversal of fortune the Vicar goes back to his old ways and has not changed in the least.

It is at this stage of the narrative that the underground satire shifts almost completely to the chapter headings. Up to the point at which he delivers his sermon Dr. Primrose

---

[57] Adelstein's thesis that Goldsmith started to write a novel stressing the virtue of prudence and then became so attached to the Vicar that he ended by lauding fortitude surely ignores the comic play in this episode as well as Goldsmith's previous satire on fortitude in *The Citizen of the World*.

has adhered to an equation of earthly prosperity with God's grace: *"I have been young, and now am old; yet never saw I the righteous man forsaken, or his seed begging their bread"* (IV, 26). Even at the beginning of his stay in jail, he praises his "heavenly corrector" (IV, 143). But the headings of Chapters Twenty-eight and Twenty-nine represent a reversal of what Dr. Primrose had previously professed. Obviously he is virtuous, and equally obviously he is living in misery and poverty; according to his previous formula he would be without grace.

> Chapter XXVIII.—Happiness and misery rather the result of prudence than of virtue in this life. Temporal evils or felicities being regarded by heaven as things merely in themselves trifling and unworthy its care in the *distribution.*
>
> (IV, 151. Italics mine.)

> Chapter XXIX.—The equal *dealings* of providence demonstrated with regard to the happy and the miserable here below. That from the nature of pleasure and pain, the wretched must be *repaid* the *balance* of their sufferings in the life hereafter.
>
> (IV, 160. Italics mine.)

By prudence Dr. Primrose means literally good business management with a regard to self-interest. It is clear that he does not consider prudence as a Christian virtue—an erroneous distinction characteristic of the sentimental optimist who by stressing the natural goodness of man consequently formulated an overscrupulous criterion of Christian virtue. It is just such a distinction that is criticized by Abraham Tucker:

> Thus prudence, the principal virtue comprehending all the rest, stands in vulgar acceptance for sagacity, penetration, experience, and clearness of judgment, which are not virtue but good fortune; or if attained by our own in-

dustry, still are the fruits of virtue rather than the tree itself: and as prudence is vulgarly understood of a cautious regard to interest, we find it often standing at the greatest variance with virtue.[58]

Dr. Primrose, now that his annuities have seemingly lost all value, no longer equates earthly prosperity with God's grace. This apparent shift, in conjunction with the sermon, would indicate that the satire has been broken and that the Vicar has rejected the materialism and complacency that made him an object of satire earlier. But the verbal irony in these chapter headings lies in the metaphors of commerce—"distribution," "dealings," "repaid," and "balance"—that reveal the Vicar's concept of heaven to be a clearinghouse or a bank that stores up credit in terms of happiness for the wretched on earth.[59] The heading of Chapter Thirty also continues the commercial metaphor: "Chapter XXX.—Happier prospects begin to appear. Let us be inflexible, and fortune will at last change in our favour" (IV, 164). The inflexibility of Dr. Primrose by this time is hardly willed. Furthermore, he has supposedly just renounced his materialistic ties, believing that he is about to die in prison. Because of his hopeless situation, when Sophia is brought back safe from her abduction, the Vicar offers her as a bride to Mr. Burchell: "'And now, Mr. Burchell, as you have delivered my girl, if you think her a recompence she is yours, if you can stoop to an alliance with a family so poor as mine, take her, ob-

---

[58] *The Light of Nature Pursued*, I, 249. For the background of *prudence* in eighteenth-century fiction, see Martin C. Battestin, "Fielding's Definition of Wisdom: Some Functions of Ambiguity and Emblem in *Tom Jones*," *ELH*, XXXV (1968), 188–217.

[59] The Vicar's theory of happiness is synonymous with what Howard Mumford Jones defines as the second of three components in eighteenth-century theories of happiness: "The virtuous Christian, by following both his religious and his commercial (or other) vocation, must become prosperous and happy, since to become both is promised to the righteous." See *The Pursuit of Happiness*, p. 105.

tain her consent, as I know you have her heart, and you have mine. And let me tell you, Sir, that I give you no small treasure, she has been celebrated for beauty it is true, but that is not my meaning, I give you up a treasure in her mind'" (IV, 166). To the reader who has been aware of the ironic wordplay on "treasure," the true sense of the sentence is: "I give you no small equivalent of wealth; she has been celebrated for her beauty and wisdom, but what I really mean is that I am giving you my daughter, who by marrying a wealthy man could have given me in turn prosperity and security for the rest of my life." The moment Dr. Primrose in despair gives up his most materialistic attitude, fortune in the sense both of good luck and of material wealth changes in his favor. The quotation on the title page, *"Sperati miseri, cavete felices"* ("Take hope, you who are in misery, let the happy beware"), contains a deeper level of meaning when the reader perceives the Vicar's materialistic ideal of happiness. In the comic frame of reference a major theme is found in George's assertion that "travelling after fortune, is not the way to secure her."

If the Vicar has renounced the pursuit of happiness alias prosperity, the heading of Chapter Thirty-one, "Former benevolence now repaid with unexpected interest," must disturb us. Dr. Primrose is the narrator telling his story after the events have taken place. The commercial metaphors in the chapter headings show that his materialism is still very much in evidence; he has not really changed after all. His chapter headings are his moral comments on the episodes after they have occurred, and his moralism is corrupted by the world of the counting-house. The Vicar's commercial morality is satirized, while simultaneously the conventional happy ending of romances, in which the hero and heroine always wind up with each other and the booty, is burlesqued. The unifying element in the satire of the narrator and of the literary form is the heavy wordplay on "fortune" in Chapter Thirty-one. The situation presents a conflict between Love and Fortune. George Primrose and Arabella Wilmot, who have a spiritual love for each other, are at last brought together in spite of seeming poverty. The wicked Squire Thornhill, who parodies the stock villain of romance and who is therefore amusing, finally admits his villainy:

"You shall know, Sir," turning to Sir William, "I am no longer a poor dependant upon your favours. I scorn them. Nothing can keep Miss Wilmot's *fortune* from me, which, I thank her father's assiduity, is pretty large. The articles, and a bond for her *fortune*, are signed, and safe in my possession. It was her *fortune*, not her person, that induced me to wish for this match, and possessed of the one, let who will take the other."

This was an alarming blow, Sir William was sensible of the justice of his claims, for he had been instrumental in drawing up the marriage articles himself. Miss Wilmot therefore perceiving that her *fortune* was irretrievably lost, turning to my son, she asked if the loss of *fortune* could lessen her value to him. "Though *fortune*," said she, "is out of my power, at least I have my hand to give."

"And that, madam," cried her real lover, "was indeed all that you ever had to give; at least all that I ever thought worth the acceptance. And now I protest, my Arabella, by all that's happy, your want of *fortune* this moment encreases my pleasure, as it serves to convince my sweet girl of my sincerity."

Mr. Wilmot now entering, he seemed not a little pleased at the danger his daughter had just escaped, and readily consented to a dissolution of the match. But finding that her *fortune*, which was secured to Mr. Thornhill by bond, would not be given up, nothing could exceed his disappointment. He now saw that his money must all go to enrich one who had no *fortune* of his own. He could bear his being a rascal; but to want an equivalent to his daughter's *fortune* was wormwood.

(IV, 176. Italics mine.)

After Arabella and George are brought together against the background of "Fortune, fortune, who's got the fortune?," Dr. Primrose is asked by the prudent Mr. Wilmot to settle six thousand pounds upon Arabella if ever he should come back into his fortune. He consents gladly, since "to one who had such little expectations as I, [it] was no great favour" (IV, 177). The return of Olivia and the surprise reversal whereby she turns out to be the Squire's legal wife lead to an even more subtle use of verbal irony: "Happiness was expanded upon every face, and even Olivia's cheek seemed flushed with *pleasure*. To be thus restored to reputation, to friends and *fortune* at once, was a rapture sufficient to stop the progress of decay and restore former health and vivacity. *But perhaps among all there was not one who felt sincerer pleasure than I*" (IV, 179; italics mine). Olivia's "pleasure" yoked with "fortune" in turn yokes the Vicar's "pleasure" to "fortune," a comical device that will be readily perceived by the reader who has been aware all along of the narrator's ulterior fortune-hunting motives. All of this wordplay on "fortune" has been prepared for by the episode of the fortune-telling Gipsy in Chapter Ten, just as the wordplay on "treasure" was prepared for by the Count Abensberg anecdote in Chapter One. The extraordinary reversal from misery to happiness exhausts the Vicar, and he retires early to bed, "exhausted by the alternation of pleasure and pain," and pours out his "heart in gratitude to the giver of joy as well as of sorrow" (IV, 181–82). This last sentence substantiates the fact that Dr. Primrose's concept of happiness has not changed, that he has not really learned his lesson—he is one of God's elect and his optimism has been justified.

That readers have managed to skim over the final chapter of *The Vicar* completely ignoring the satire in the text is perhaps testimony to the great power that erroneous criticism may exert over generations of readers. The Vicar's benevolence is by no means supported by the moral choice he makes at the start of this chapter:

> The next morning as soon as I awaked I found my eldest son sitting by my bedside, who came to encrease my joy with another *turn of fortune* in my favour. First having released me from the settlement that I had made the day before in his favour, he let me know that my merchant who had failed in town was arrested at Antwerp, and there had given up effects to a much greater amount than what was due to his creditors. *My boy's generosity pleased me almost as much as this unlooked for good fortune.* But I had some doubts whether I ought in justice to accept his offer. While I was pondering upon this, Sir William entered the room, to whom I communicated my doubts. His opinion was, that as my son was already possessed of a *very affluent fortune* by his marriage, I might accept his offer without any hesitation.
>
> (IV, 182. Italics mine.)

Surely Goldsmith did not insert this passage into the novel without purpose. The Vicar's good fortune is not only the recovery of his original sum of money but also his not having to give his son six thousand pounds. We should notice how the Vicar tries to evade responsibility for his choice (most unheroic) by having Sir William decide for him, and if this is to make too much of his choice, why did it trouble Dr. Primrose so much in the first place? The answer is that his renunciation of his materialism was only momentary. In prison we were shown a glimpse of what he might be capable of accomplishing, but in the concluding chapter we discover that the Vicar has not had the moment of self-realization which is absolutely necessary in order to break the satire. The narrative has come full circle: we are back at the point where the novel began and the Primrose family indulged "in a moral or rural amusement." The Vicar reads "two homilies, and a thesis of my own composing" to the bridal couples. He tattles to Sir William about the proper parishioners who attempted to come to the Vicar's aid when he was taken to prison. His action, analogous to an English schoolboy's telling on his classmates, embodies an observation made by Goldsmith elsewhere: "The Great, in themselves, perhaps, are not so bad as they are generally represented; but I have almost ever found the dependents and favourites of the Great, strangers to every sentiment of honour and generosity. Wretches, who, by giving up their own dignity to those above them, insolently exact the same tribute from those below" (III, 198). Even in the final sentence of *The Vicar of Wakefield* Goldsmith calls attention to Dr. Primrose's pursuit of fortune: "It now only remained that my gratitude in *good fortune* should exceed my former submission in adversity" (IV, 184; italics mine). The sentimental view of life with its materialistic concept of happiness (most alarming in a clergyman) has never been more subtly satirized than in this novel. Goldsmith's original intention in writing *The Vicar*, an intention which was never changed, may be summed up in a quatrain by William Blake:

> Since all the Riches of this World
> May be gifts from the Devil & Earthly Kings,
> I should suspect that I worship'd the Devil
> If I thank'd my God for Worldly things.

The Vicar of Wakefield *and Fortune*

No critic can maintain that *The Vicar* is a sentimental novel without also recognizing that it is an artistic failure.

Morris Golden, taking the traditional view of the novel, writes with complete candor, "The first twenty-seven chapters present Goldsmith at his prose best; the last five, at his dullest." [60] But if *The Vicar* is interpreted as a satire and as burlesque, the narrative structure will meet all the requirements of great art.[61] Dr. Primrose is an object of satire because he is a clergyman whose complacency and materialism detract from his spiritual vocation. And yet Goldsmith treats him gently enough. We deplore Primrose's shallow optimistic belief that virtue will always win out; nonetheless, we are amused because in this story virtue *does* win out. The happy ending does not diminish the satire on optimism at all, for, as Dryden once observed, "there is still a vast difference betwixt the slovenly butchering of a man, and the fineness of a stroke that separates the head from the body, and leaves it standing in its place."

It may well be that the germinal idea for *The Vicar of Wakefield* was derived from Samuel Johnson's attack on optimism in *The Adventurer* No. 120: "It has been the boast of some swelling moralists, that every man's fortune was in his own power, that prudence supplied the place of all other divinities, and that happiness is the unfailing consequence of virtue. But surely, the quiver of Omnipotence is stored with arrows, against which the shield of human virtue, however adamantine it has been boasted, is held

[60] "Image Frequency and the Split in the *Vicar of Wakefield*," *Bulletin of the New York Public Library*, LXIII (1959), 476. Golden ignores the problem of Goldsmith's own self-consciousness as to what was going on in the novel. The extraordinary repetition of *fortune* in Chapter Thirty-one and the hurried treatment of potentially sentimental situations may be far more easily explained as verbal irony and structural burlesque rather than as mere hasty writing.

[61] *The Vicar* has an affinity, I believe, with Menippean satire as defined by Northrop Frye: "The Menippean satire deals less with people as such than with mental attitudes. . . . The Menippean satire . . . differs from the novel in its characterization, which is stylized rather than naturalistic, and presents people as mouthpieces of the ideas they represent." See his *Anatomy of Criticism*, p. 309.

up in vain: we do not always suffer by our crimes; we are not always protected by our innocence." [62] In Chapter Thirty-one of *The Vicar,* words like "transport" and "rapture" mark Dr. Primrose as a "swelling moralist." Such words, I submit, were still pejorative to Goldsmith and Johnson. It is clear from a reading of *The Citizen of the World* and *The Life of Richard Nash* that Goldsmith was no hero-worshiper and was not inclined to treat characters panegyrically. When Goldsmith writes in the "Advertisement" that "The hero of this piece unites in himself the three greatest characters upon earth," we may well suspect that he is ironically exaggerating. And those who insist that *The Vicar* is a prose *Deserted Village* fail to see that Dr. Primrose suffers in comparison with Goldsmith's brother, "who despising fame and fortune, has retired early to happiness and obscurity, with an income of forty pounds a year." In the interpretation of the novel as sustained satire presented in this chapter, the Vicar has not made a voluntary retirement to the country, he is most assuredly not a despiser of fortune, and by his writing of pedantic tracts he is not avoiding fame. He is in fact an embodiment of Goldsmith's theory of humor. As Goldsmith created Beau Tibbs to caricature the manners of the decadent aristocracy, so he created Dr. Primrose to satirize the complacency and material corruption of a type of clergy. In a very real sense the Primroses were a threat to their age, as Wesley and Blake well knew.

Although Goldsmith never seems to reveal in his life the deep religious devotion to Christianity that we associate with Johnson, his works do show traces of indignation at clerical complacency:

> . . . it is very obvious, that the clergy are no where so little thought of by the populous as here, and though

[62] *The Yale Edition of the Works of Samuel Johnson,* 7 vols. to date (New Haven, 1958———), II, 468.

our divines are foremost, with respect to abilities, yet they are found last in the effects of their ministry; the vulgar, in general, appearing no way impressed with a sense of religious duty. I am not for whining at the depravity of the times, or for endeavouring to paint a prospect more gloomy than in nature, but certain it is, no person who has travelled will contradict me, when I aver, that the lower orders of mankind in other countries, testify on every occasion the profoundest awe of religion, while in England they are scarcely awakened into a sense of its duties, even in circumstances of the greatest distress.

This dissolute and fearless conduct, foreigners are apt to attribute to climate and constitution; may not the vulgar being pretty much neglected in our exhortations from the pulpit be a conspiring cause? Our divines seldom stoop to their mean capacities, and they who want instruction most, find least in our religious assemblies.

(III, 150.)

Another passage, from *An Enquiry*, portrays the corrupting influence of wealth on the clergy:

The beneficed divine, whose wants are only imaginary, expostulates as bitterly as the poorest author, that ever snuffed his candle with finger and thumb. Should interest or good fortune, advance the divine to a bishopric, or the poor son of Parnassus into that place which the other has resign'd; both are authors no longer, the one goes to prayers once a day, kneels upon cushions of velvet, and thanks gracious heaven for having made the circumstances of all mankind so extremely happy; the other battens on all the delicacies of life, enjoys his wife and his easy chair, and sometimes, for the sake of conversation, deplores the luxury of these degenerate days.

(I, 307–8.)

That there was *some* basis for Goldsmith's concern is evident in Norman Sykes's assertion that "the spectacle of episcopal opulence and nepotism contrasting with the immobility of the parish system, its inability to cope with the new civic populations, and the relative poverty of the majority of the inferior clergy, seemed an argument for reform rather than thanksgiving." [63]

On a more universal level of meaning, the verbal irony on "fortune" in *The Vicar of Wakefield* links Goldsmith's work to what Lionel Trilling has seen to be historically the central function of the novel as an art form, the dealing "with reality and illusion in relation to questions of social class, which in relatively recent times are bound up with money." [64] What Goldsmith was doing in *The Vicar* preceded what nineteenth-century novelists were later to do. As Harry Levin so beautifully puts it:

> Speaking in terms of quantity and of its perennial encroachment on quality, we see values converted to prices. When Jane Austen speaks of "fortune"—a word which connotes so many vicissitudes—or when Trollope speaks of "living"—which should be limitless in its connotations —what is denoted, in either case, is simply "income." It is this process of cultural deflation, as it withers ideals and reduces individuals to a state of disillusionment, which the novelist—whether he considers himself a realist or a naturalist—makes it his task to comprehend and interpret. [65]

A modern analogy to *The Vicar* in twentieth-century literature is James Joyce's short story "Grace," in *Dubliners*, which has been described as "a study of rotarianism in

[63] *Church and State in England in the Eighteenth Century* (Cambridge, 1934), p. 408. Again I must caution that Goldsmith's view should not be mistaken for historical reality. The eighteenth-century Anglican Church was probably no better or worse than the Church in any other century.
[64] *The Liberal Imagination* (Garden City, N.Y., 1957), p. 249.
[65] *Contexts of Criticism* (Cambridge, Mass., 1957), p. 180.

Irish religion." [66] The story concludes with a seemingly straightforward sermon the irony of which lies in its use of the language of commerce so as to adapt the message of Christianity to the listeners, who are businessmen participating in a religious retreat.

That readers may have been misinterpreting *The Vicar of Wakefield* for over 175 years is not a legitimate reason for calling it a failure as satire. This would be itself a quantitative argument; and, as we have already observed, Swift himself was badly misinterpreted for almost as long. Nor should we have expected Goldsmith to declare overtly that his novel was a satire. Edmund Burke waited a year before proclaiming in a preface to the second edition that his anonymous pamphlet *Vindication of Natural Society* (1756) was a satire and a parody of Bolingbroke.[67] Sir Joshua Reynolds wrote of Goldsmith that "he would in a shorter time write the poem in his closet than give a satisfactory account in company of the plan or conduct of the work, or give any satisfactory explanation of a passage." [68] Indeed, had that anonymous critic in the *Monthly Review* explored more thoroughly why Goldsmith was "so strangely under-writing himself," this interpretation of *The Vicar* as sustained satire would perhaps not seem startling. Past interpretations have placed *The Vicar* in the category of homily and fiction extolling emotion for emotion's sake or else have seen the second half and conclusion to be a failure. Surely now, if we recognize

---

[66] Richard Levin and Charles Shattuck, "First Flight to Ithaca," in *James Joyce: Two Decades of Criticism,* ed. Seon Givens (New York, 1948), p. 84.

[67] See John C. Weston, "The Ironic Purpose of Burke's *Vindication* Vindicated," *Journal of the History of Ideas,* XIX (1958), 434–41.

[68] *Portraits by Sir Joshua Reynolds,* p. 55. My very close explication of *The Vicar* must of necessity be an anatomy of the work itself. It is not a substitute for a fresh reading of *The Vicar,* which is a complex and organic experience.

the irony and satire in this novel from beginning to end, we can read and enjoy it intelligently with the same mature interest that we take in *Tom Jones* and *Tristram Shandy*. And we shall realize that—for reasons different from those given in the past—*The Vicar of Wakefield* remains one of the truly great prose works of eighteenth-century English literature.

CONCLUSION

Versatility and an engaging prose style that enabled him to write interestingly on almost any subject or topic were what made Goldsmith a major writer in his own lifetime. If these virtues were possible only at the expense of profundity or depth of learning—say of a Johnson or a Carlyle—they nonetheless were uniquely eighteenth century. One of the great episodes in Boswell's *Life of Johnson* is the first meeting of John Wilkes and Samuel Johnson. On the surface it is doubtful if two more diametrically opposite human beings could have been selected to be brought together. Certainly only Boswell could have actually brought them together. Once they did meet, Wilkes's charming graciousness and deference, Johnson's determination not to be outdone in politeness, and Boswell's sly direction of conversation—all combined to make a most enjoyable evening. Later, Boswell summarized the significance of how these two men so "widely different, had *so many things in common*—classical learning, modern literature, wit, and humour, and ready repartee." [1] It was this commonality—this centripetal locus of eighteenth-century English culture grounded not in a compartmentalized or specialized body of knowledge or in a narrow professionalism but in the universal humanness which every man shared, or ought to have shared,

[1] Boswell, *Life*, III, 79. Italics mine.

with one another—that enabled such diverse figures as Wilkes and Johnson to come together in lively but amiable discourse. It is this same commonality that characterizes Goldsmith at his best. "The man of taste," in Goldsmith's words, is placed in "a middle station, between the world and the cell, between learning and *common* sense" (I, 306; italics mine). As mediator, the writer has an obligation to write not merely for the intellectual but for the largest possible audience. If Goldsmith was a popularizer and appeared to sacrifice depth for his newspaper readers, his very attempt to reach the common man was not a vice but a virtue. The writer is also "the monitor" of his age, whose obligation it is to seek out "new fashions, follies, and vices" and attack them either by "ridicule, or reproof," "persuasion, or satire" (I, 315).

Goldsmith could easily be accused of being a mere amuser, a dilettante who wrote off the top of his head. It was George Saintsbury—ironically, of all critics—who, unintentionally perhaps, patronized Goldsmith by concluding that he lacked "the critical *ethos*," that he was "always too careless" as well as "ignorant," and that he must be thought of, therefore, as an "amuser." [2] Oliver W. Ferguson has perceptively observed, however, that Goldsmith possessed "a substantial fund of self-knowledge," "a capacity for self-judgment," "a sure comic sense," and "a view of his world that was as free from illusions as it was from cynicism." [3] The whole import of the analysis of Goldsmith's genius in this book has been to show that he was a craftsman, that in his desire to mediate between the traditional, aristocratic patterns of discriminating qualitative values and the crude, mass media–directed, quantitative values of a growing middle-class audience, Goldsmith achieved a lucid prose, the very

[2] *The Peace of the Augustans* (London, 1916), p. 208.
[3] "Goldsmith," *South Atlantic Quarterly*, LXVI (1967), 472.

readability of which has caused generations of readers to miss completely its subtle nuances and refined irony. We have been taught to look for more than surface-level meanings in every other major comic writer of the age, with the exception, it seems, of Goldsmith. The late Frank O'Connor attributed the scandalous twentieth-century neglect of Goldsmith to Goldsmith's gift of "absolute pitch, of being always able to give out the middle C of literature," and to the fact that the "middle C's" of literature tend to be consigned to the back shelves where they are unnoticed and unread.[4] No wonder that Goldsmith—preceded by Swift, Gay, Pope, and Fielding, and contemporaneous with Johnson, Smollett, and Sterne—has been relegated by critical default to the second or even third rank of eighteenth-century writers, where he is equated less with literary genius and more with mediocrity.

It has been a traditional dictum that one should read *all* of a man's work before judging him. Few commentaries on individual works, such as *The Vicar*, indicate any such familiarity with Goldsmith. The entire corpus of Goldsmith's work read chronologically in the order in which it was written shows an underlying unity and development. Very early Goldsmith revealed his commitment to a conservative set of values and to a view of his comic artistry as a species of virtue. Irony became the instrument of Goldsmith's compromise with the commercially oriented reading audience of the *Bee* and the *Public Ledger*. Without sacrificing the integrity of his perceptive point of view, Goldsmith could satirize the pride of a dehumanizing rationalism, the propagandists' attempts to impose words for ideas upon others, the pathological narcissism of universal benevolence, and the false taste of conspicuous consumption. Such irony could both use and exploit sur-

[4] "Shadows on the Artist's Portrait," *New York Times Book Review* (Aug. 24, 1958), p. 1.

face-level meanings so that the discriminating reader could laugh at the foibles of the age and even at himself. If nondiscriminating readers missed the point, Goldsmith could still personally experience the private satisfaction of writing a subtle satire that had made its point. Goldsmith's theory of humor was also worked into a remarkable instrument of satire in his portrayals of Beau Tibbs and Richard Nash, who, as low characters, parody and mimic the divorce between morals and manners in the mid-eighteenth-century Whig aristocracy of the *nouveau riche*. All of Goldsmith's previous satire in the *Bee* and *The Citizen of the World* culminates logically in the antiromance of *The Vicar of Wakefield,* a magnificently constructed work that satirizes the complacency and the materialism of a certain type of Anglican clergyman and plays on a favorite eighteenth-century theme that the moral actions of men more often than not depend on their fortunes. Such a theme ultimately focuses on the fallibility of human nature.

No longer should it be necessary to puzzle over Goldsmith's self-conscious antisentimentalism toward weeping comedy and trite romances and his seeming contradiction in writing a sentimental novel. No longer should it be necessary to view Goldsmith as turning soft—as one of the first pre-Romantics. If *The Traveller* and *The Deserted Village* are no longer read as autobiographical you-can't-go-home-again poems and are recognized as deliberately rhetorical, then the view of Goldsmith as becoming a man of sensibility is untenable. It is here, however, that one may take issue with those who have made as strong a case as it is possible to make for these two poems. Given the two prime modes of writing as Goldsmith saw them—the craft of persuasion and the craft of satire—one can little doubt that Goldsmith's craft of satire is what still speaks to us directly today. Despite the very able analyses of

The Traveller and *The Deserted Village* made in the last decade or so, I do not think that we can suspend our taste and maintain the greatness of Goldsmith's verse and then use another set of poetic values to read contemporary verse. Swift's verse and Pope's verse do not require such a shift. Their poetry is still contemporary. To restate the issue, many works once thought to be great now seem moribund and are studied as literary history and even sociologically as cultural documents. Other works require historical exegesis but can be taught as contemporary works because they are not dated. To maintain that *The Traveller* and *The Deserted Village* have endured the test of time seems questionable. Their rhetoric is worthy of study, as are their poetic structures, but there must be discrimination between literary history for the purposes of understanding an era and those works that genuinely endure beyond that era. To overrate Goldsmith's "persuasive strain" would be harmful in the long run. Goldsmith's real strength lies in his prose satire and in his stage comedy.

Rather than labeling Goldsmith an "amuser," we may instead interpret him as an amiable satirist. Goldsmith himself, as we have seen, would not think of this label as a contradiction in terms. For some, no doubt, satire must be corrosive—must be the lashing mode of Juvenal or Swift—but this is to limit its range too narrowly. Satire should be conceived as a spectrum in which the color is determined by the technique and by the ends for which a particular work is designed.[5] In the past critics have called Goldsmith a comic writer, forgetting that comedy is a criticism of life and ignoring exactly what it is Goldsmith is criticizing. Goldsmith-as-amiable-satirist demands

[5] David Worcester observes that the "spectrum-analysis of satire runs from the red of invective at one end to the violet of the most delicate irony at the other." See *The Art of Satire*, p. 16.

that his moral motives as they are expressed in the structures of the works themselves be defined as well as his means; indeed, aesthetic understanding is impossible without an understanding of function. If Swift is placed at one pole of eighteenth-century English satire and Goldsmith at the other, we will have a much better grasp of the mode's surprising range, refinement, and versatility. We will no longer think of Goldsmith as merely an amuser but second only to Chaucer as a master of the art of amiable satire.

INDEX

tacked in, 76–77; and narrator's increasing emotional involvement, 75, 86, 87–88, 89–90; as "prospect" poem, 68–69; sound patterns in, 71–73, 81–82
—*Vicar of Wakefield:* 166; author of, "strangely under-writing himself," 166–67, 229; chapter headings as clues to satire, 217–19; character manipulation, legitimate satirical technique in, 184, 192–93; children, use for pathetic effects, burlesqued in, 196; commercial language, intentionally ironical in, 187–88, 209, 216, 218–20; and Dr. Primrose: as actor, 195–97; commercial morality of, 220; his "hard measure" in, 177–78; his hypocrisy on marriage in, 191; as "lesser gentry" in, 182; his pedantry in, 192; Falkland allusion in, 178–79; Fortune, irony of in, 190, 221–23, 228; fortune hunting in, 190; Hooker-Bishop jewel allusion in, 180–81; levels of meaning in, 207–8; and missing chapter hypothesis, 176; narrative structure as burlesque in, 199–207; Primrose family, mirror function of in, 191–96; prudence in, 218–19; retrospective reading process essential to a complete interpretation of, 185; survey of past criticism of, 166–72; title of as clue to satire, 173; unreliable narration of as clue to satire, 172–98
Gosse, Edmund, 158n
Gothic, 30–31
Gray, Thomas, 38, 54, 57–61
Greene, Donald, 22n, 27n, 105, 139–40
Griffin, Robert J., 23n

Haig, Robert, 18
Happiness: as virtue, 90, 94–95
Heilman, Robert B., 51, 128
Helvétius, Claude Adrian, 25

Hilles, Frederick W., 15, 67, 80, 170, 184, 200
Hipple, Walter J., Jr., 35n
Hoarding, 76–77
Hodson, Daniel, 181
Hogarth, William, 6, 16, 142, 146
Hooker, Edward N., 27n, 138–39
Hughes, Helen L., 200
Hume, David, 34–35
Humor: Goldsmith's theory of, 138–43
Humphrey Clinker, 4–5, 154–55
Hutcheson, Francis, 126

Idler, 198
Irony, 6, 8–9, 9–11, 12, 32–33, 50–52, 59–60, 97–98, 100–37 *passim,* 166–230 *passim,* 233–34

Jack, Ian, 69
Jaeger, Werner, 112n
Jefferson, D. W., 169–70, 182, 201, 212n
Jenyns, Soame, 104, 111, 120
Johnson, James W., 24n
Johnson, Maurice, 21
Johnson, Samuel, 1, 2, 3, 64–67, 104, 111, 118, 129, 152, 198, 213, 225–26, 231
Jones, Howard Mumford, 94–95, 219n
Joyce, James, 228

Langhorne, John, 45
Levin, Harry, 228
Lewis, C. S., 139
Literature: as a business, 1–4
"Little," 155–57
Locke, John, 110
Lovejoy, Arthur O., 105
Lovett, Robert M., 200
"Low," 140–43
Lucas, F. L., 67, 113–14, 150
Lucretius, 96–97

Macaulay, Thomas, 91, 199
Magdalene Hospital for Reformed Prostitutes, 19–20, 56–57
Mandeville, Bernard, 125

Designed by Edward D. King

Composed in Caledonia by The Colonial Press Inc.

Printed offset by The Colonial Press Inc.
on 60-lb. Warren 1854, Regular Finish

Bound by The Colonial Press Inc.
in Fictionette Natural Finish-FNV-3442